MW00709963

Bright Kids Core Concepts Workbook

Illustrations by: Kenneth Sommer
Written and published by: Bright Kids NYC

Copyright © 2010 by Bright Kids NYC Inc. All of the questions in this book have been created by the staff and consultants of Bright Kids NYC Inc.

Bracken® Basic Concept Scale: Receptive (BBCS:R) is a registered trademark of NCS Pearson Inc. Pearson Inc. neither endorses nor supports the content of the Bright Kids Core Concepts Practice Test.

All rights reserved. No part of this book may be reproduced or transmitted in any form or by any means without written permission from the author. ISBN (978-1-935858-06-5)

Corporate Headquarters:
Bright Kids NYC Inc.
225 Broadway, Suite 1504
New York, NY 10007
www.brightkidsnyc.com
info@brightkidsnyc.com
917-539-4575

TABLE OF CONTENTS

About Bright Kids NYC

Bright Kids NYC was founded in New York City to provide language arts and math enrichment for young children and to educate parents about standardized tests through workshops and consultations, as well as to prepare young children for such tests through assessments, tutoring and publications. Our philosophy is that regardless of age, test-taking is a skill than can be acquired and mastered through practice.

At Bright Kids NYC, we strive to provide the best learning materials. Our publications are truly unique. First, all of our books have been created by qualified psychologists, learning specialists and teachers. Second, our books have been tested by hundreds of children in our tutoring practice. Since children can make associations that many adults cannot, testing of materials by children is critical to creating successful test preparation guides. Finally, our learning specialists, and teaching staff have provided practical strategies and tips so parents can best help their child prepare to compete successfully on standardized tests.

Feel free to contact us should you have any questions or concerns.

Corporate Headquarters:
Bright Kids NYC Inc.
225 Broadway, Suite 1504
New York, NY 10007
www.brightkidsnyc.com
info@brightkidsnyc.com
917-539-4575

Introduction

Bright Kids NYC created the Core Concepts Practice Workbook to ensure that children are familiar with all core concepts that are key to succeeding on all standardized tests.

The Bright Kids Core Concepts Practice Workbook is based on the Bracken® Basic Concept Scale: Receptive (BBCS: R). This is an expanded version of the Bracken® School Readiness Assessment (BSRA), which is administered in various school districts and early childhood programs across the country.

The objective of the Bright Kids Core Concepts Workbook is to identify your child's strengths and weaknesses and test-taking ability so you can prepare your child adequately for the actual test. Our Core Concepts Practice Workbook can be utilized prior to taking our Core Concepts Practice Test or afterwards to work on areas where your child needs the most help.

In order to maximize the effectiveness of the Bright Kids Core Concepts Workbook, it is important to first familiarize yourself with the Workbook. In addition, it is recommended that you designate a quiet place to work with your child, ideally in a neutral environment, free of noise and clutter. Finally, provide a comfortable and proper seating arrangement to enable your child to focus and concentrate to the best of his or her ability.

Children will be taking many standardized tests throughout their school years. Our philosophy is that regardless of age, test-taking is a skill that can be acquired and mastered through practice.

Bright Kids Core Concepts Practice Workbook Overview

Our Core Concepts Practice Workbook is based on the Bracken® Basic Concept Scale: Receptive (BBCS: R) and has a total of ten subtests and 456 questions.

The first five sections of our Core Concepts Practice Workbook focus on all the skills tested on the Bracken® School Readiness Assessment (BSRA), which is essentially the School Readiness Assessment portion of the BBCS: R. The BSRA is designed to evaluate children's knowledge of 85 fundamental academic concepts in the categories of colors, letters, numbers/counting, sizes/comparisons, and shapes. The BSRA is typically administered to children ages three years to six years and eleven months. Just like the BSRA, the first five subtests of our Core Concepts Practice Workbook consists of colors, letters, numbers/counting, sizes/comparisons, and shapes subtests. There are 207 items in the first five subtests.

The second part of the Bright Kids Core Concepts Workbook includes additional categories that are not on the Bracken School Readiness Test but are on the BBCS: R. We have included these concepts because the additional concepts that are on the BBCS: R are rigorously tested in many other aptitude tests like the Stanford-Binet (direction/position, quantity, time/sequence) and the OLSAT® (position/direction and self/social awareness). In addition, these concepts are critical to success in any early childhood development program and need to be mastered by children entering kindergarten or early elementary grades.

Core concepts are an important part of language development for children and are deemed necessary to succeed in early formal education.

The following core concepts are tested in our Core Concepts Workbook:

1. **Colors:** This subtest tests a child's knowledge of all primary and secondary colors.
2. **Letters:** This subtest includes both uppercase and lowercase letters.
3. **Numbers/Counting:** This subtest includes both single-digit and double-digit numbers. Children must be able to count items up to ten.
4. **Sizes/Comparisons:** This subtest includes one; two; and three-dimensional comparatives such as tall, short, and big or small. This measures a child's ability to match and compare objects based on their characteristics.
5. **Shapes:** This subtest includes two and three-dimensional shapes as well as linear shapes, such as a curve.
6. **Direction/Position:** This subtest includes descriptions of the placement of an object relative to another such as below, above, inside, next to, over and under or placement of an object relative to itself, such as upside down or closed. It also includes the direction of the placement of an object such as left or right.
7. **Social Awareness (listed as Social/Self Awareness on BBCS:R):** This subtest includes emotional states such as happy, sad, angry, or mad.
8. **Texture/Material:** This subtest includes concepts such as wood, metal, rough, smooth, etc.
9. **Math Concepts (Listed as Quantity on the BBCS:R)**: These concepts are critical to grasping fundamental math topics including descriptions of the degree to which objects exist and the space they occupy, such as double and full. This subtest also includes items that measure how children can manipulate quantity, e.g. less than and except.
10. **Time/Order (Listed as Time/Sequence on the BBCS:R):** This subtest includes concepts related to time and order such as fast, slow, third, and fourth.

In the Bright Kids Core Concepts Workbook, we cover all concepts on the BSRA in the first five subtests and most of the concepts on subtest six through ten. There are 207 practice items on subtests one through five and 249 practice items on subtests six through ten. Please note that the Bright Kids Core Concepts Workbook includes additional concepts and items that are not in our Core Concepts Practice Test.

Bracken® Basic Concept Scale: Receptive (BBCS:R) Overview

The Bracken® Basic Concept Scale: Receptive (BBCS:R) consists of ten subtests that help evaluate a child's basic concept development and the child's ability to express basic concepts that are core to learning. There are a total of 282 items on the BBCS:R:

1) Colors
2) Letters
3) Numbers/Counting
4) Sizes/Comparisons
5) Shapes
6) Direction/Position
7) Self/Social Awareness
8) Texture/Material
9) Quantity
10) Time and Sequence

The first five subtests make up the School Readiness Composite, which measures educationally relevant concepts children need to master for formal early childhood education. These first five concepts are also tested on the Bracken® School Readiness Assessment (BSRA).

The BBCS:R is typically administered to children who are three years and zero months to six years and eleven months. The administration time is typically 30-40 minutes.

Table 1: Description of the BBCS:R

The subtests that are in bold are a part of the Bracken® School Readiness Assessment (BSRA).

Subtest	Description	Number of Items
Colors	Includes primary colors as well as secondary colors.	10
Letters	Includes uppercase and lowercase letters and sounds that correspond to letters.	15
Numbers/Counting	Contains single-digit and double-digit numbers (Numbers) and assigning a value to objects (Counting).	18
Sizes/Comparisons	Includes concepts that describe in one, two and three dimensions such as deep, short, long, big, and small. This subtest also tests a child's ability to match and compare objects based on common characteristics.	22
Shapes	Includes two-dimensional and three-dimensional shapes such as triangle and pyramid, as well as linear shapes such as a curve.	20
Direction/Position	Includes relational terms that describe spatial positioning of objects such as behind and in front of, or the positioning of an object relative to itself, like open, as well as a placement of an object such as right or middle.	62
Self/Social Awareness	Includes concepts referring to an emotional state of mind, such as happy and angry, as well as relative ages such as old and young.	33
Texture/Material	Includes concepts that describe salient characteristics of objects, such as hot and cold as well as the material composition of an object such as glass.	29
Quantity	Includes concepts that help identify quantity of objects such as more or less and space that objects occupy such as full or double.	43
Time/Sequence	Includes temporal items like night and day and sequential items such as first and third.	30

Bright Kids NYC Inc ©

Bracken® Basic Concept Scale: Receptive (BBCS:R) Administration

The BBCS:R starts with a few sample items to help familiarize the child with the structure of the test. The sample items can be prompted and explained as much as possible to ensure that the child has a good understanding of what is asked of him or her.

School Readiness Composite Score (SRC) Subtests 1-5

The subtests one through five on the BBCS:R create a School Readiness Composite Score (SRC). Correct answers are awarded one point and incorrect ones are given zero points. An individual subtest is discontinued if the child incorrectly answers three items in a row. The total score is the raw score for the SRC.

Subtests 6-10

Subtests six through ten have a different starting point for the subtests depending on the SRC score of the child. Then, all the subtests are administered until each subtest is complete or until the child obtains three consecutive zeros for each subtest.

For this section, a basal is also established. The basal is defined as the point in which a child answers three questions in a row correctly. If the child fails to answer three questions in a row correctly, the previous questions will be administered in reverse order until the child answers three consecutive questions correctly. Even if a basal is not established, all raw scores can still be converted into scaled scores. Scaled score is defined as the score that ranks a child relative to his or her peers based on norm-referenced age appropriate tables.

In order to scale a child's score relative to his or her peer group, the child's chronological age must be calculated by subtracting his or her birth date from the test date. When borrowing days from months, only 30 days is borrowed regardless of the length of the month. In addition, age is not rounded up or down to the nearest month. For example, if a child is tested on September 19th, 2010 and the child's birthday is September 20th, 2006, the child's chronological age is calculated to be 3 years, 11 months, and 29 days.

The BBCS:R is normed in three-month age bands. This means that children born within the same three-month band will be compared to children only in that age band. For example, a child who is born January 4th, 2004 will be in the same group as a child born on March 15th, 2004, if they both take the test the same day, for example on January 5th, 2010. These children will both be normed with other children in the six years to six years and three months age band.

Composite Scores

There are two types of composite scores that can be obtained from the BBCS:R:

1) Receptive Total Composite (Receptive RTC)

   This is a measure of a child's use of all of the foundational concepts in all ten categories of the BBCS:R. Receptive Total Composite is calculated by adding the SRC scaled score (not the raw score) and the individual subtest scaled scores (6-10).

2) Receptive School Readiness Composite (Receptive SRC)

   The receptive SRC is an independent assessment of the child's school learning ability and is similar to the Bracken School Readiness Assessment (BSRA).

The composite scores can then be converted into percentile ranks. For example, if a child receives a 97% rank on the BBCS:R, this means that the child scored better than 97% of the children who took the test in his or her age band.

Bracken® School Readiness Assessment (BSRA) Overview

The Bracken® School Readiness Assessment (BSRA) is designed to evaluate children's knowledge of 85 fundamental academic concepts in the categories of colors, letters, numbers/counting, sizes/comparisons, and shapes. The BSRA is administered to children ages three years to six years and eleven months.

Table 2: Description of the BSRA

Subtest	Description	Number of Items
Colors	Includes primary colors as well as secondary colors.	10
Letters	Includes uppercase and lowercase letters.	15
Numbers/Counting	Contains single and double digit numbers (Numbers) and assigning a value to objects (Counting).	18
Sizes/Comparisons	Includes concepts that describe items in one, two, and three dimensions such as deep, short, long, big, and small. This subtest also tests a child's ability to match and compare objects based on common characteristics.	22
Shapes	Includes two-dimensional and three-dimensional shapes such as triangle and pyramid as well as linear shapes such as a curve.	20

BSRA General Administration Guidelines

The Bracken® School Readiness Assessment (BSRA) is typically administered in one sitting and takes about 15-20 minutes to administer. The first five sections of our Core Concepts Workbook include all the concepts tested on the BSRA, which are:

- Colors
- Letters
- Numbers/Counting
- Sizes/Comparisons
- Shapes

There are four sample items on the BSRA. Three of the sample items include pantomime-like directions where the child practices pointing and showing items the examiner asks for. The last trial is from the Stimulus Book, where the tester asks the child to identify an item among four pictures. The children can ask to repeat an item and testers can repeat an item after 10 seconds if the child does not respond. Self-correction is allowed as long as it happens prior to administration of the next item. The child must only select one answer; if the child points to multiple items, the score will be counted as a zero.

All 85 items on the Bracken® School Readiness Assessment (BSRA) are scored one point for correct answers and zero points for wrong answers. If a child answers three questions in a row in a given subtest incorrectly, that subtest is immediately discontinued.

BSRA is also normed within three-month intervals. This means that children born within the same three-month band will be compared to children only in that age band. For example, a child who is born January 4th, 2004 will be in the same group as a child born on March 15th, 2004 if they both take the test on the same day, for example on January 5th, 2010. These children will both be normed with other children in the six years to six years and three months age band.

Just like in the BBCS: R, the raw scores are converted to scaled scores, which can then be converted to percentile ranks.

How to Use this Book

The objective of this book is to help children practice core concepts. In each section, many of the concepts are repeated multiple times utilizing different pictures to ensure that children have enough repetition to master the concepts.

While the instructions say: "Mark the item….", this book can be used as a coloring book by simply changing the instruction from "mark" to "color". This will enable you to create an activity book for your child while teaching him or her important core concepts.

Given that this book has 456 questions, it is important to pace through the book and focus on the concepts your child has the most trouble with. The Bright Kids Core Concept Workbook can also be used in conjunction with the Bright Kids Core Concepts Practice Test. First, the Core Concepts Practice Test can be utilized to identify your child's strengths and weaknesses. Afterwards, your child can work on the concepts he or she had the most trouble with using the Bright Kids Core Concepts Workbook. You can also work through this book first to practice all the concepts with your child, and then administer the Core Concepts Practice Test to evaluate his or her skills.

There are ten subtests that cover the following concepts:

- Colors
- Letters
- Numbers/Counting
- Sizes/Comparisons
- Shapes
- Direction/Position
- Social Awareness
- Texture/Material
- Math Concepts
- Time/Order

The concepts covered in ten subtests are summarized below:

Table 3: Concepts Covered in the Bright Kids Core Concepts Workbook

Subtest	Concepts Covered	Number of Items
Colors	Red, blue, green, black, yellow, pink, orange, purple, white, and brown.	20
Letters	All uppercase and lowercase letters.	28
Numbers/ Counting	All single-digit and double-digit numbers up to 100 and counting objects up to 10.	81
Sizes/ Comparisons	Big, small, long, little, not the same, short, match, different, tall, deep, large, same, alike, wide, exactly, other than, similar, equal, thin, narrow, unequal, shallow, identical, and medium.	48
Shapes	Star, heart, circle, line, square, triangle, cone, round, diamond, oval, rectangle, check mark, row, pyramid, cylinder, cube, sphere, straight, curve, column, diagonal, and angle.	30
Direction/ Position	On, open, closed, off, under, up, upside down, behind, top, out, high, apart, close, around, next to, outside, near, in front, together, away, middle, bottom, into, down, side, through, between, front, backward, beside, edge, back, low, corner, toward, end, still, below, above, across from, forward, sideways, inside-out, ahead, center, level, close, opposite, right, left, and far.	87
Social Awareness	Crying, laughing, sad, afraid, angry, happy, relaxing, resting, tired, old, excited, sleepy, friendly, frowning, worried, right, healthy, sick, exhausted, easy, difficult, disappointed, young, and curious.	36
Texture/ Material	Wet, loud, dark, quiet, soft, wood, sharp, hard, glass, shiny, light, flat, bright, metal, smooth, cloth, rough, clear, dry, tight, loose, light, dull, hot, cold, and warm.	39
Math Concepts	Many, whole, empty, full, none, nothing, both, all, most, alone, every, with, missing, piece, almost, each, left, greatest, part, little, except, dozen, without, half, more than, several, least, less than, pair, another, double, twice, single, add, subtract, divide, multiply, neither, couple, some, few, as many as, triple, pair and least.	60
Time/Order	Last, daytime, nighttime, before, first, second, third, fourth, slow, fast, late, after, and fall, winter, summer, and spring.	27

Bright Kids
Core Concepts Workbook

Bracken® Basic Concept Scale: Receptive (BBCS: R) and Bracken® School Readiness Assessment (BSRA) are registered trademarks of NCS Pearson Inc. Pearson Inc. neither endorses nor supports the content of the Bright Kids Core Concepts Workbook. All rights reserved. No part of this Workbook may be reproduced or transmitted in any form or by any means without written permission from Bright Kids NYC Inc. ISBN (978-1-935858-06-5).

123
ABC

SECTION ONE:
COLOR

1. **Mark the blue cup.**

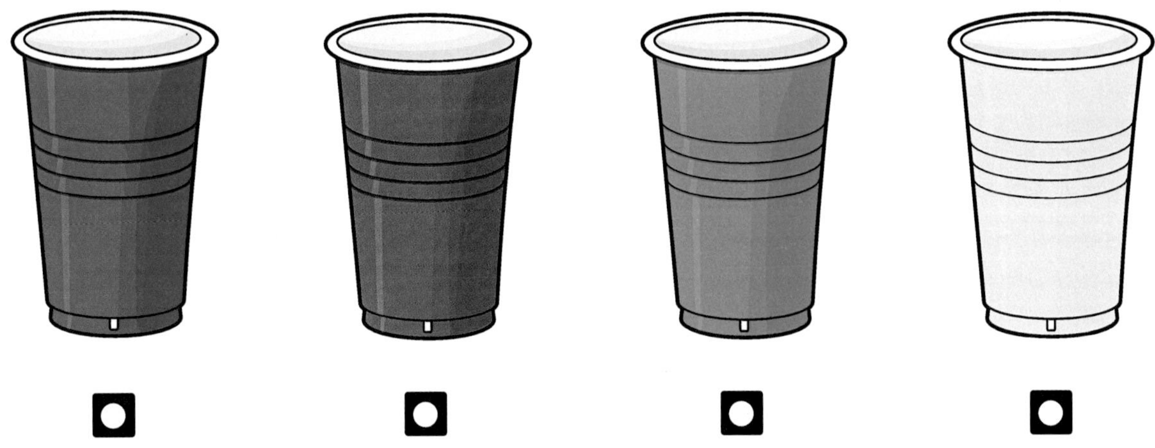

2. **Mark the purple fruit.**

3. **Mark the pink dress.**

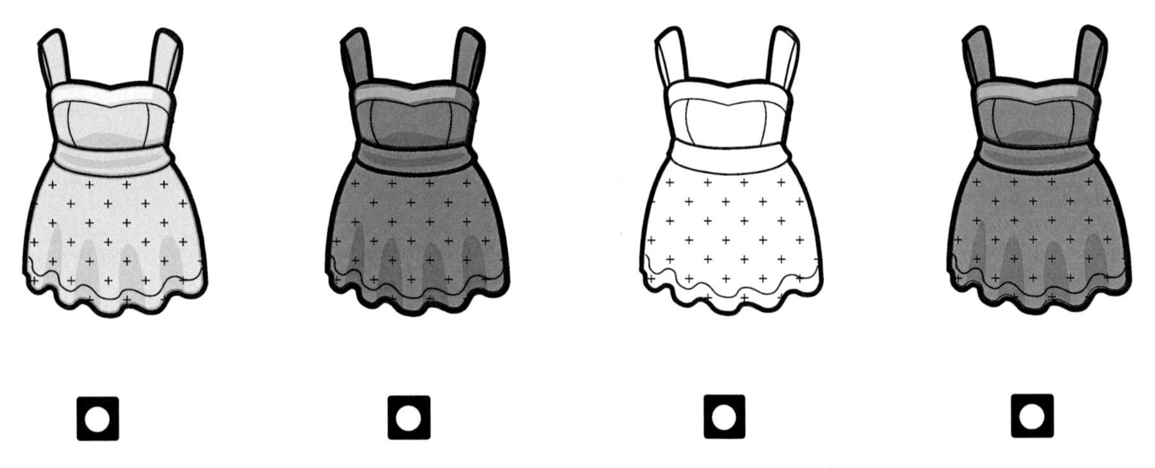

4. Mark the red hat.

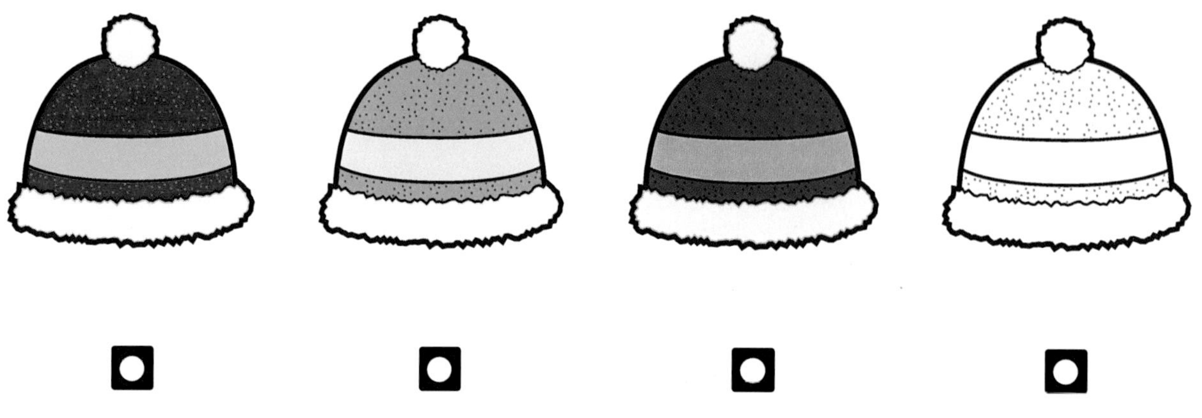

5. Mark the white bowl.

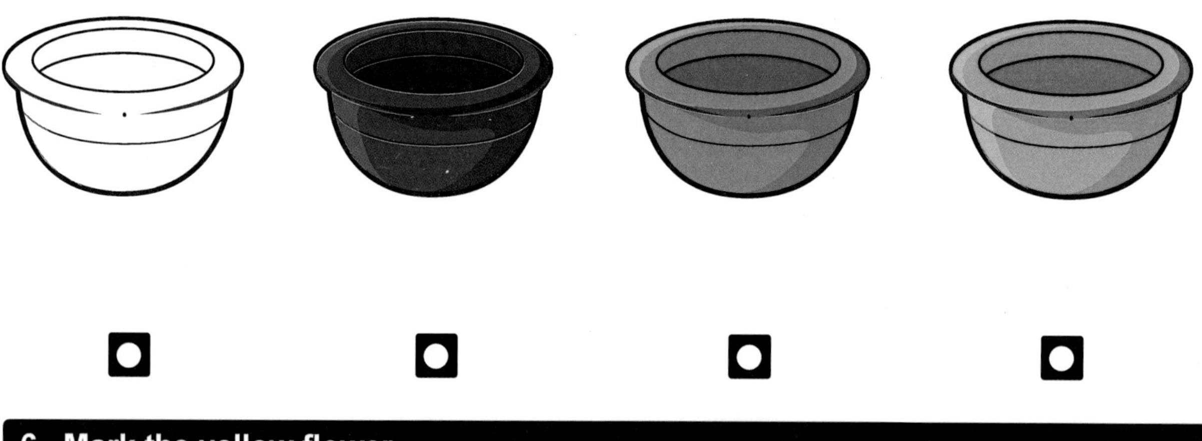

6. Mark the yellow flower.

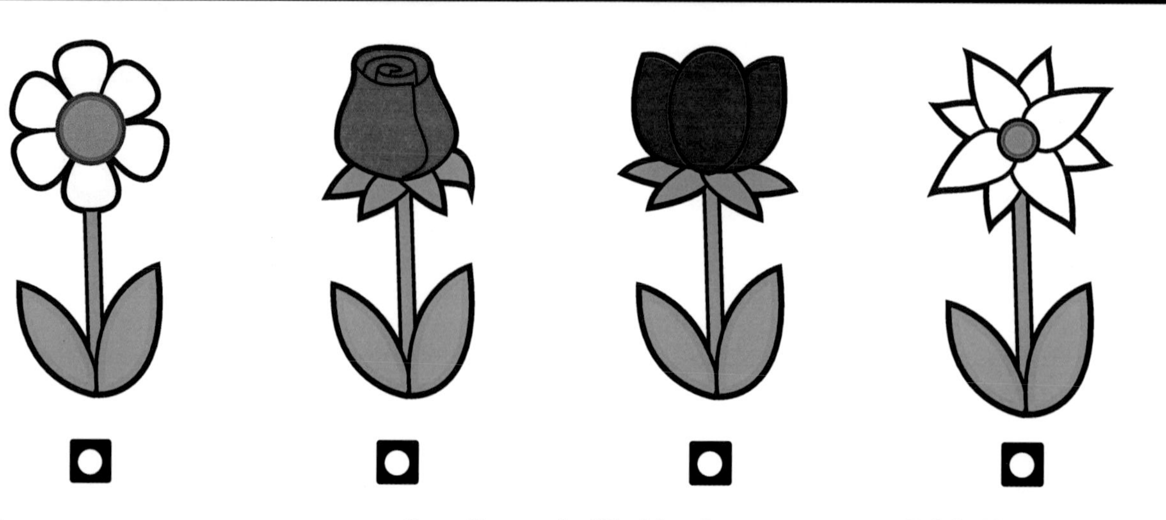

Bright Kids NYC Inc ©

7. Mark the black chair.

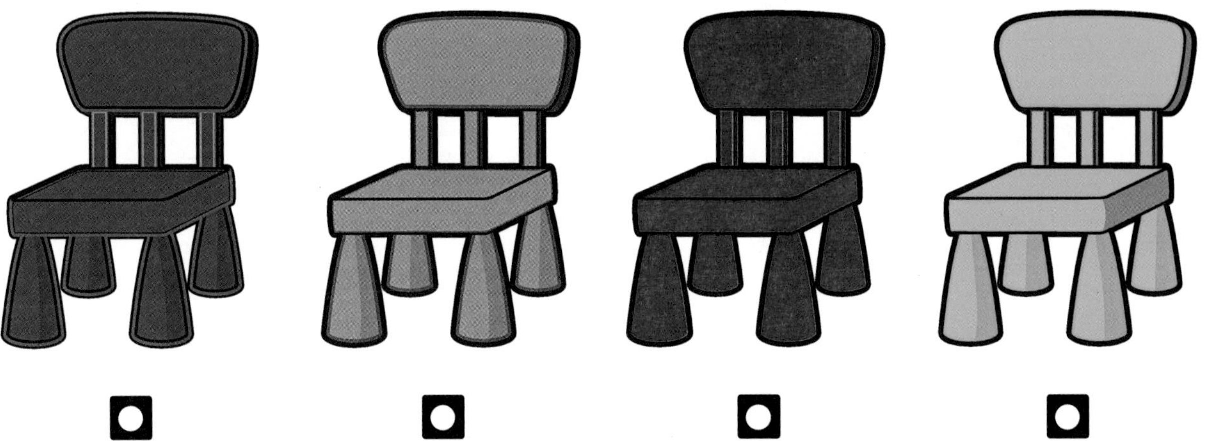

8. Mark the brown teddy bear.

9. Mark the green vegetable.

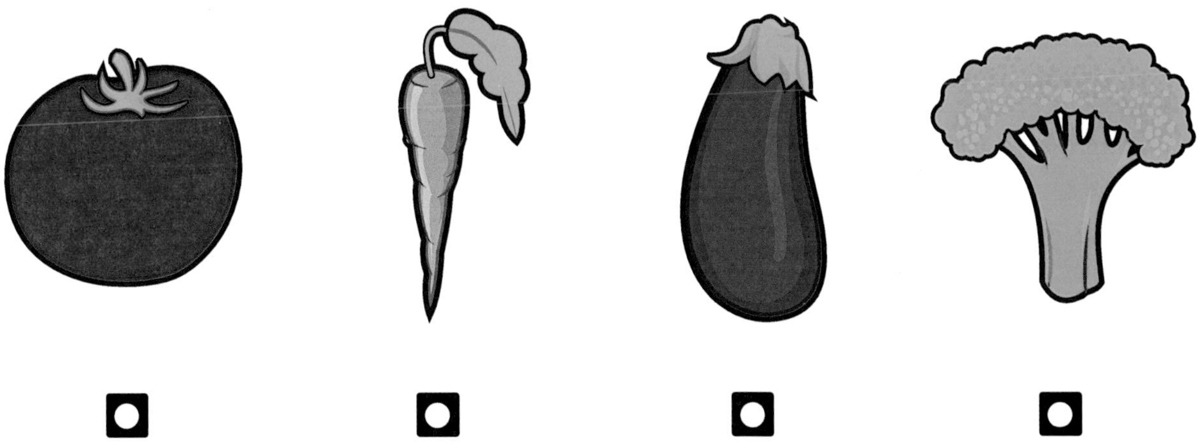

10. Mark the blue balloon.

11. Mark the white cup.

12. Mark the red fruit.

 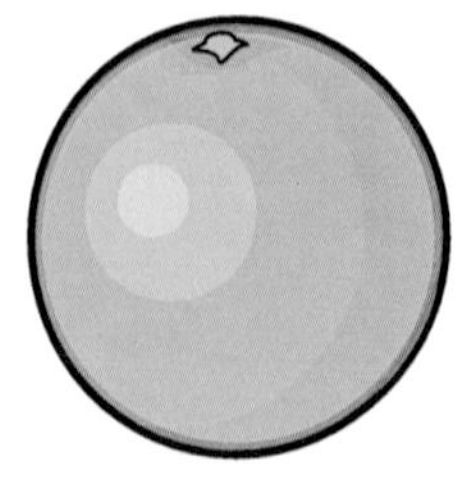  

13. Mark the purple dress.

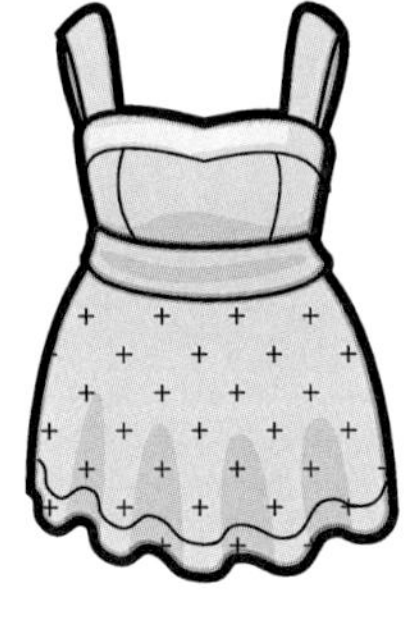
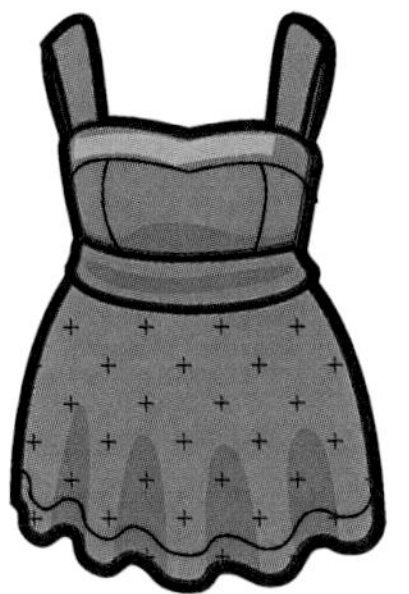
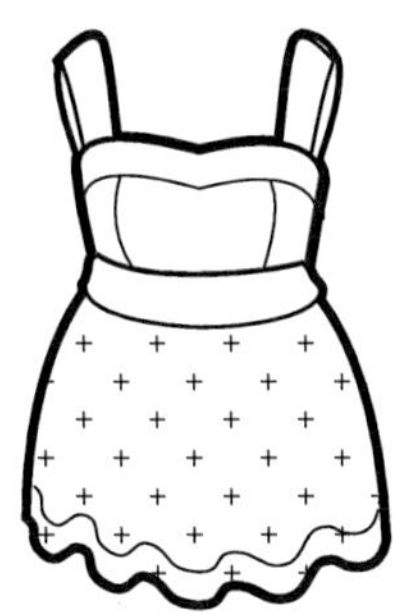
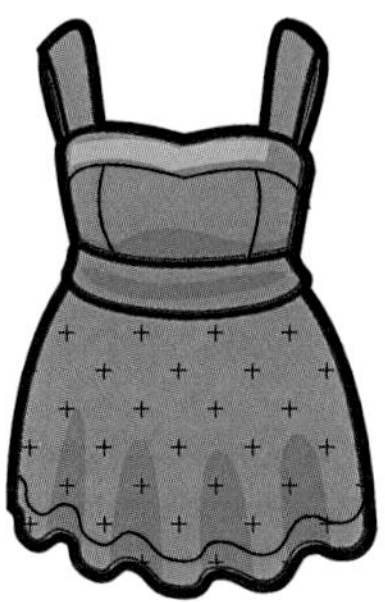

14. Mark the blue hat.

15. Mark the brown bowl.

16. Mark the pink flower.

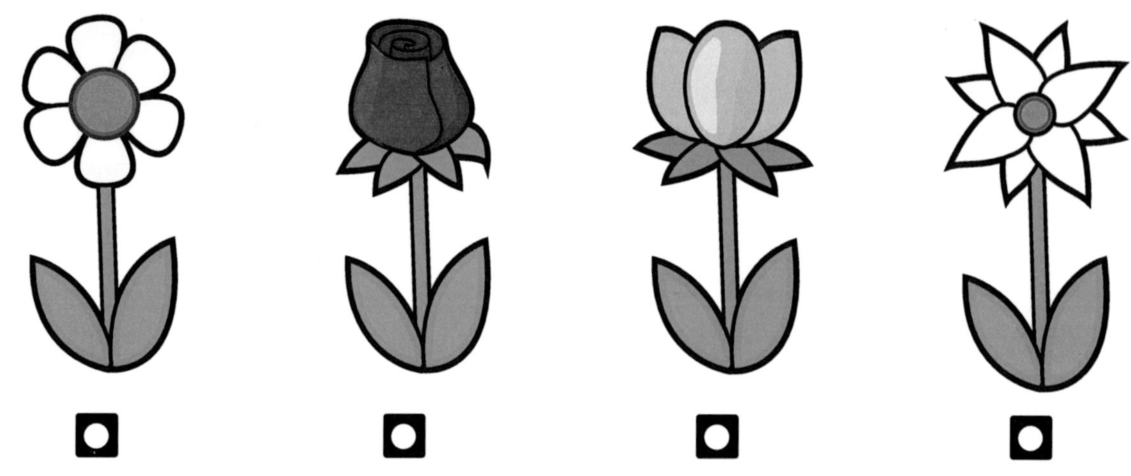

17. Mark the green chair.

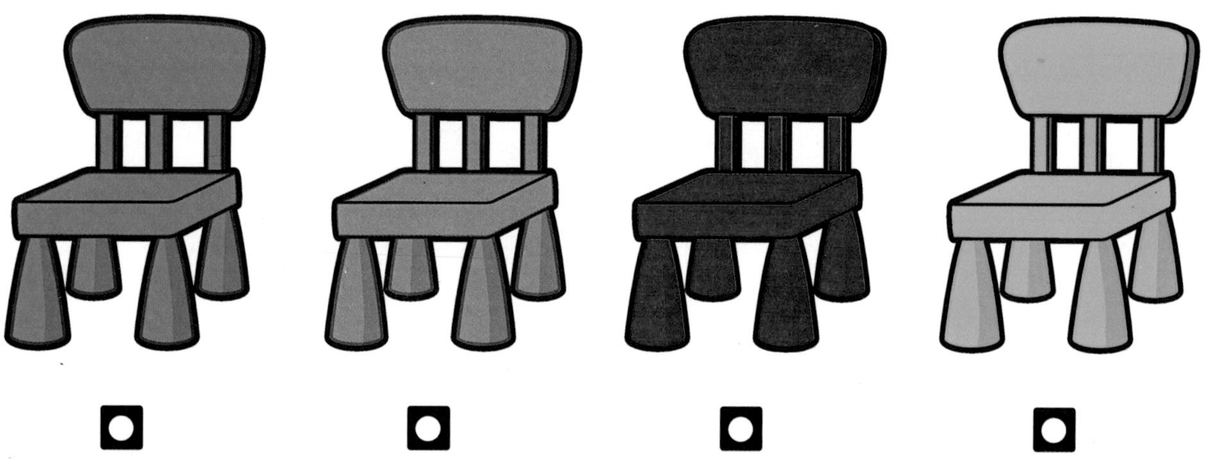

18. Mark the yellow teddy bear.

19. Mark the orange vegetable.

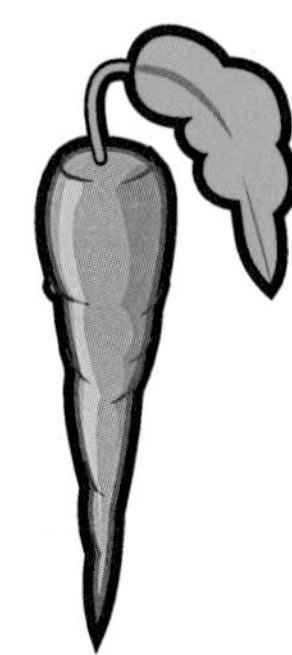

20. Mark the white balloon.

ANSWER KEY

1.	Picture 1	-	Blue cup
2.	Picture 4	-	Grapes
3.	Picture 1	-	Pink dress
4.	Picture 1	-	Red hat
5.	Picture 1	-	White bowl
6.	Picture 1	-	Yellow flower
7.	Picture 1	-	Black chair
8.	Picture 1	-	Brown bear
9.	Picture 4	-	Broccoli
10.	Picture 4	-	Blue balloon
11.	Picture 1	-	White cup
12.	Picture 3	-	Apple
13.	Picture 2	-	Purple dress
14.	Picture 2	-	Blue hat
15.	Picture 3	-	Brown bowl
16.	Picture 3	-	Pink flower
17.	Picture 4	-	Green chair
18.	Picture 3	-	Yellow teddy bear
19.	Picture 2	-	Carrot
20.	Picture 2	-	White balloon

SECTION TWO:
LETTERS

A	B	C	D
is for apple	is for bird	is for cake	is for dog

1. Identify all the letters below.

A B C D

2. Identify all the letters below.

B D C A

a is for apple

b is for bird

c is for cake

d is for dog

3. Identify all the letters below.

a b c d

4. Identify all the letters below.

b d c a

 Bright Kids NYC Inc ©

E	**F**	**G**	**H**
is for elephant	is for fan	is for grapes	is for house

5. Identify all the letters below.

G H F E

6. Identify all the letters below.

F G H E

e	f	g	h
is for elephant	is for fan	is for grapes	is for House

7. Identify all the letters below.

e h g f

8. Identify all the letters below.

g e f h

I	J	K	L
is for ice cream	is for jacket	is for kitten	is for lamp

9. Identify all the letters below.

K J I L

10. Identify all the letters below.

J I L K

i

is for ice cream

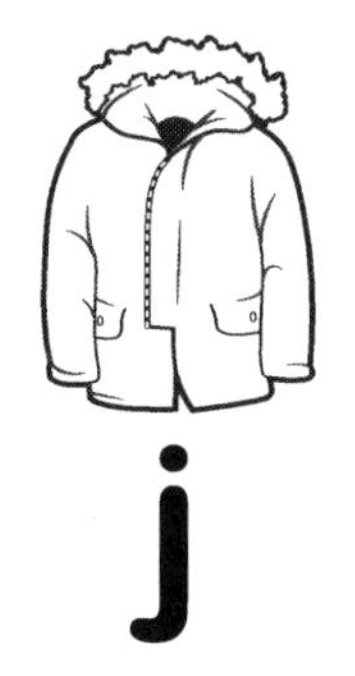

j

is for jacket

k

is for kitten

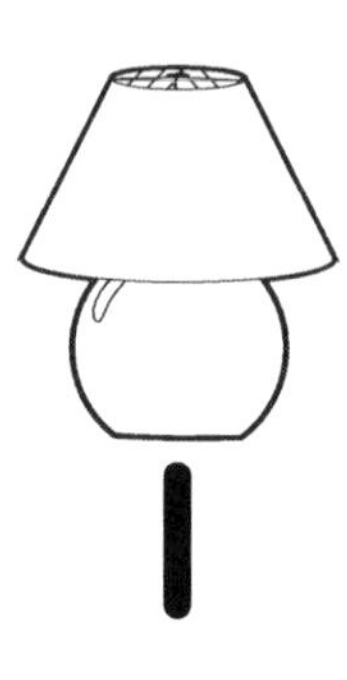

l

is for lamp

11. Identify all the letters below.

l i k j

12. Identify all the letters below.

k i j l

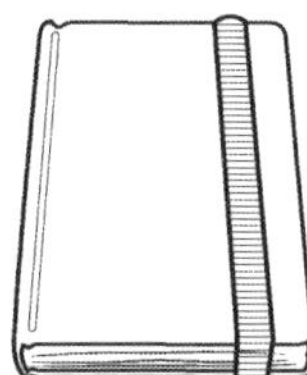

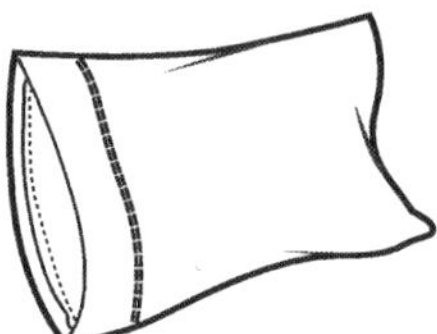

M	N	O	P
is for mouse	is for notebook	is for octopus	is for pillow

13. Identify all the letters below.

N O M P

14. Identify all the letters below.

M N P O

	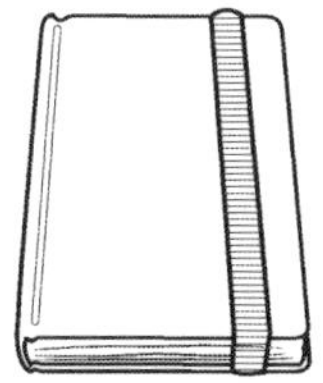		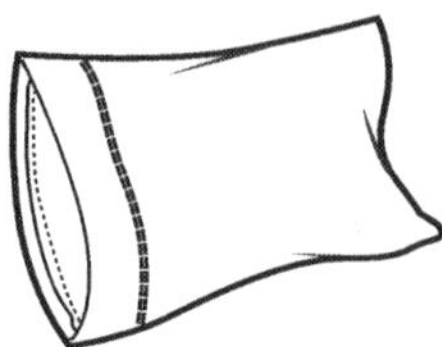
m	**n**	**o**	**p**
is for mouse	is for notebook	is for octopus	is for pillow

15. Identify all the letters below.

o ◘ **n** ◘ **p** ◘ **m** ◘

16. Identify all the letters below.

p ◘ **o** ◘ **n** ◘ **m** ◘

Q	R	S	T
is for queen	is for rabbit	is for spoon	is for turtle

17. Identify all the letters below.

Q T R S

18. Identify all the letters below.

S R Q T

q	r	s	t
is for queen	is for rabbit	is for spoon	is for turtle

19. Identify all the letters below.

t q s r

20. Identify all the letters below.

s t q r

Bright Kids NYC Inc ©

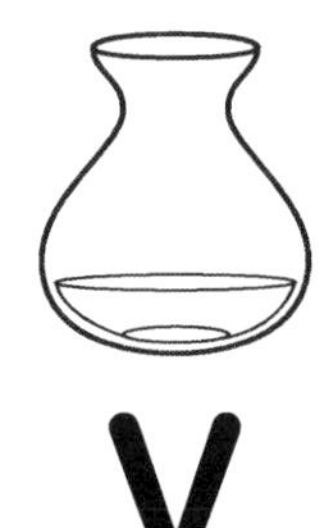

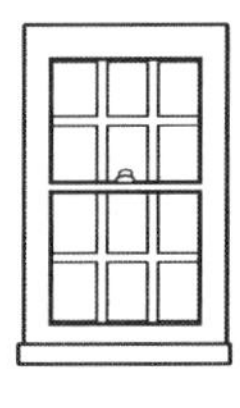

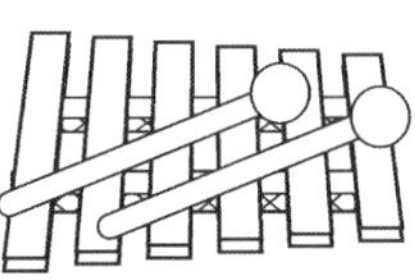

U	V	W	X
is for unicorn	is for vase	is for window	is for xylophone

21. Identify all the letters below.

U W V X

22. Identify all the letters below.

W X U V

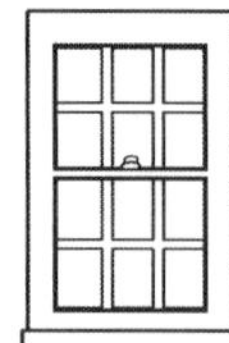

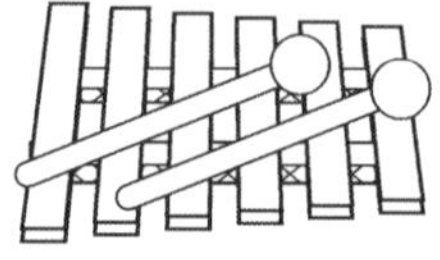

u	v	w	x
is for unicorn	is for vase	is for window	is for xylophone

23. Identify all the letters below.

w x v u

24. Identify all the letters below.

x v u w

Y

is for yarn

Z

is for zebra

25. Identify all the letters below.

Y T Z H

□ □ □ □

26. Identify all the letters below.

Q B Z Y

□ □ □ □

y

is for yarn

z

is for zebra

27. Identify all the letters below.

u z a y

28. Identify all the letters below.

g y z o

123
ABC

SECTION THREE:
NUMBERS/COUNTING

1. Mark the three.

1 2 3 4

2. Mark the card with three stars.

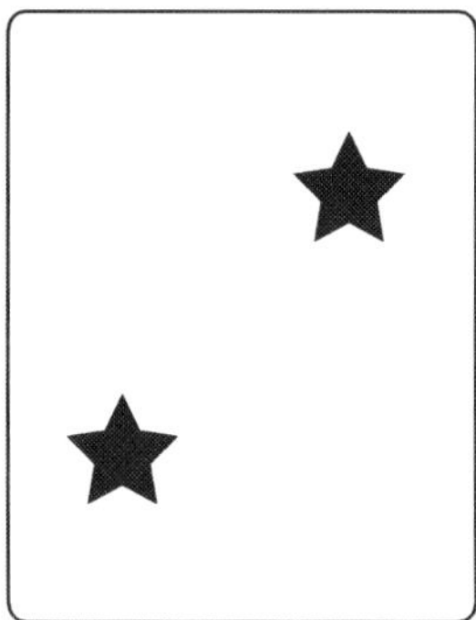

3. Mark the four.

1 2 3 4

4. Mark the one.

1 2 3 4

5. Mark the group of three ducks.

6. Mark the two.

1 2 3 4

 Bright Kids NYC Inc ©

7. Mark the five.

5 6 7 8

8. Mark the group of six turtles.

9. Mark the eight.

5 6 7 8

10. Mark the seven.

5 6 7 8

11. Mark the card with eight stars.

12. Mark the six.

5 6 7 8

13. Mark the eleven.

9 10 11 12

14. Mark the group of nine apples.

15. Mark the ten.

9 10 11 12

16. Mark the nine.

9 10 11 12

17. Mark the group of eleven soccer balls.

18. Mark the twelve.

9 10 11 12

19. Mark the fourteen.

10 11 12 13 14

20. Mark the baseball helmet with the number sixteen.

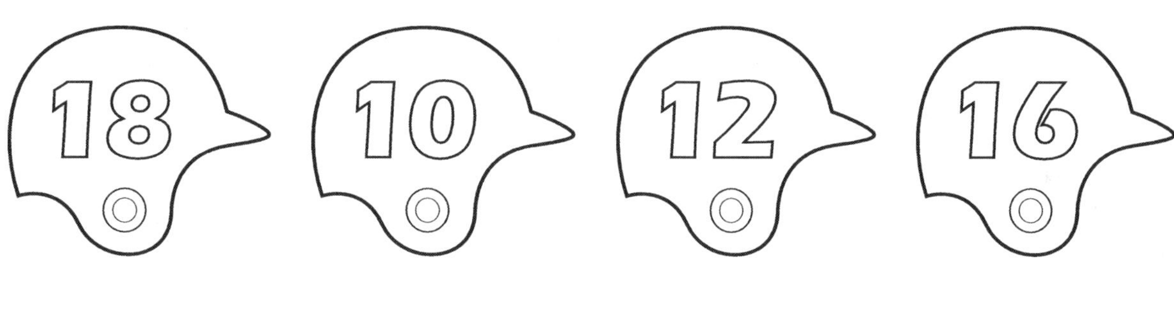

21. Mark the nineteen.

15 16 17 18 19

22. Mark the ten.

10 11 12 13 14

23. Mark the race car with the number twelve.

24. Mark the seventeen.

15 16 17 18 19

25. Mark the twenty.

20 21 22 23 24

26. Mark the football shirt with the number twenty-five.

27. Mark the twenty-seven.

25 26 27 28 29

28. Mark the twenty-three.

20 21 22 23 24

29. Mark the price tag with the number twenty-one.

30. Mark the twenty-eight.

25 26 27 28 29

Bright Kids NYC Inc ©

31. Mark the thirty-two.

30 31 32 33 34

32. Mark the race car with the number thirty-four.

33. Mark the thirty-eight.

35 36 37 38 39

34. Mark the thirty-three.

30 31 32 33 34

35. Mark the ball with the number thirty-two.

36. Mark the thirty-five.

35 36 37 38 39

37. Mark the forty-three.

40 41 42 43 44

38. Mark the basketball shirt with the number forty-one.

39. Mark the forty-nine.

45 46 47 48 49

40. Mark the forty-two.

40 41 42 43 44

41. Mark the football helmet with the number forty-eight.

42. Mark the forty-six.

45 46 47 48 49

43. Mark the fifty.

50 51 52 53 54

44. Mark the sign with the number fifty-five.

SPEED LIMIT 55	SPEED LIMIT 50	SPEED LIMIT 57	SPEED LIMIT 56

45. Mark the fifty-eight.

55 56 57 58 59

46. Mark the fifty-three.

50 51 52 53 54

47. Mark the basketball shirt with the number fifty-six.

48. Mark the fifty-nine.

55 56 57 58 59

49. Mark the sixty-four.

60 61 62 63 64

☐ ☐ ☐ ☐ ☐

50. Mark the ball with the number sixty-seven.

☐ ☐ ☐ ☐

51. Mark the sixty-eight.

65 66 67 68 69

☐ ☐ ☐ ☐ ☐

52. Mark the sixty-one.

60 61 62 63 64

53. Mark the shirt with the number sixty-six.

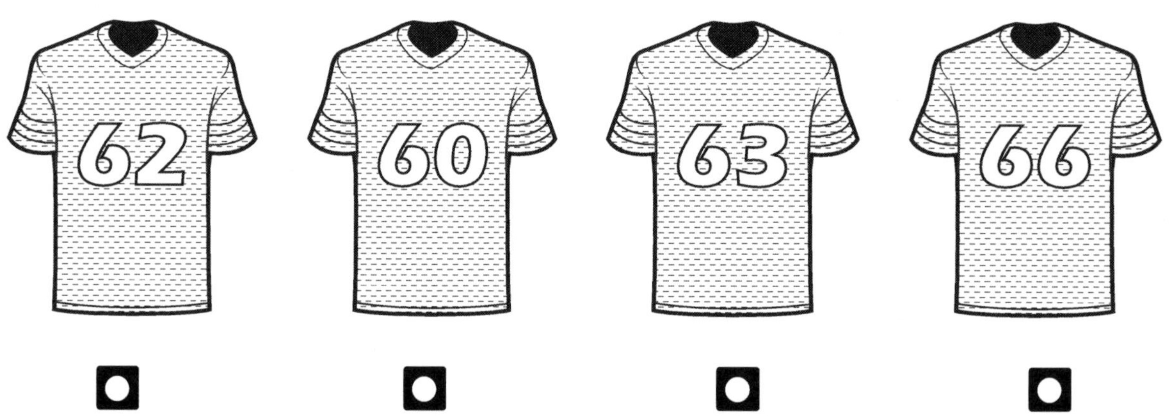

54. Mark the sixty-five.

65 66 67 68 69

55. Mark the seventy-three.

70 71 72 73 74

56. Mark the price tag with the number seventy-eight.

57. Mark the seventy-seven.

75 76 77 78 79

58. Mark the seventy.

70 71 72 73 74

59. Mark the sign with the number seventy-five.

SPEED LIMIT 75

SPEED LIMIT 70

SPEED LIMIT 76

SPEED LIMIT 71

60. Mark the seventy-nine.

75 76 77 78 79

 Bright Kids NYC Inc ©

61. Mark the eighty-one.

80 81 82 83 84

62. Mark the football helmet with the number eighty-eight.

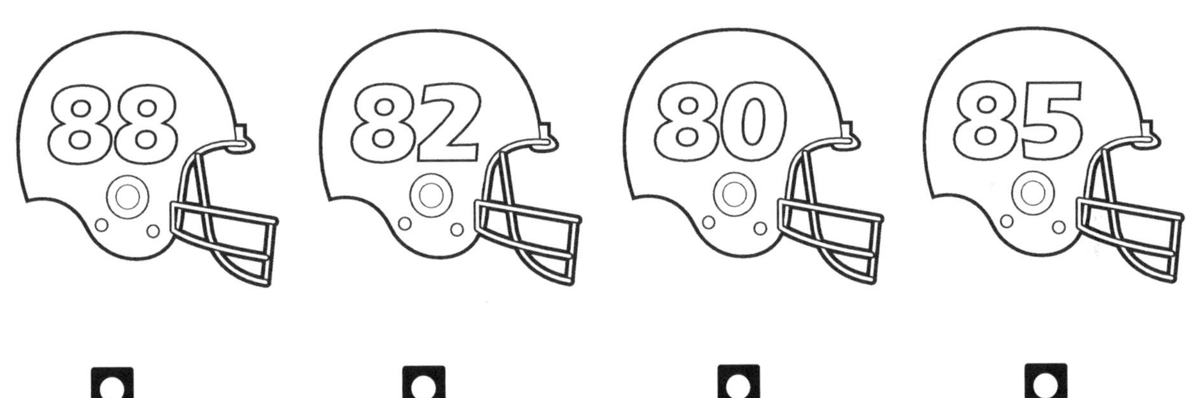

63. Mark the eighty-six.

85 86 87 88 89

64. Mark the eighty.

80 81 82 83 84

65. Mark the shirt with the number eighty-one.

66. Mark the eighty-five.

85 86 87 88 89

67. Mark the ninety.

90 91 92 93 94

68. Mark the shirt with the number ninety-one.

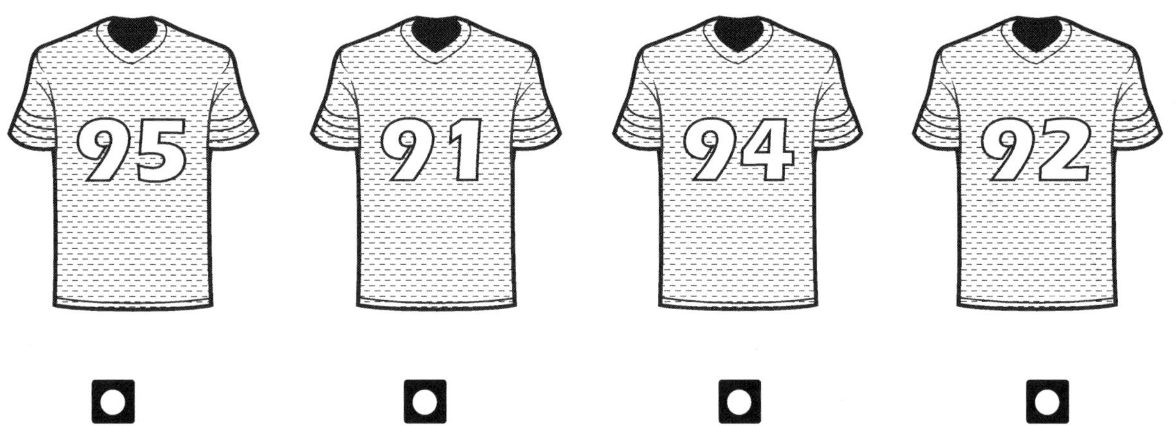

69. Mark the ninety-eight.

95 96 97 98 99

70. Mark the ninety-three.

90 91 92 93 94

71. Mark the baseball helmet with the number ninety-four.

72. Mark the ninety-six.

95 96 97 98 99

Bright Kids NYC Inc ©

73. Mark the two fish.

  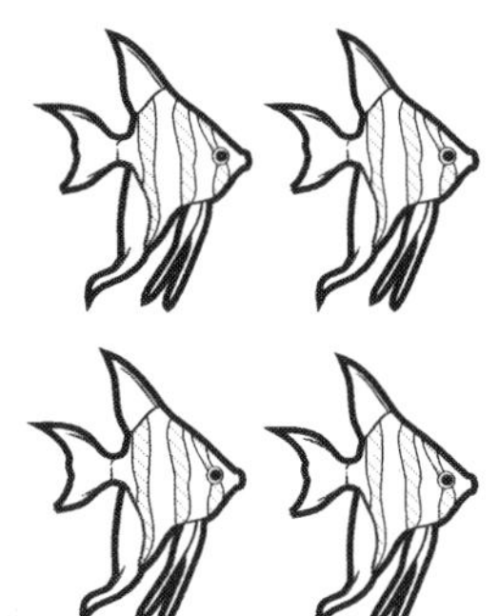 

74. Mark the four stars.

75. Mark the three balls.

   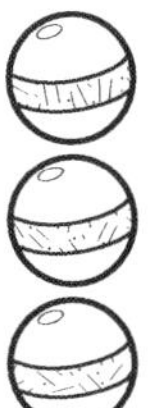

76. Mark the six ladybugs.

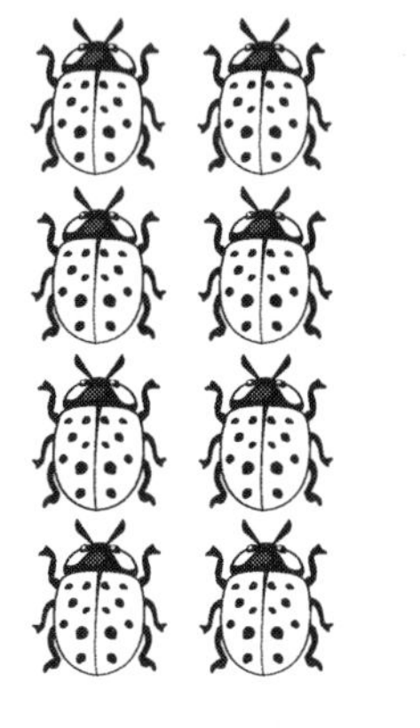

77. Mark the five marbles.

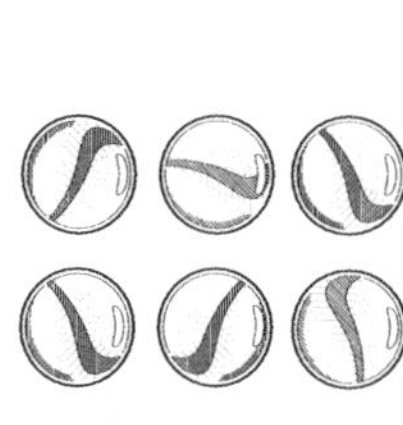
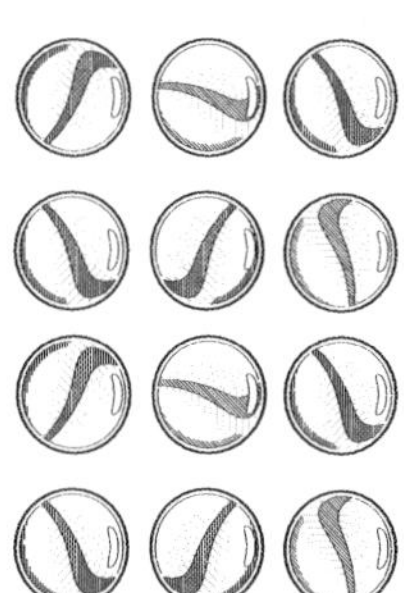
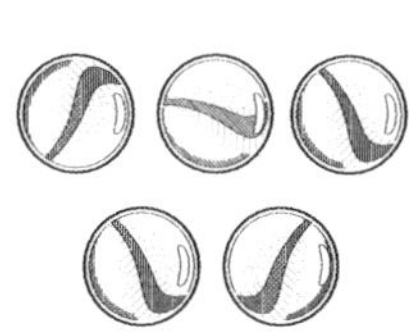
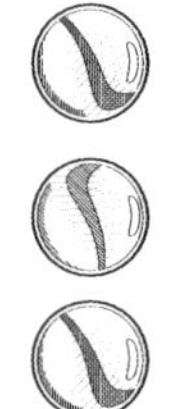

78. Mark the eight flowers.

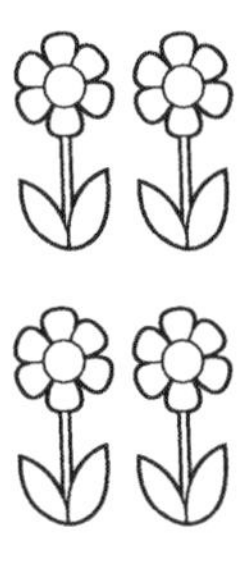

Bright Kids NYC Inc ©

79. Mark the group with seven cupcakes.

80. Mark the nine butterflies.

81. Mark the ten birds.

 Bright kids NYC Inc ©

ANSWER KEY

1. Number 3
2. Picture 1 - Card with three stars
3. Number 4
4. Number 1
5. Picture 2 - Three ducks
6. Number 2
7. Number 5
8. Picture 1 - Six turtles
9. Number 8
10. Number 7
11. Picture 4 - Card with eight stars
12. Number 6
13. Number 11
14. Picture 2 - Nine apples
15. Number 10
16. Number 9
17. Picture 1 - Eleven soccer balls
18. Number 12
19. Number 14
20. Picture 4 - Helmet marked sixteen
21. Number 19
22. Number 10
23. Picture 3 - Race car marked twelve
24. Number 17
25. Number 20
26. Picture 1 - Jersey marked twenty-five
27. Number 27
28. Number 23
29. Picture 1 - Price tag marked twenty-one
30. Number 28
31. Number 32
32. Picture 3 - Race car marked thirty-four
33. Number 38
34. Number 33
35. Picture 1 - Ball marked thirty-two
36. Number 35
37. Number 43
38. Picture 1 - Jersey marked fourty-one
39. Number 49
40. Number 42

41.	Picture 4	-	Helmet marked forty-eight
42.	Number 46		
43.	Number 50		
44.	Picture 1	-	Sign marked fifty-five
45.	Number 58		
46.	Number 53		
47.	Picture 1	-	Jersey marked fifty-six
48.	Number 59		
49.	Number 64		
50.	Picture 3	-	Ball marked sixty-seven
51.	Number 68		
52.	Number 61		
53.	Picture 4	-	Jersey marked sixty-six
54.	Number 65		
55.	Number 73		
56.	Picture 4	-	Price tag marked seventy-eight
57.	Number 77		
58.	Number 70		
59.	Picture 1	-	Sign marked seventy-five
60.	Number 79		
61.	Number 81		
62.	Picture 1	-	Helmet marked eighty-eight
63.	Number 86		
64.	Number 80		
65.	Picture 4	-	Jersey marked eighty-one
66.	Number 85		
67.	Number 90		
68.	Picture 2	-	Jersey marked ninety-one
69.	Number 98		
70.	Number 93		
71.	Picture 3	-	Helmet marked ninety-four
72.	Number 96		
73.	Picture 2	-	Two fish
74.	Picture 2	-	Four stars
75.	Picture 4	-	Three balls
76.	Picture 4	-	Six ladybugs
77.	Picture 3	-	Five marbles
78.	Picture 2	-	Eight flowers
79.	Picture 3	-	Seven cupcakes
80.	Picture 1	-	Nine butterflies
81.	Picture 2	-	Ten birds

 Bright Kids NYC Inc ©

123
ABC

SECTION FOUR:
SIZES/COMPARISONS

1. Mark the shoes that are equal size.

2. Mark the boxes that are identical.

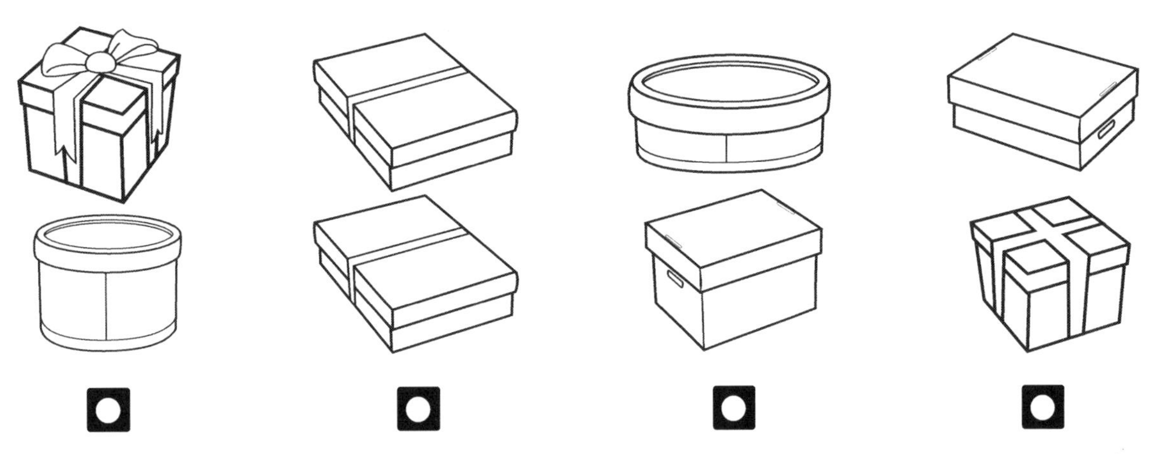

3. Mark the person eating something other than a carrot.

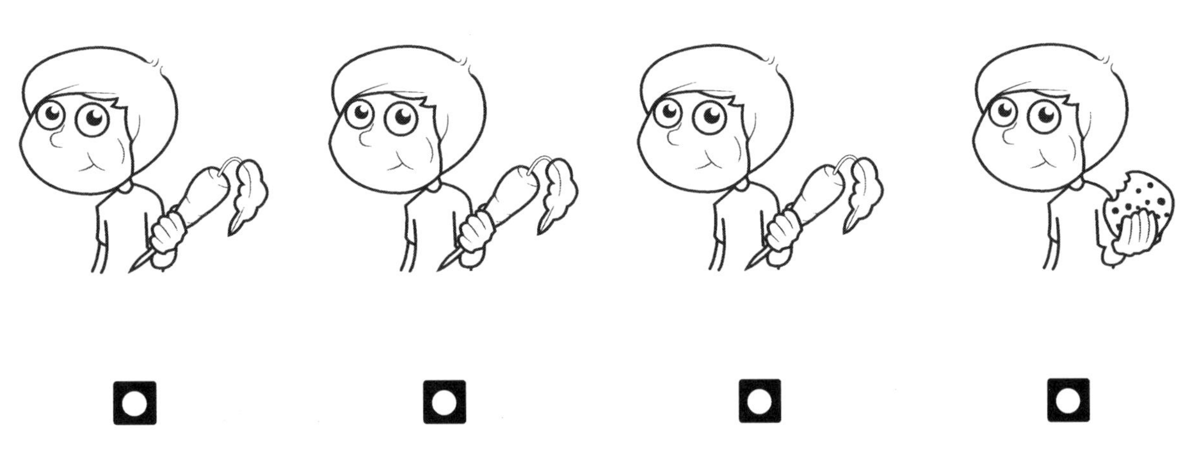

4. Mark the fruits that are the same.

5. Mark the stool that is different.

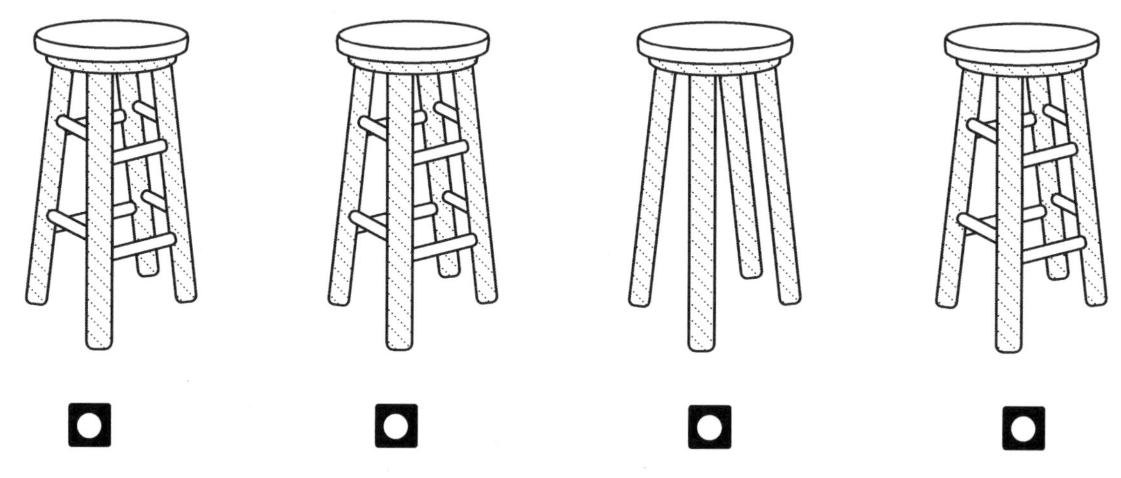

6. Mark the books that are identical.

7. Mark the shoes that match.

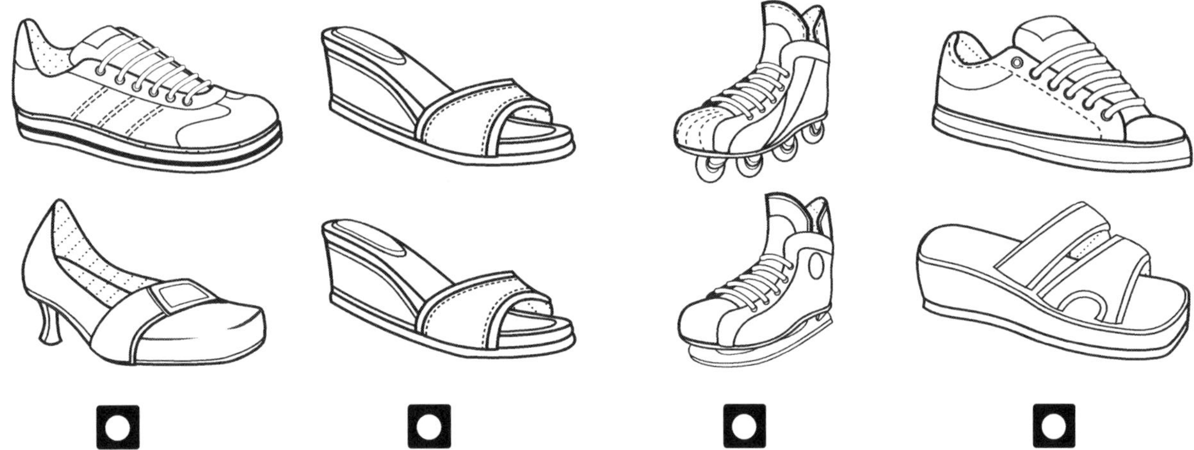

8. Mark the vegetables that are the same.

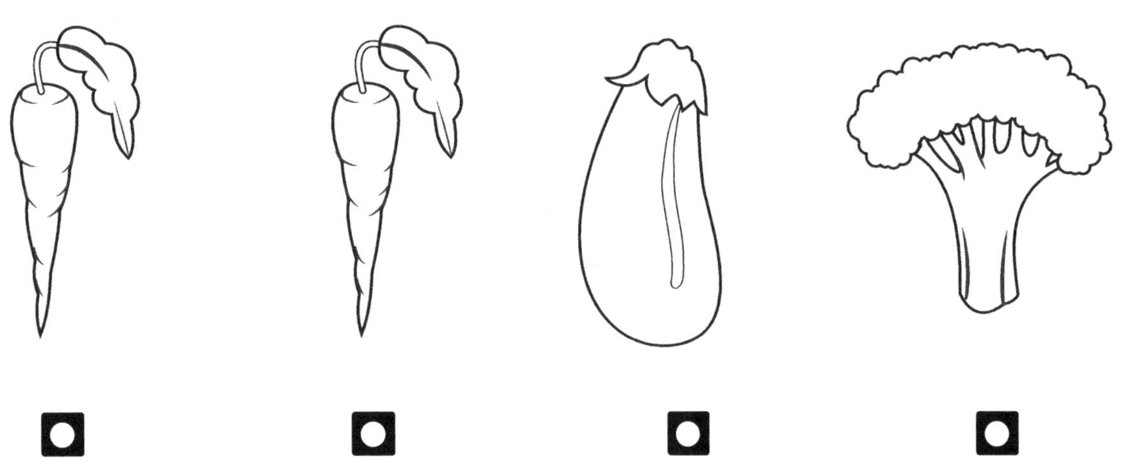

9. Mark the dog that is not the same as the others.

10. Mark the bird that is not the same as the others.

11. Mark the presents that are similar.

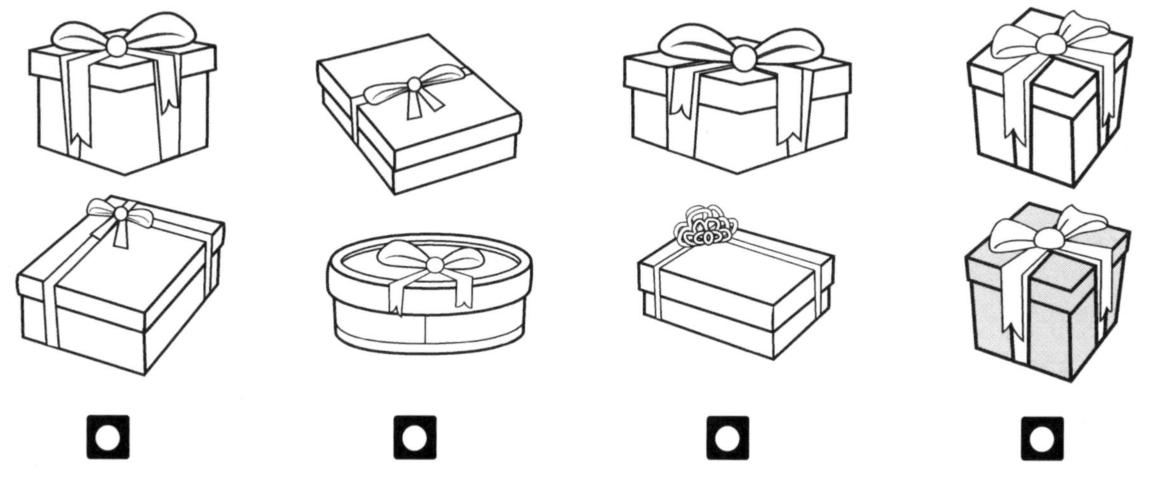

12. Mark the cat that is different.

13. Mark the fish that is not the same as the others.

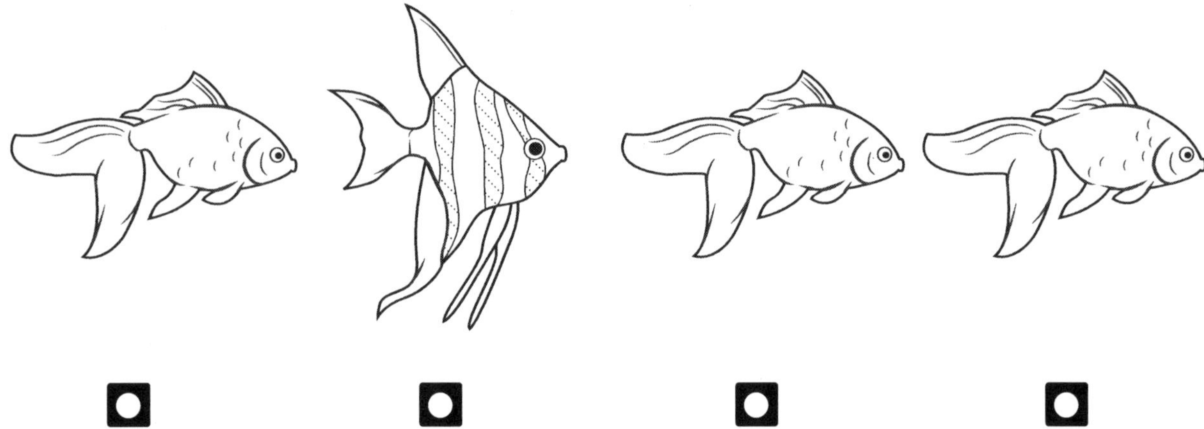

14. Mark the mittens that match.

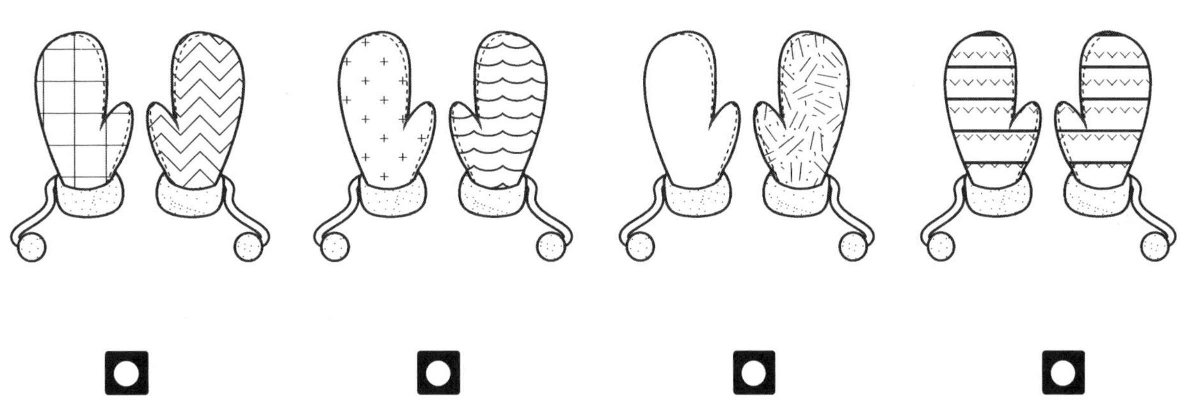

15. Mark the toy that is different.

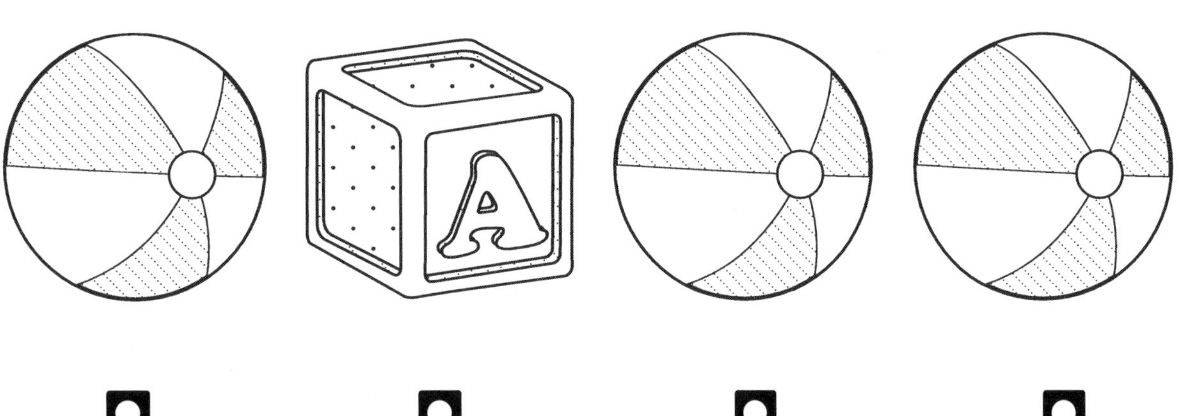

16. Mark the shallow water.

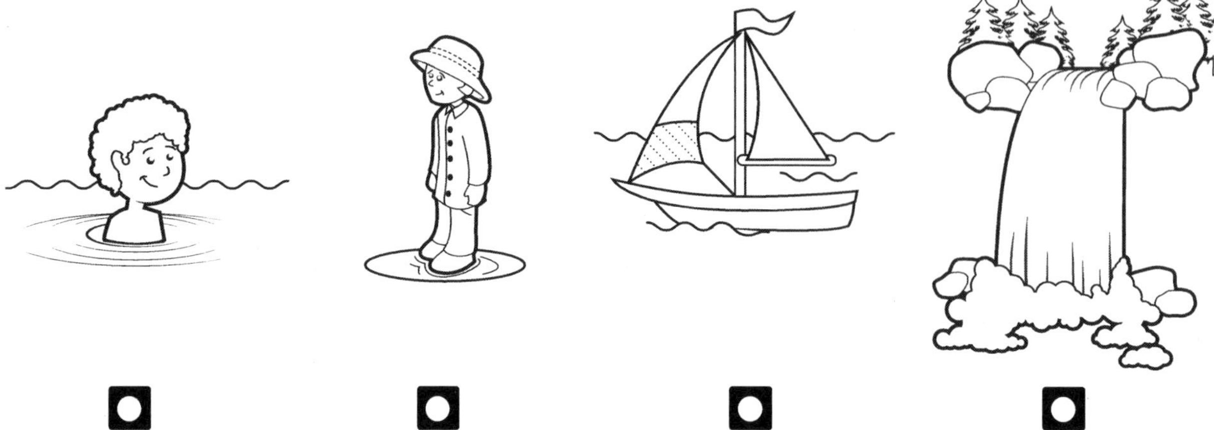

17. Mark the unequal glasses.

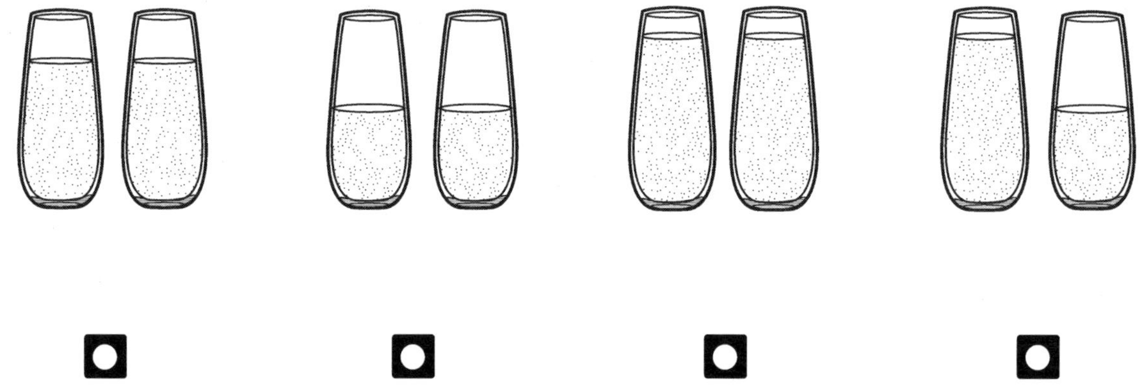

18. Mark the deep water.

19. Mark the narrow bookshelf.

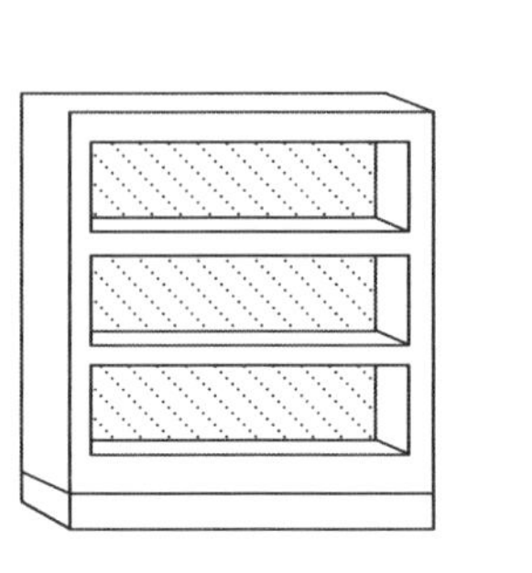 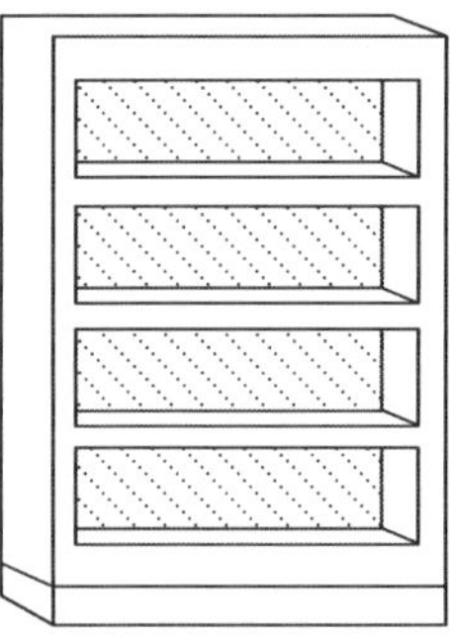 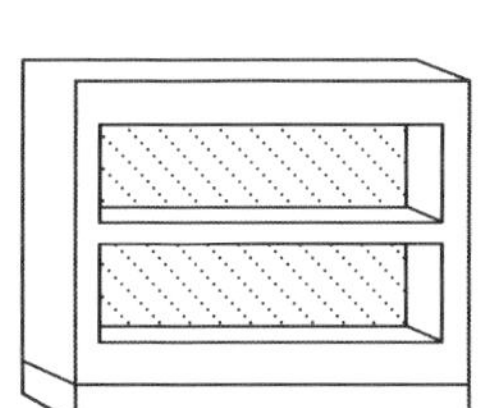 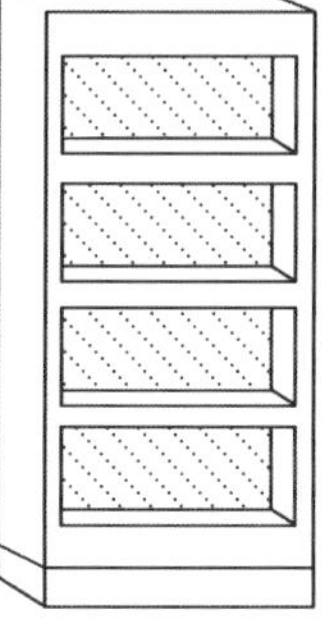

20. Mark the narrow ribbon.

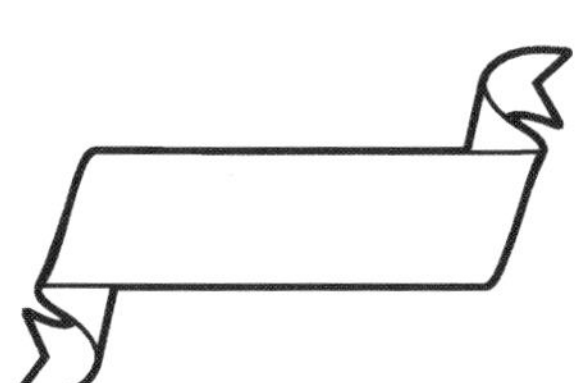 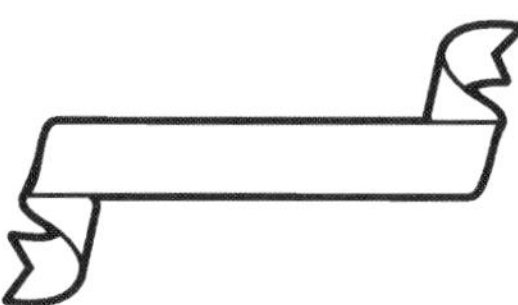  

21. Mark the deep water.

 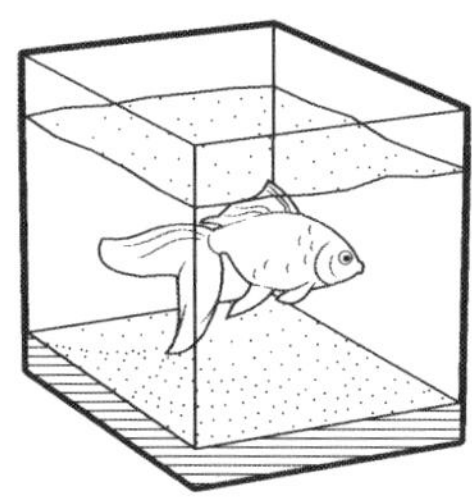  

22. Mark the little bird.

23. Mark the small balloon.

24. Mark the large hotdog.

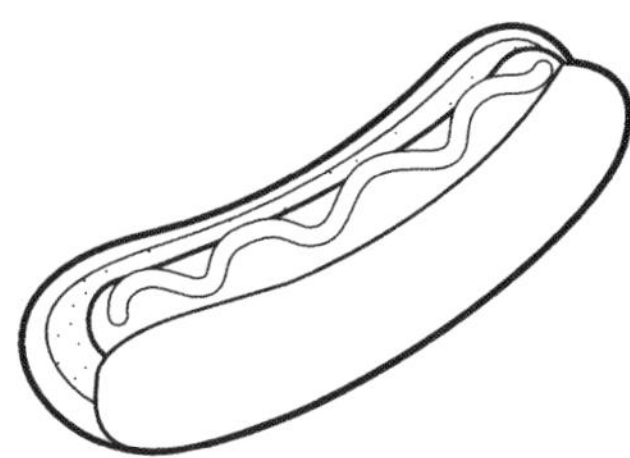  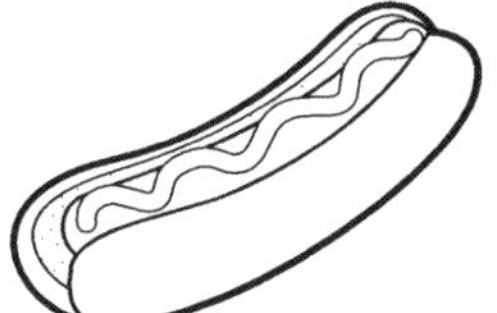 

 Bright Kids NYC Inc ©

25. Mark the little crayon.

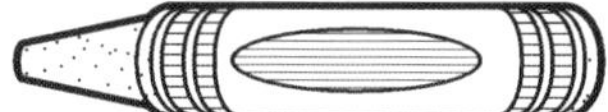
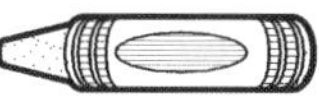
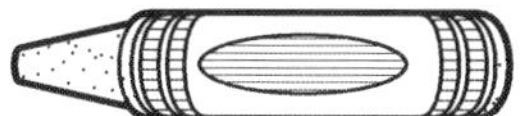
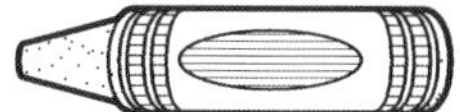

26. Mark the big tree.

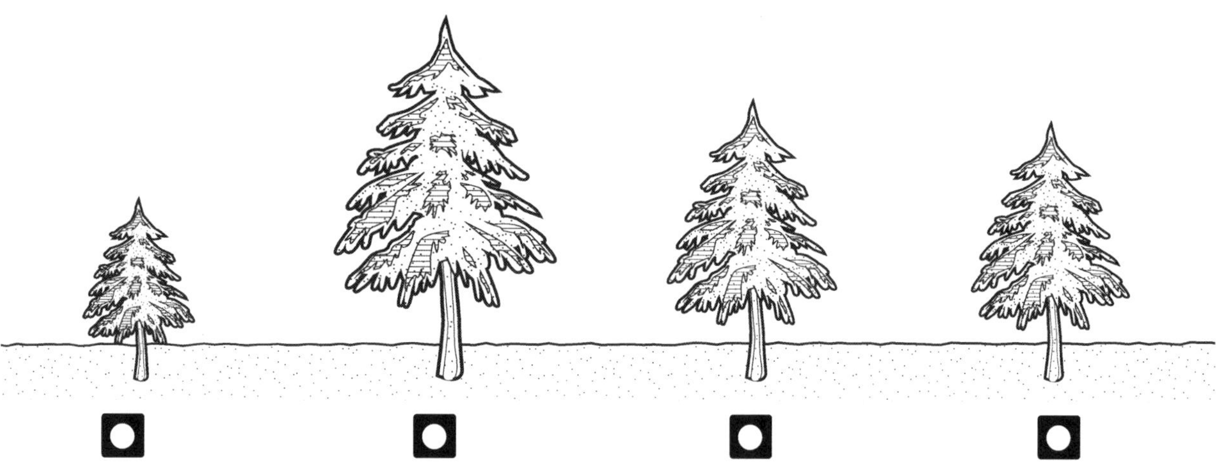

27. Mark the small vase.

28. Mark the large balloon.

29. Mark the tall child.

30. Mark flowers that are similar.

 Bright Kids NYC Inc ©

31. Mark the medium size ball.

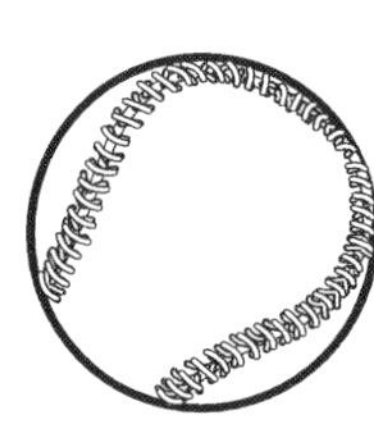

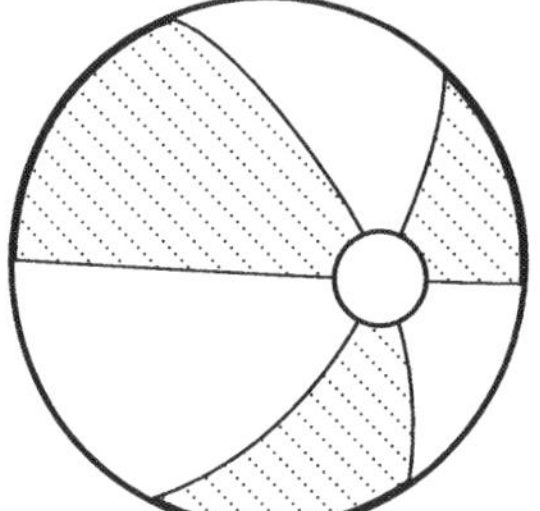

32. Mark the wide paint brush.

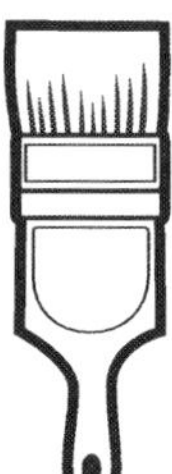

33. Mark the short person.

34. Mark the medium size cup.

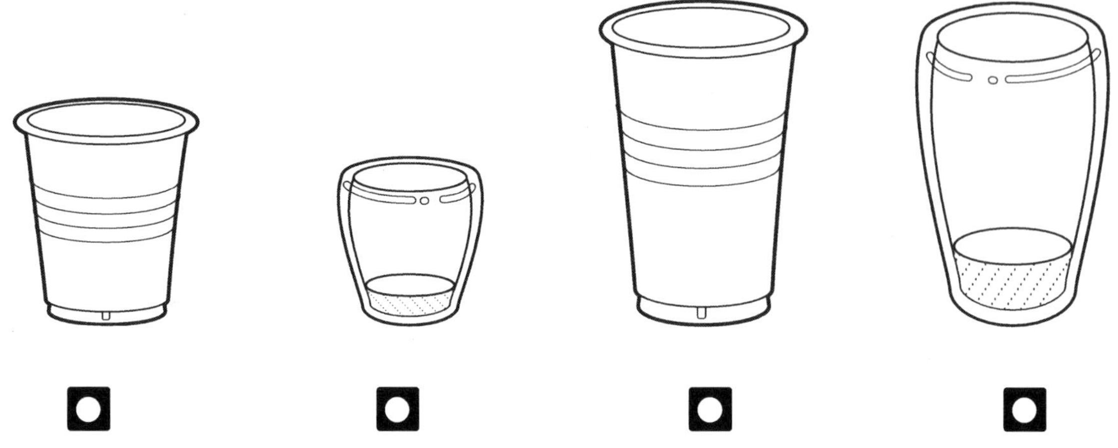

35. Mark the wide board.

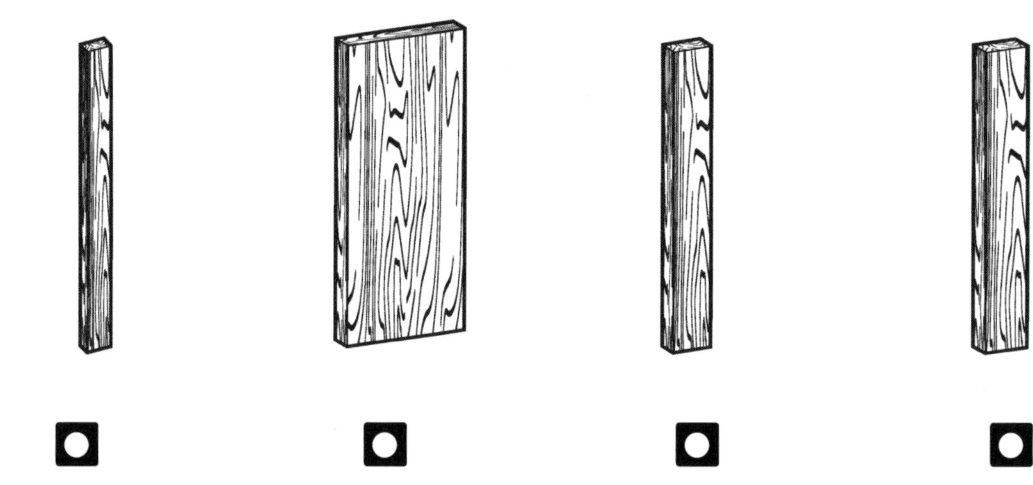

36. Mark the short tree.

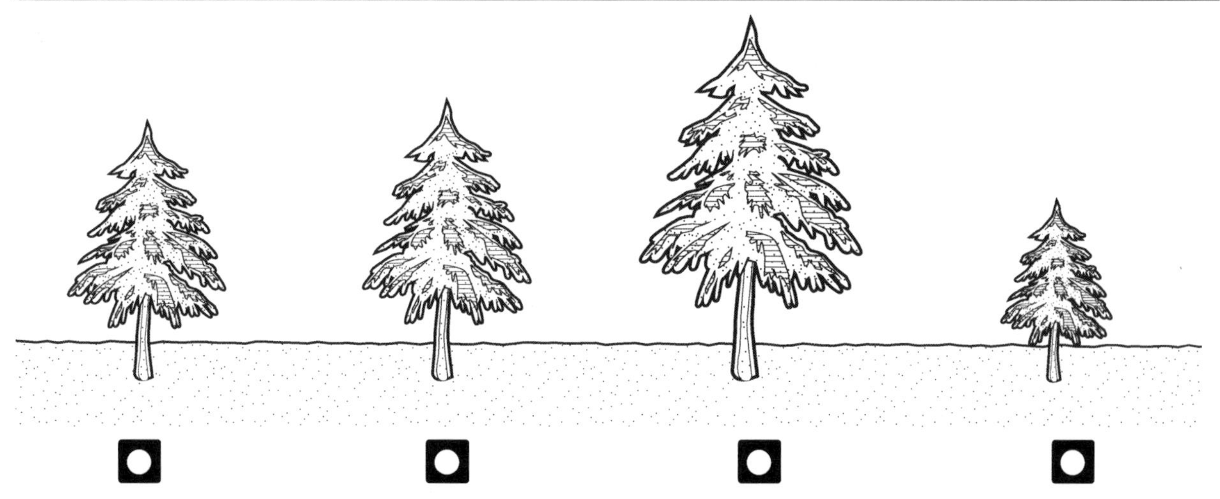

 Bright Kids NYC Inc ©

37. Mark the tall fence.

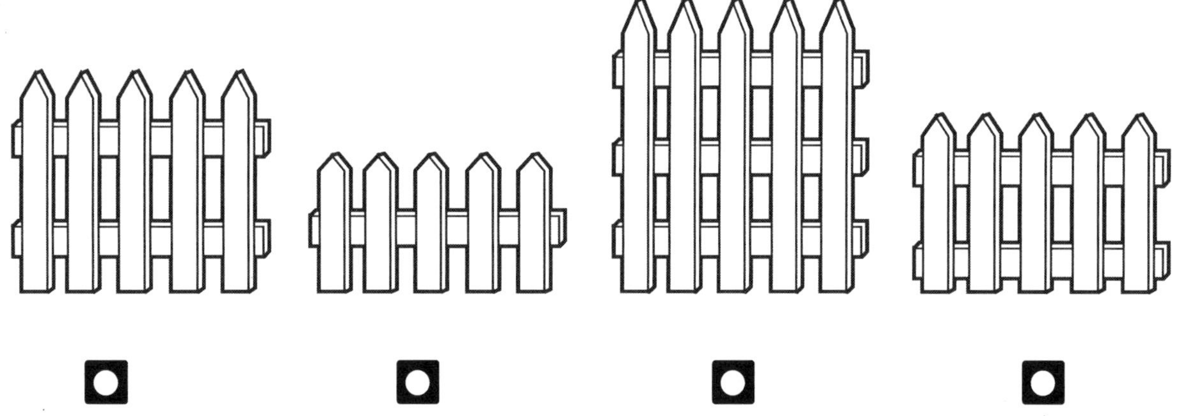

38. Mark the crayons that are alike.

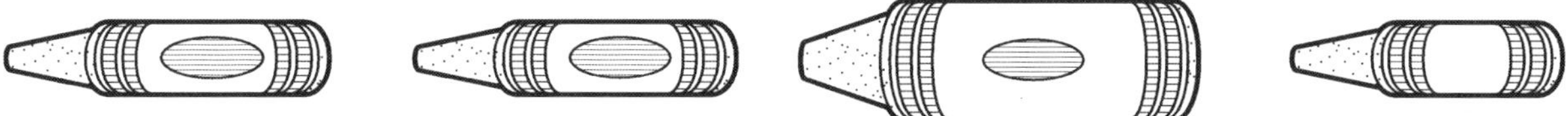

39. Mark the long crayon.

40. Mark the thick sandwich.

41. Mark the thin bottle.

 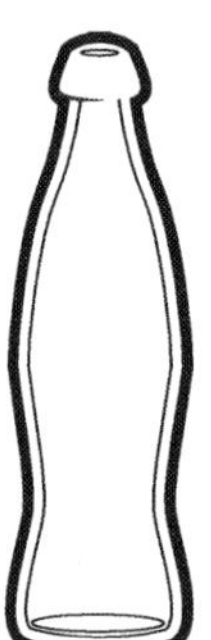  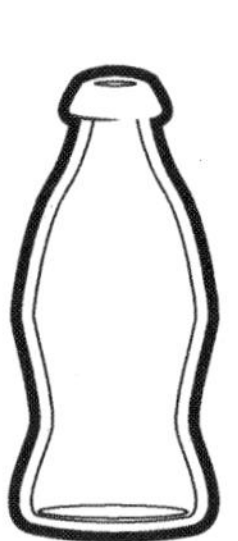

42. Mark the long ribbon.

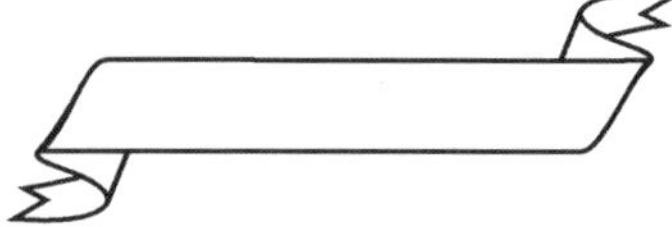 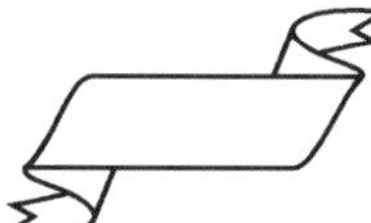 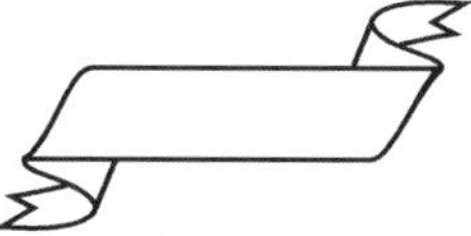 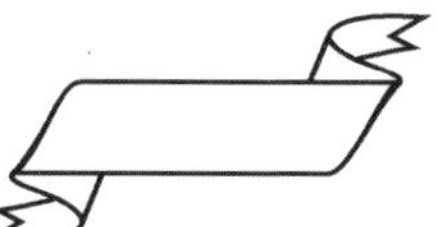

Bright Kids NYC Inc ©

43. Mark the thick notebook.

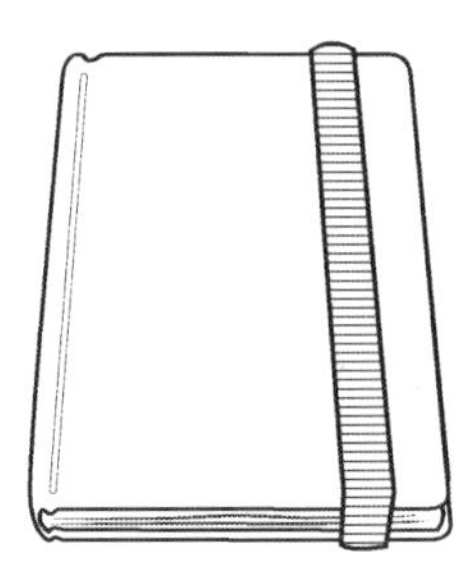
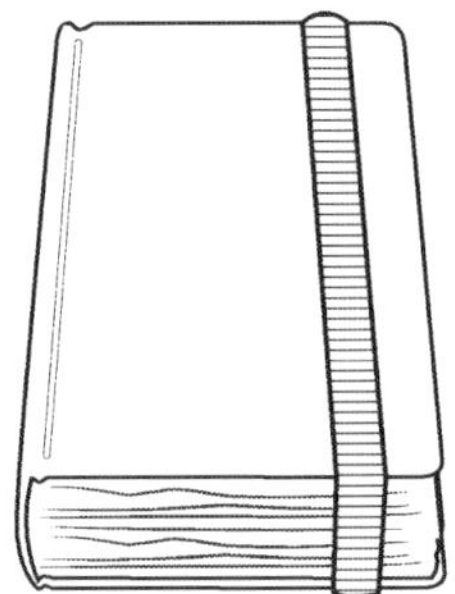
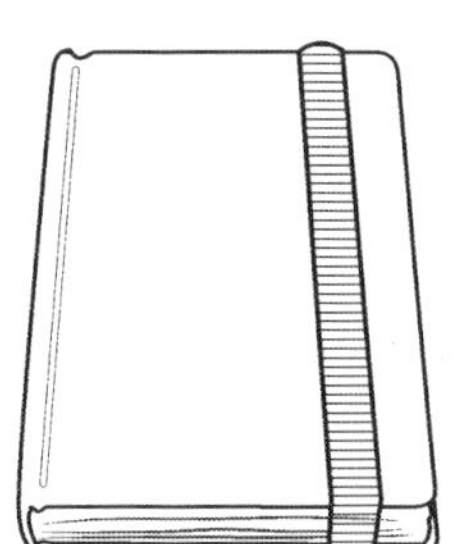
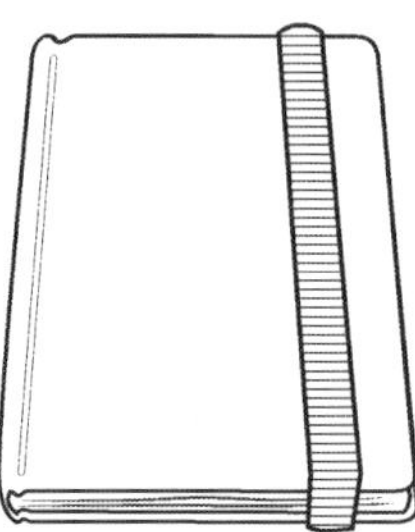

44. Mark the thin person.

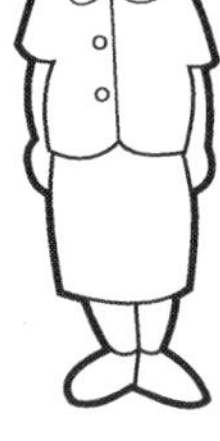

45. Mark the shallow water.

46. Mark the person playing something other than a piano.

47. Mark the pants that fit exactly.

  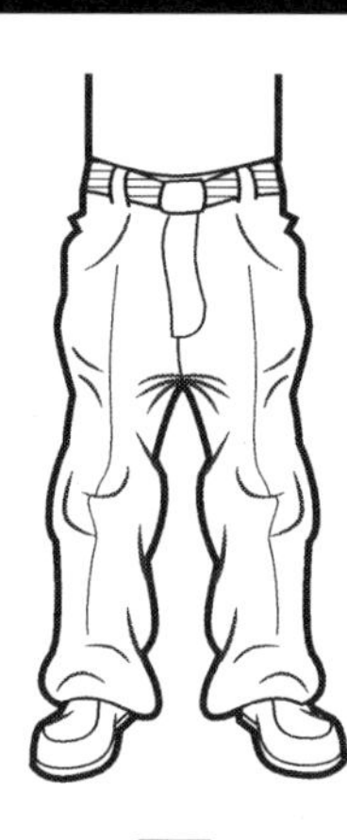 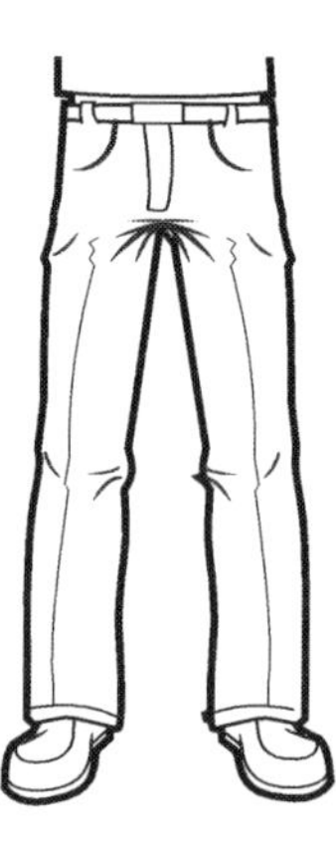

48. Mark the hat that fits exactly.

ANSWER KEY

1.	Picture 3	-	Equal sized sneakers
2.	Picture 2	-	Flat boxes
3.	Picture 4	-	Boy holding cookie
4.	Pictures 1/2	-	Two apples
5.	Picture 3	-	Third stool
6.	Pictures 1/2	-	Two books with cats on the cover
7.	Picture 2	-	Two sandals
8.	Pictures 1/2	-	Two carrots
9.	Picture 2	-	Second dog
10.	Picture 1	-	Parrot
11.	Picture 4	-	Grey present and white present
12.	Picture 3	-	Third cat
13.	Picture 2	-	Second fish
14.	Picture 4	-	Fourth pair of mittens
15.	Picture 2	-	Toy block
16.	Picture 2	-	Child standing in puddle
17.	Picture 4	-	Fourth pair of glasses
18.	Picture 2	-	Sailboat in deep water
19.	Picture 4	-	Fourth bookshelf
20.	Picture 2	-	Second ribbon
21.	Picture 4	-	Sailboat in deep water
22.	Picture 2	-	Second parrot
23.	Picture 3	-	Third balloon
24.	Picture 1	-	First hotdog
25.	Picture 2	-	Second crayon
26.	Picture 2	-	Second tree
27.	Picture 1	-	First vase
28.	Picture 4	-	Fourth balloon
29.	Picture 4	-	Fourth child
30.	Picture 1/2	-	First and second flower
31.	Picture 2	-	Second ball
32.	Picture 4	-	Fourth paint brush
33.	Picture 2	-	Second person
34.	Picture 1	-	First cup
35.	Picture 2	-	Second board
36.	Picture 4	-	Fourth tree
37	Picture 3	-	Third fence
38.	Picture 1/2	-	First and second crayon
39.	Picture 1	-	First crayon
40.	Picture 1	-	First sandwich

41.	Picture 2	-	Second bottle
42.	Picture 1	-	First ribbon
43.	Picture 2	-	Second notebook
44.	Picture 3	-	Third person
45.	Picture 2	-	Girl standing in puddle
46.	Picture 2	-	Boy playing congas
47.	Picture 4	-	Fourth pair of pants
48.	Picture 4	-	Person wearing wool hat

123
ABC

SECTION FIVE:
SHAPES

1. Mark the cone.

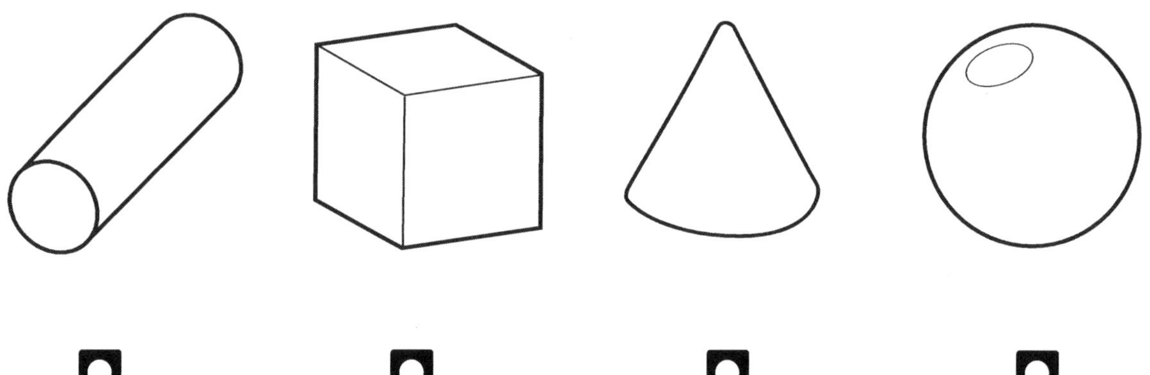

2. Mark the heart.

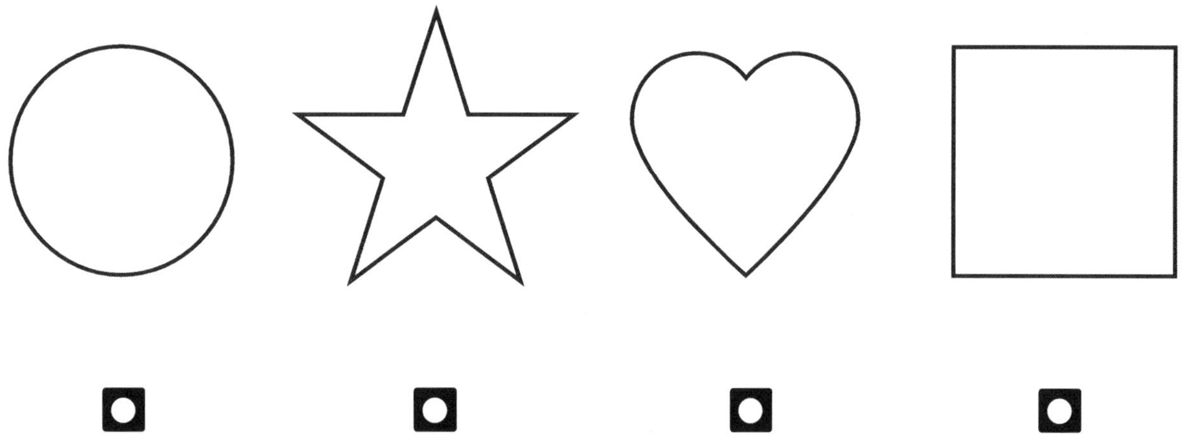

3. Mark the star.

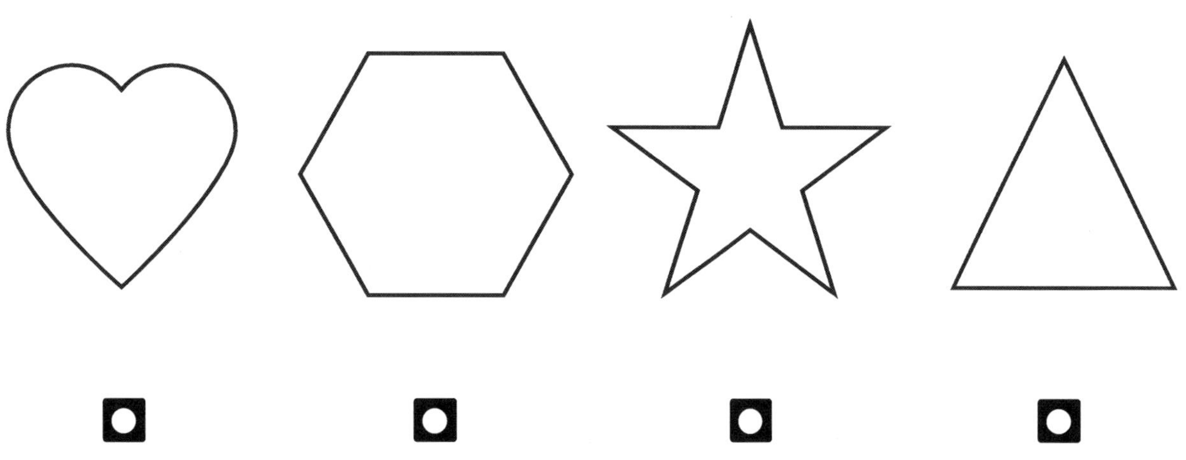

4. Mark the circle.

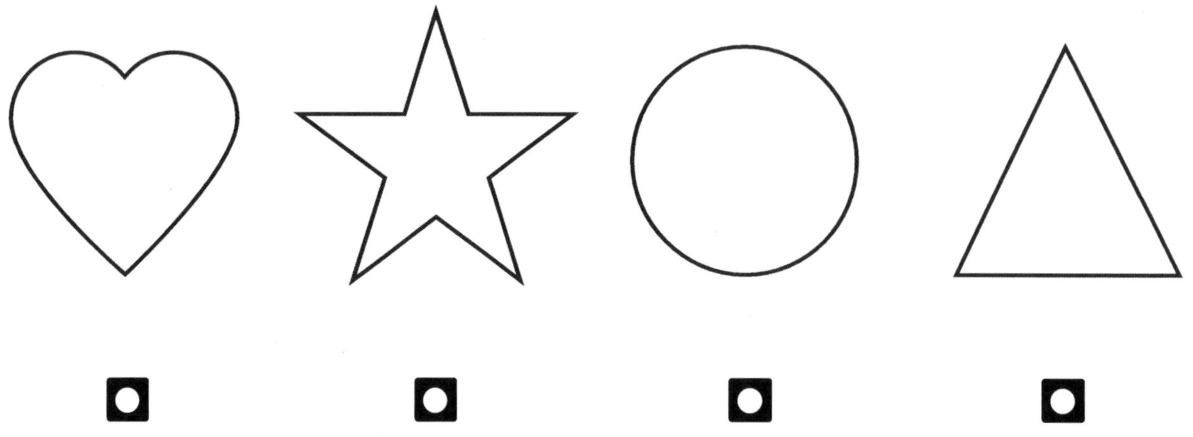

5. Mark the column.

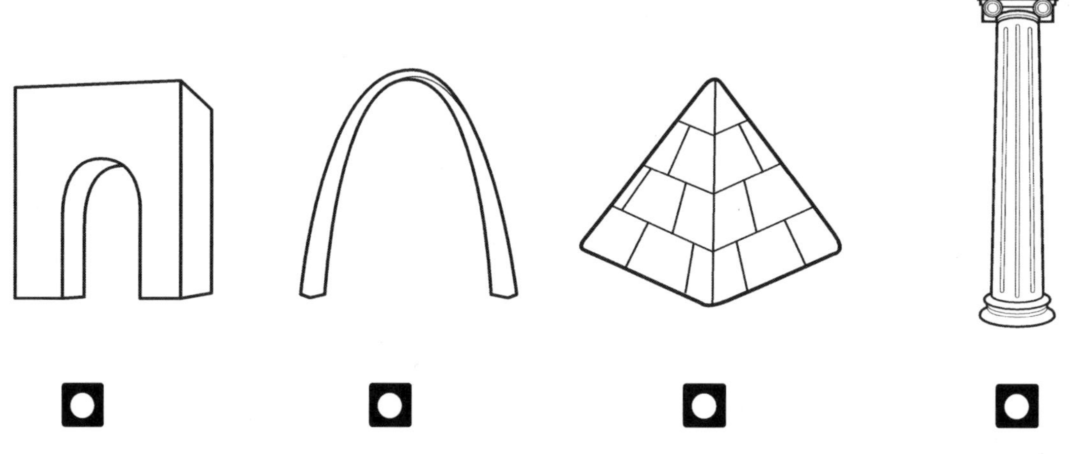

6. Mark the triangle.

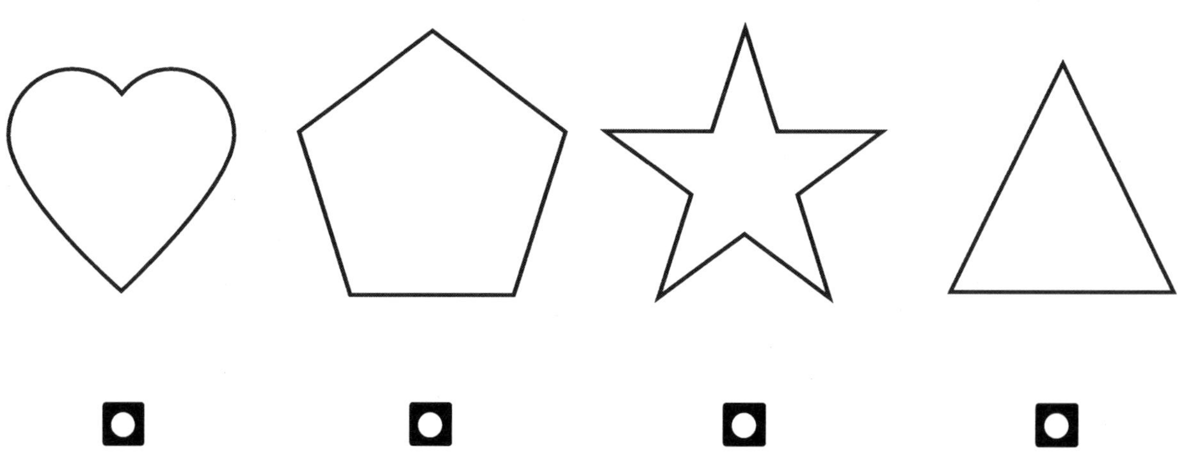

7. Mark the rectangle.

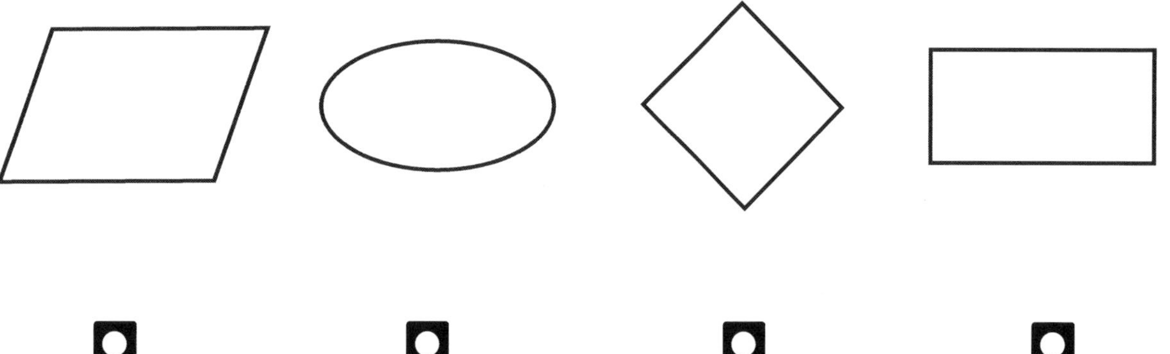

8. Mark the oval sticker.

9. Mark the sign that is shaped like a diamond.

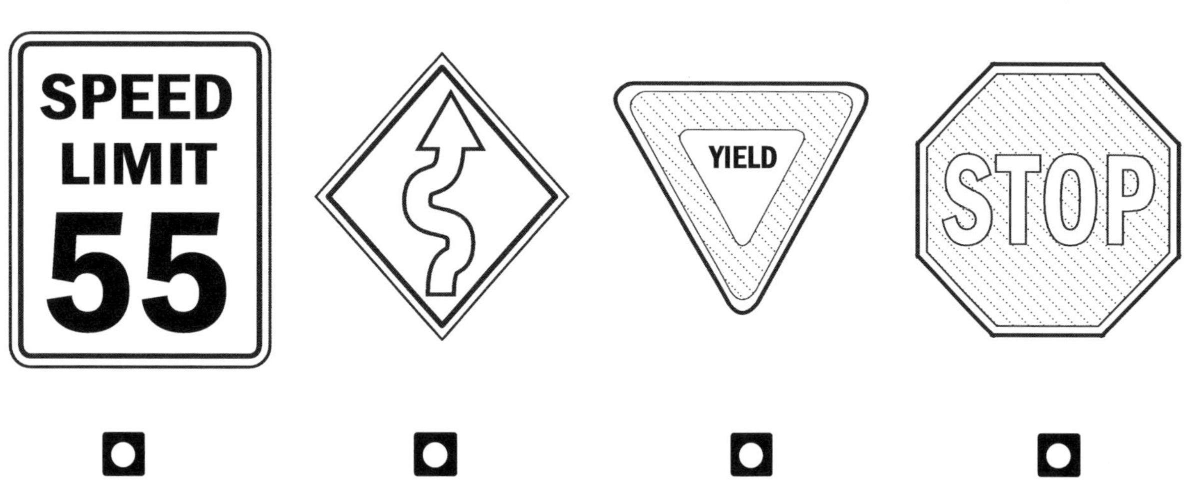

10. Mark the sign that is shaped like a rectangle.

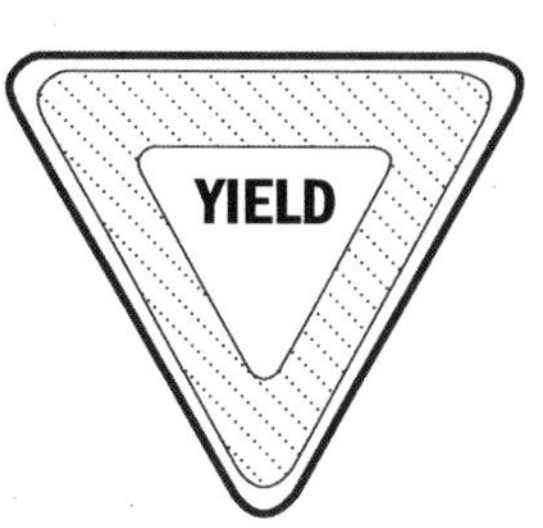

11. Mark the oval.

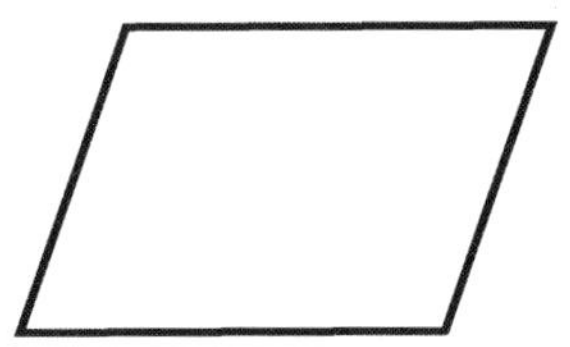
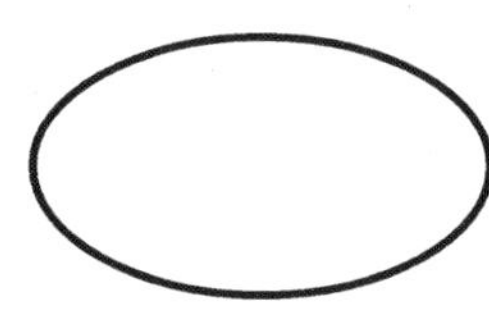
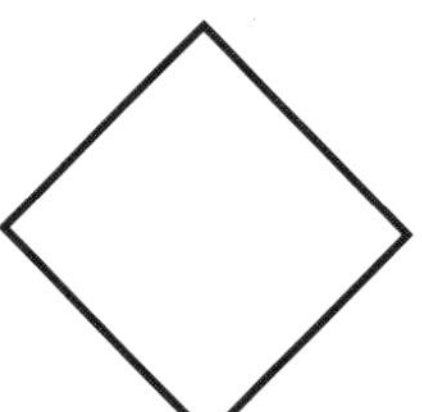

12. Mark the circle shaped sticker.

 Bright Kids NYC Inc ©

13. Mark the oval frame.

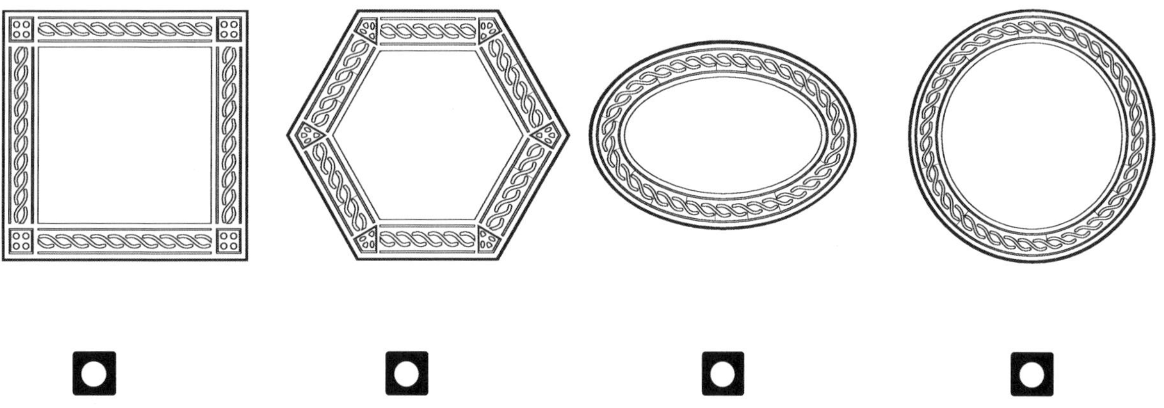

14. Mark the diamond.

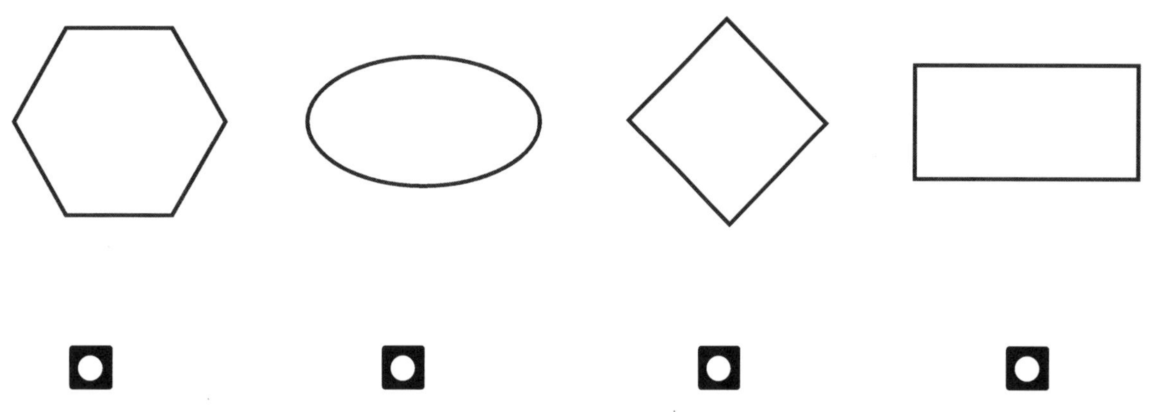

15. Mark the item shaped like a sphere.

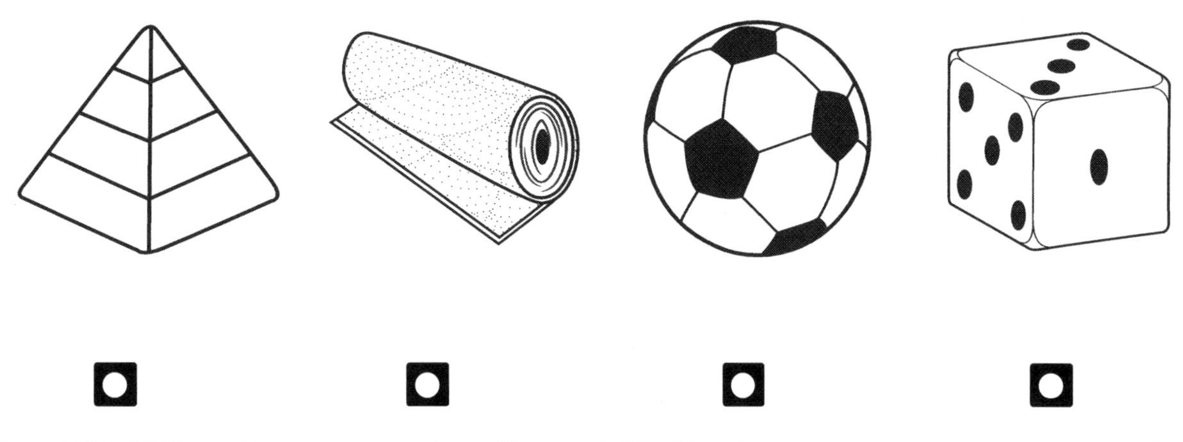

16. Mark the item shaped like a cube.

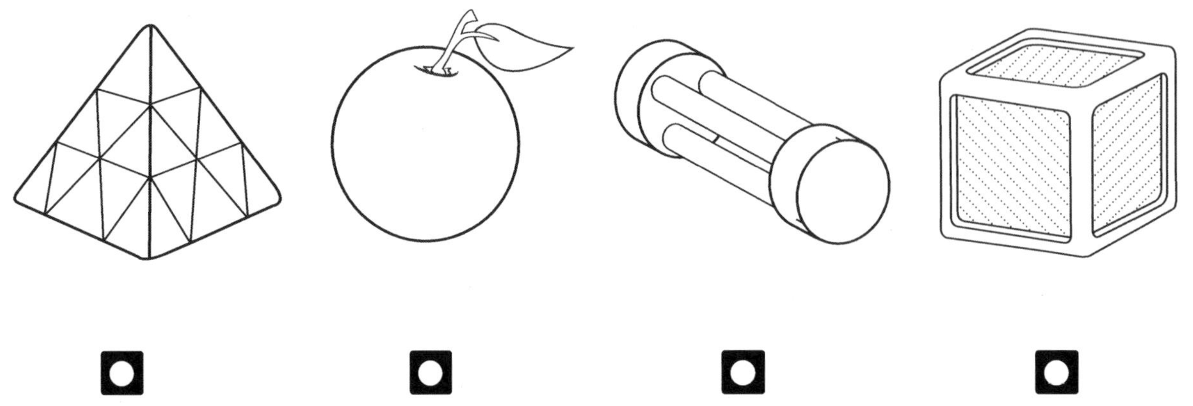

17. Mark the item shaped like a pyramid.

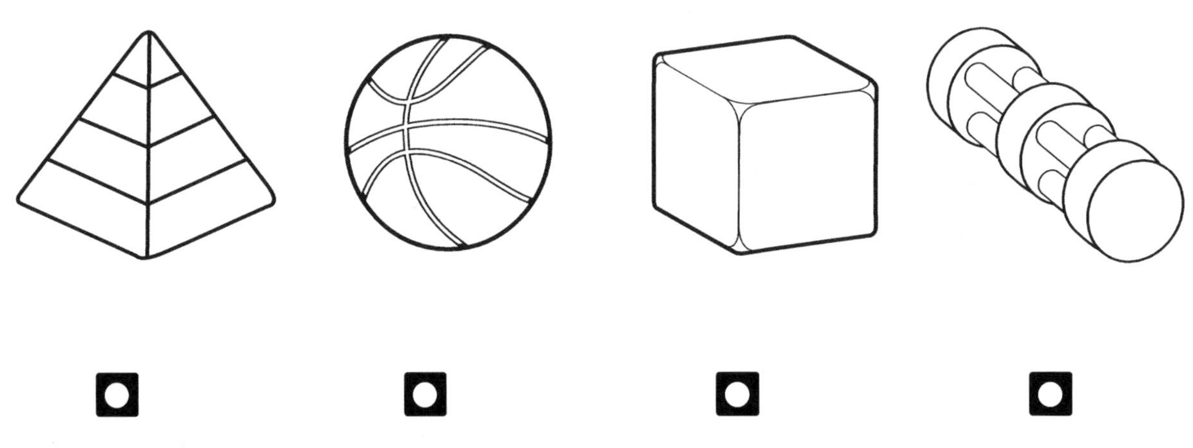

18. Mark the item shaped like a cylinder.

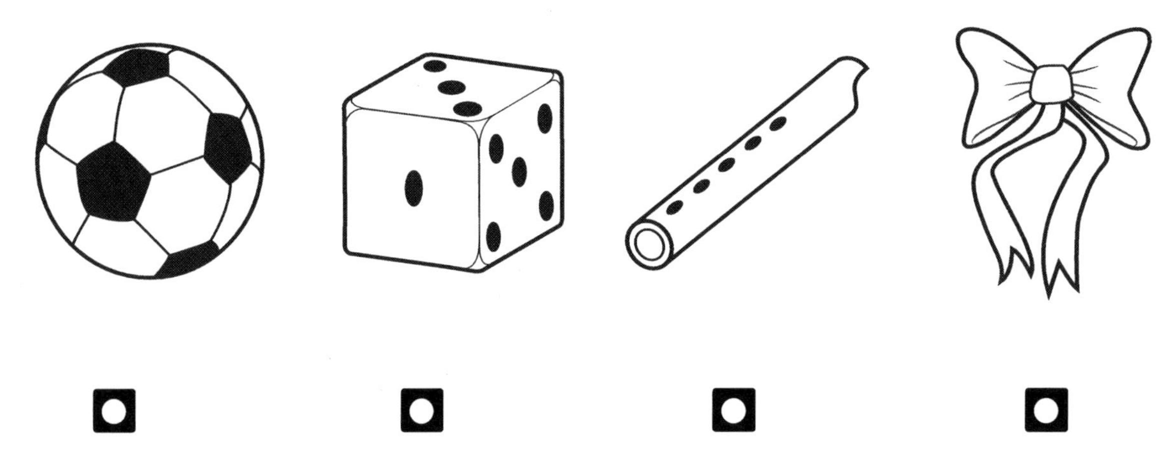

Bright Kids NYC Inc ©

19. Mark the item shaped like a sphere.

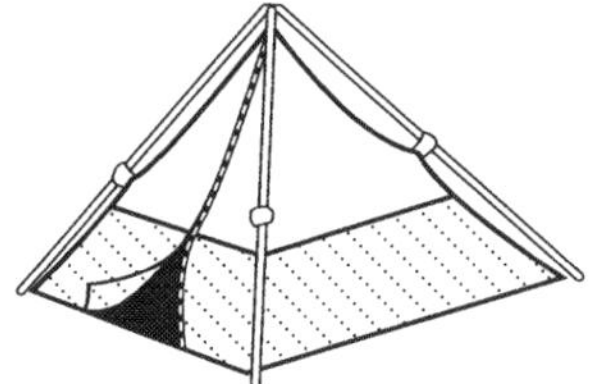
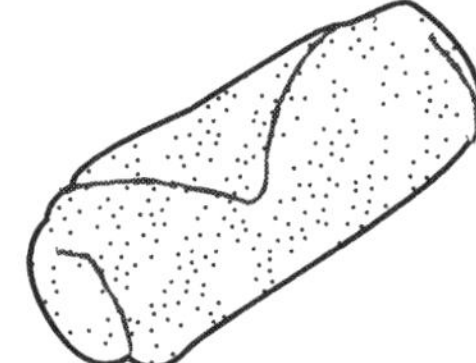

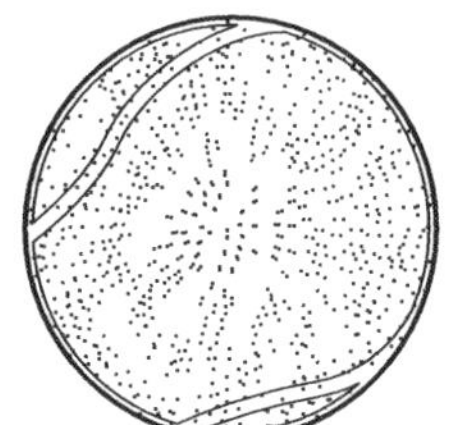

20. Mark the cube.

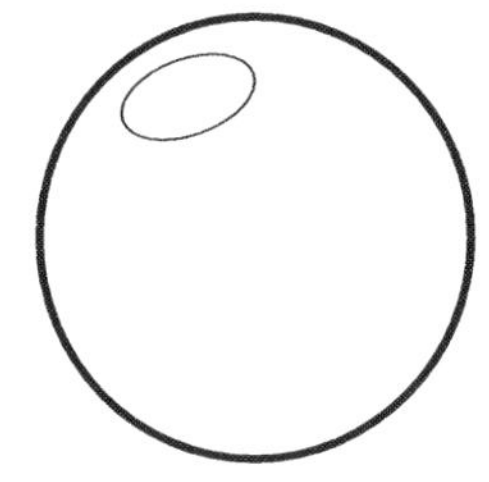
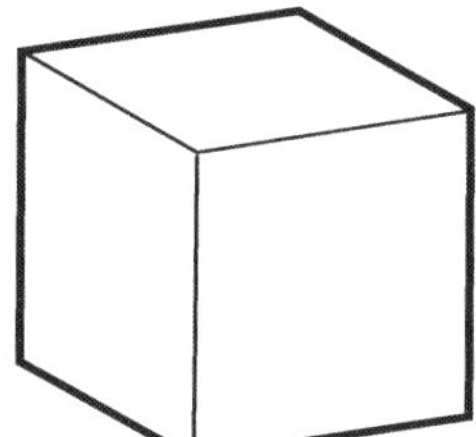
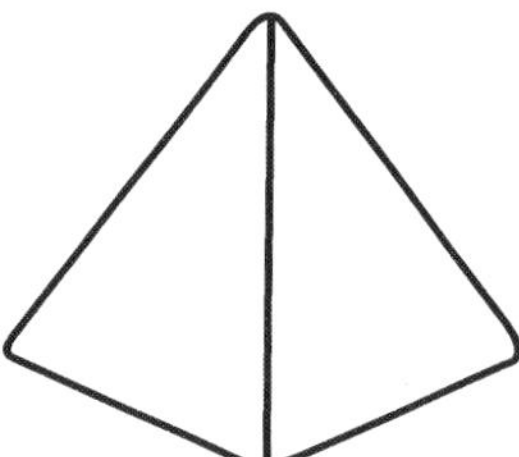
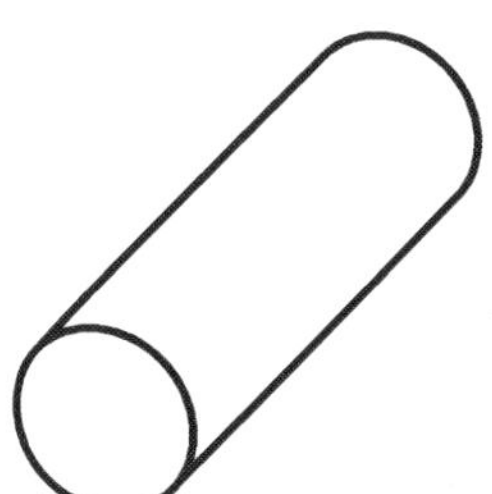

21. Mark the item shaped like a pyramid.

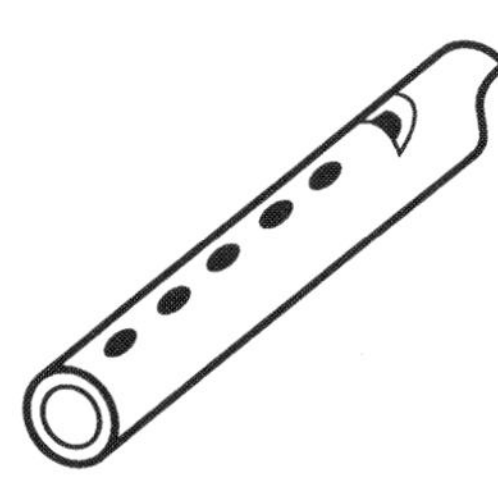

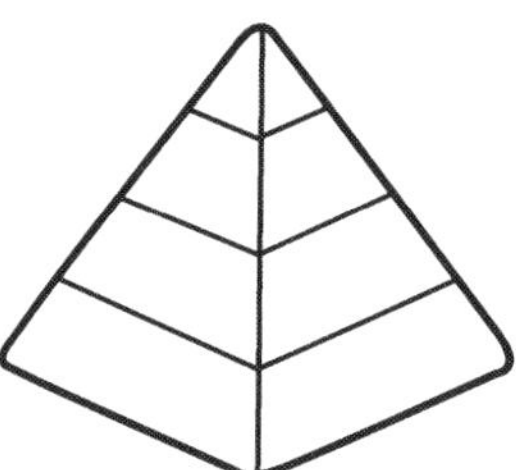

22. Mark the item shaped like a cylinder.

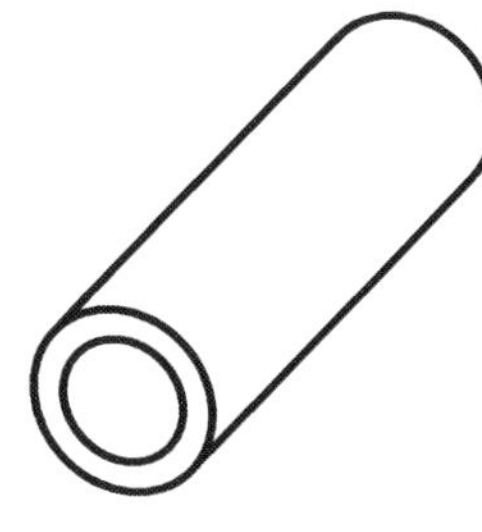
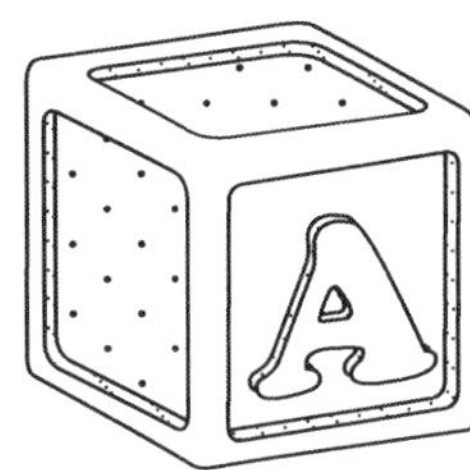

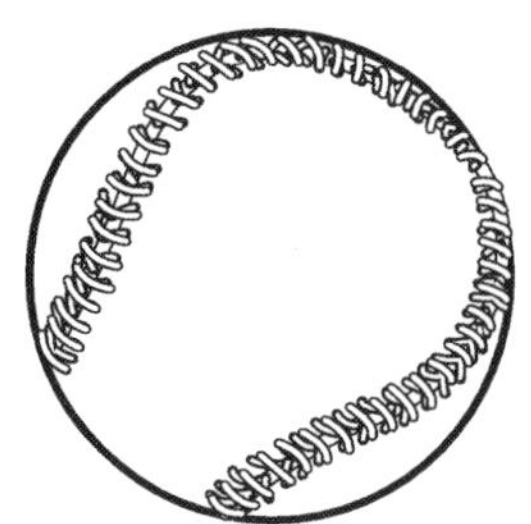
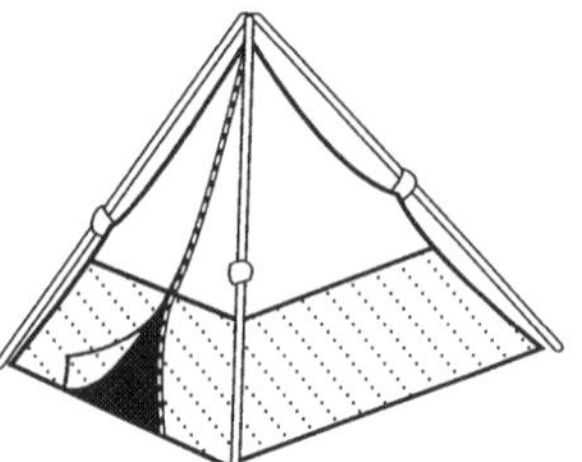

23. Mark the straight ruler.

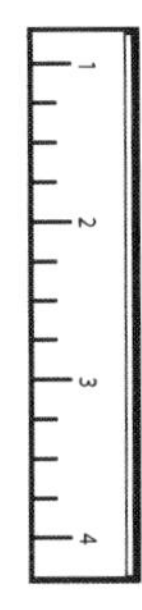
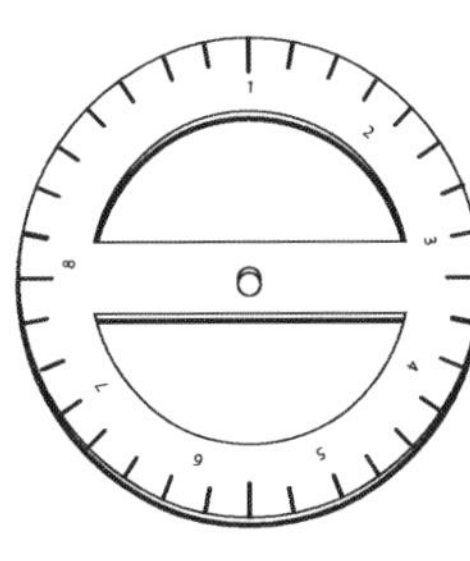
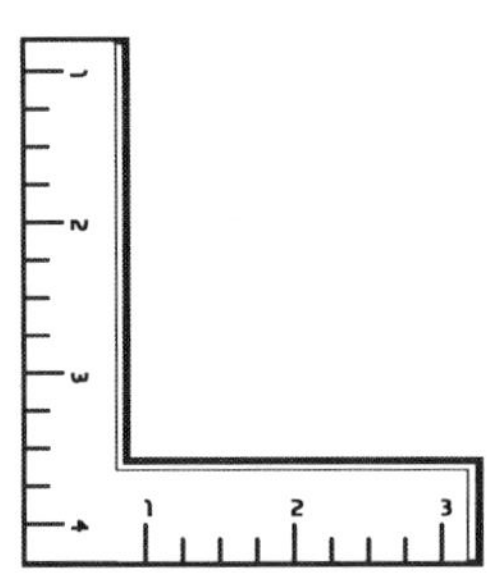
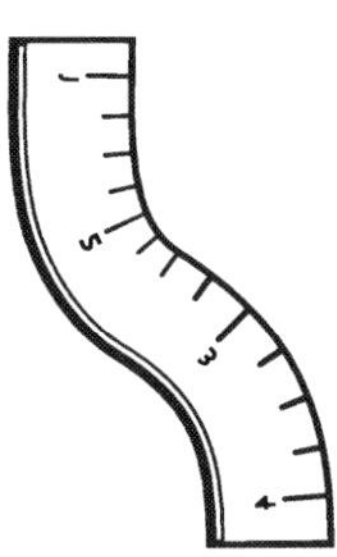

24. Mark the round cracker.

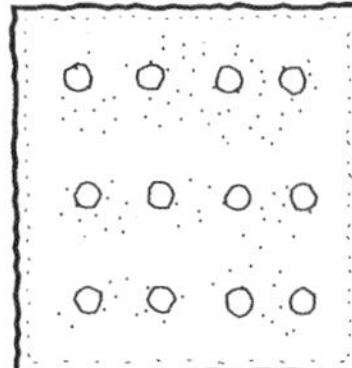
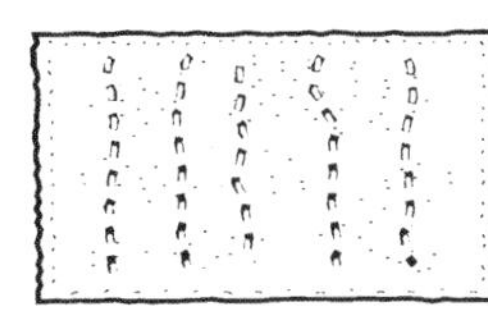
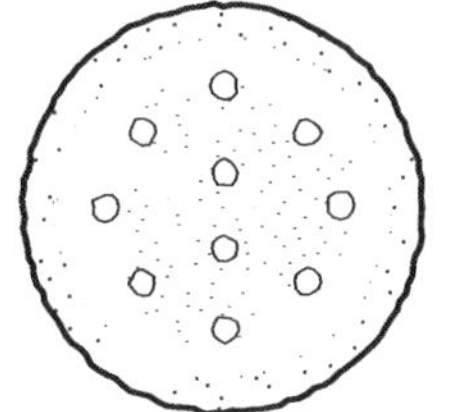
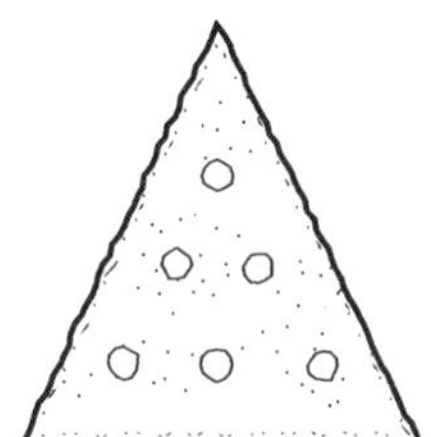

25. Mark the curved ruler.

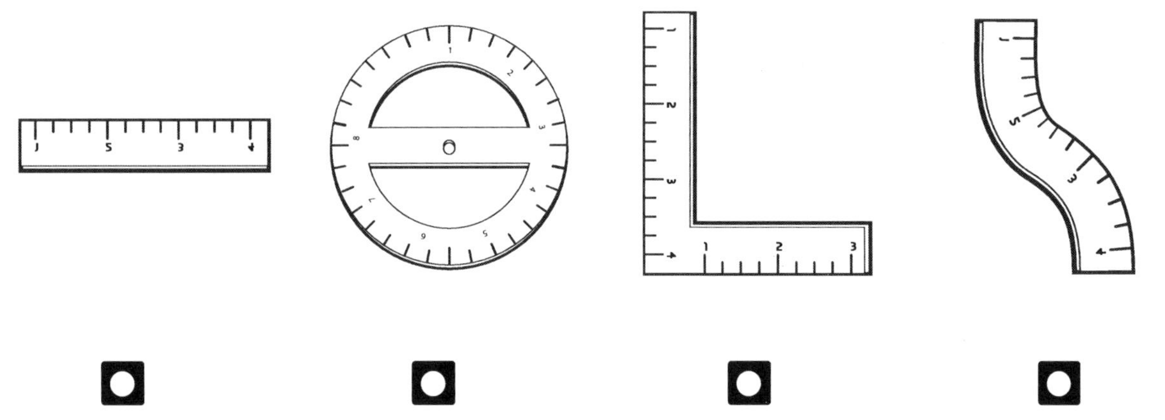

26. Mark the ribbon that is at an angle.

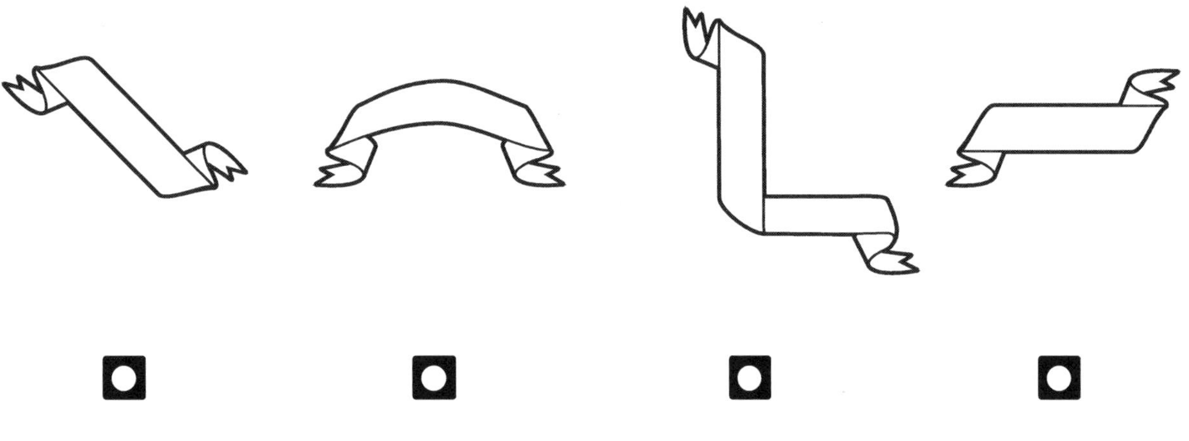

27. Mark the square mirror.

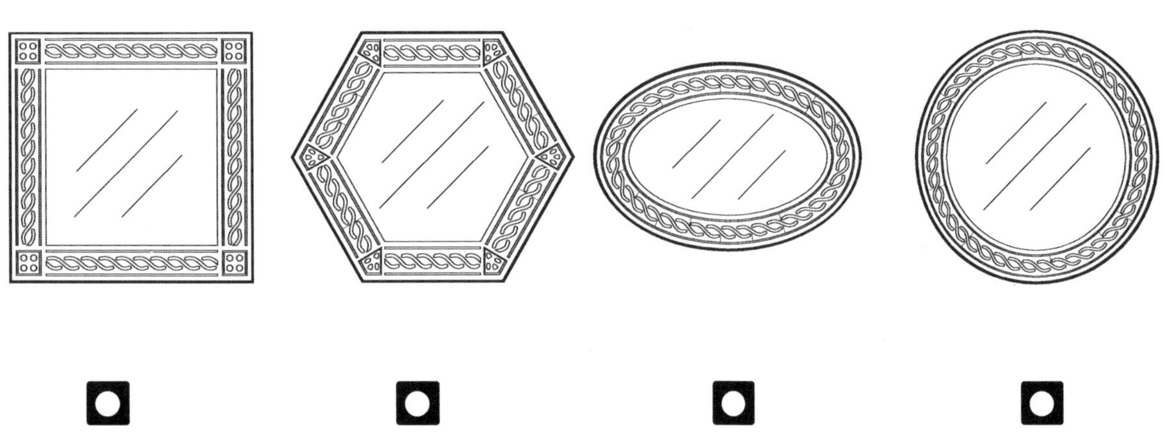

28. Mark the check mark.

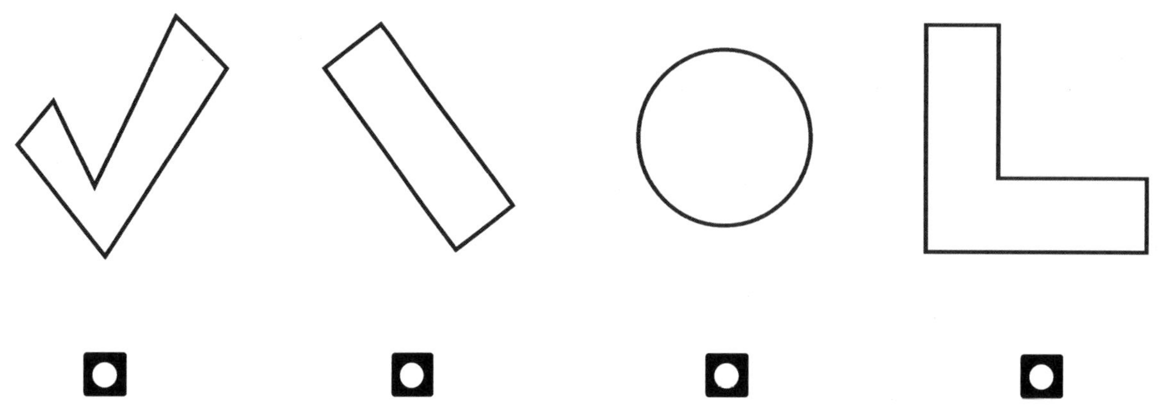

29. Mark the diagonal line.

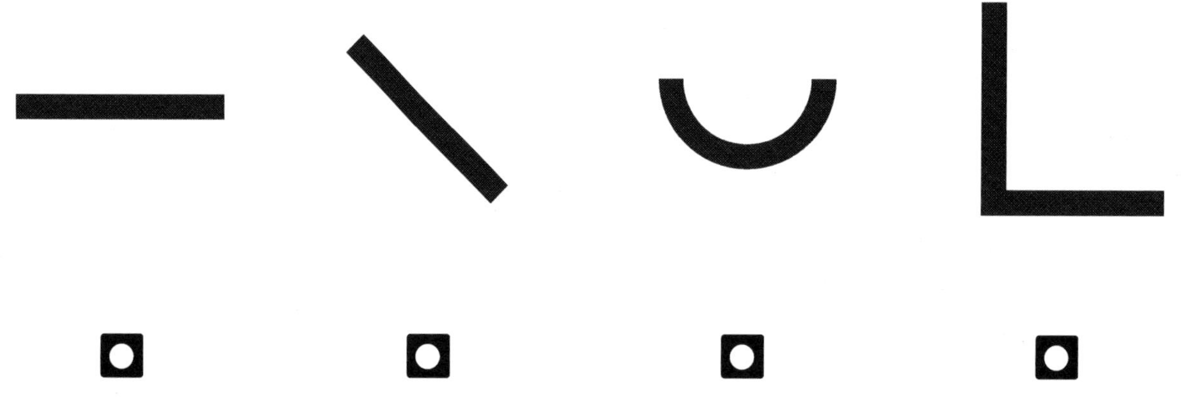

30. Mark the chickens in a row.

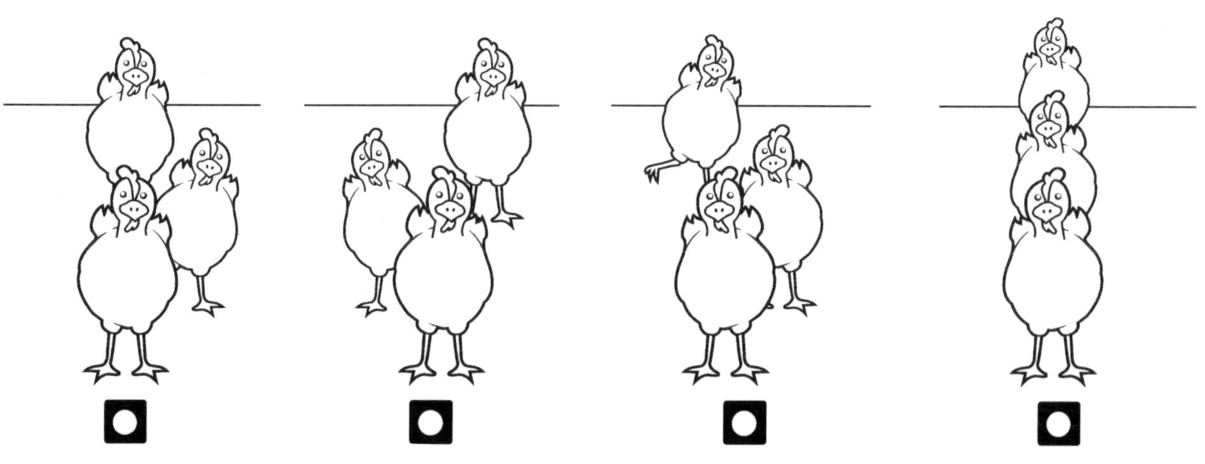

 Bright Kids NYC Inc ©

ANSWER KEY

1.	Picture 3	-	Cone
2.	Picture 3	-	Heart
3.	Picture 3	-	Star
4.	Picture 3	-	Circle
5.	Picture 4	-	Column
6.	Picture 4	-	Triangle
7.	Picture 4	-	Rectangle
8.	Picture 2	-	Oval cat sticker
9.	Picture 2	-	Curved road sign
10.	Picture 1	-	Speed limit sign
11.	Picture 2	-	Oval
12.	Picture 1	-	Circle shaped sticker
13.	Picture 3	-	Oval frame
14.	Picture 3	-	Diamond
15.	Picture 3	-	Soccer ball
16.	Picture 4	-	Toy block
17.	Picture 1	-	Pyramid toy
18.	Picture 3	-	Flute
19.	Picture 4	-	Tennis ball
20.	Picture 2	-	Cube
21.	Picture 4	-	Pyramid toy
22.	Picture 1	-	Tube
23.	Picture 1	-	First ruler
24.	Picture 3	-	Third cracker
25.	Picture 4	-	Fourth ruler
26.	Picture 1	-	First ribbon
27.	Picture 1	-	Square mirror
28.	Picture 1	-	Check mark
29.	Picture 2	-	Diagonal line
30.	Picture 4	-	Chickens in a row

123
ABC

SECTION SIX:
DIRECTION/POSITION

1. Mark the items that are open.

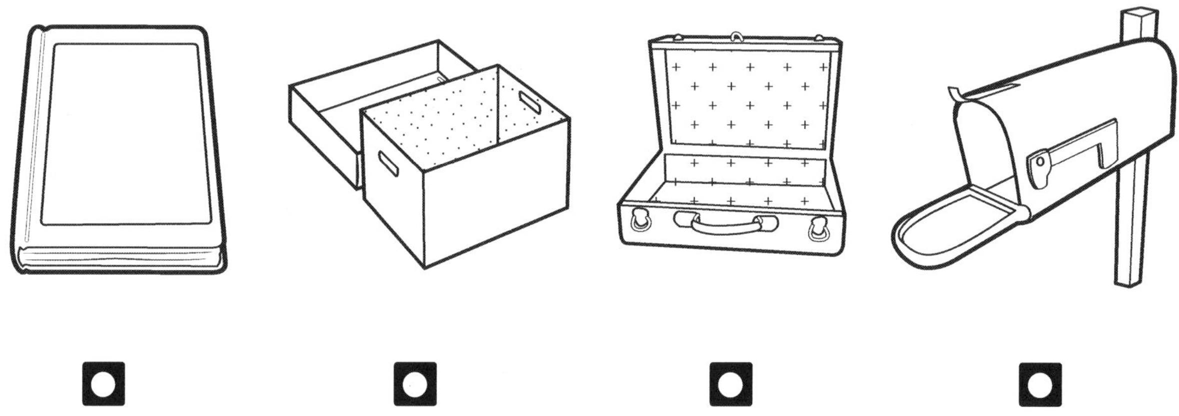

2. Mark the cat that is on the table.

3. Mark the items that are closed.

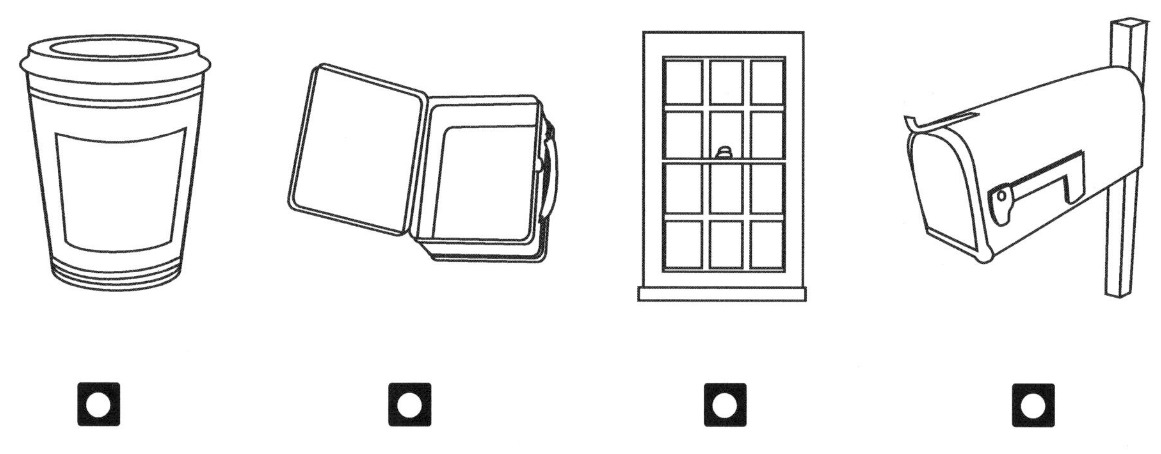

4. Mark the items that are open.

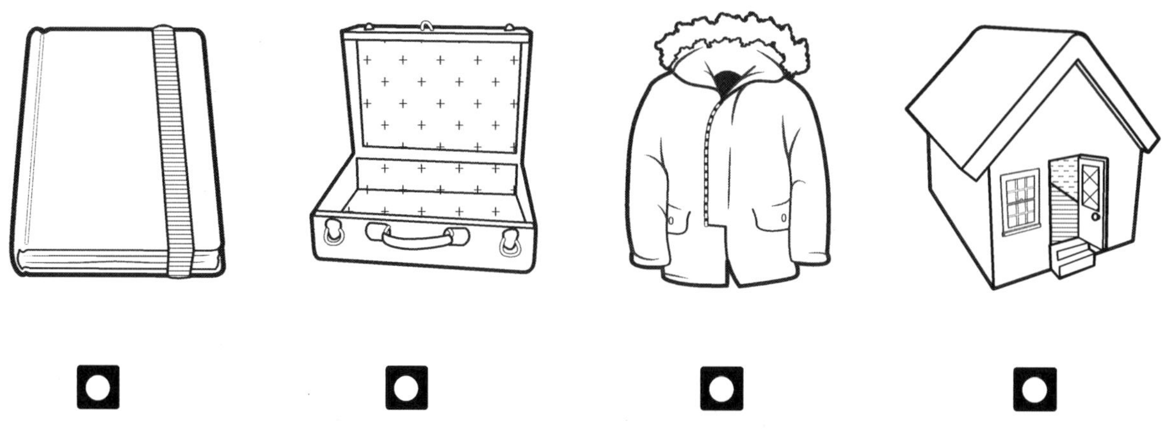

5. Mark the items that have something in them.

6. Mark the animals that are out of their cages.

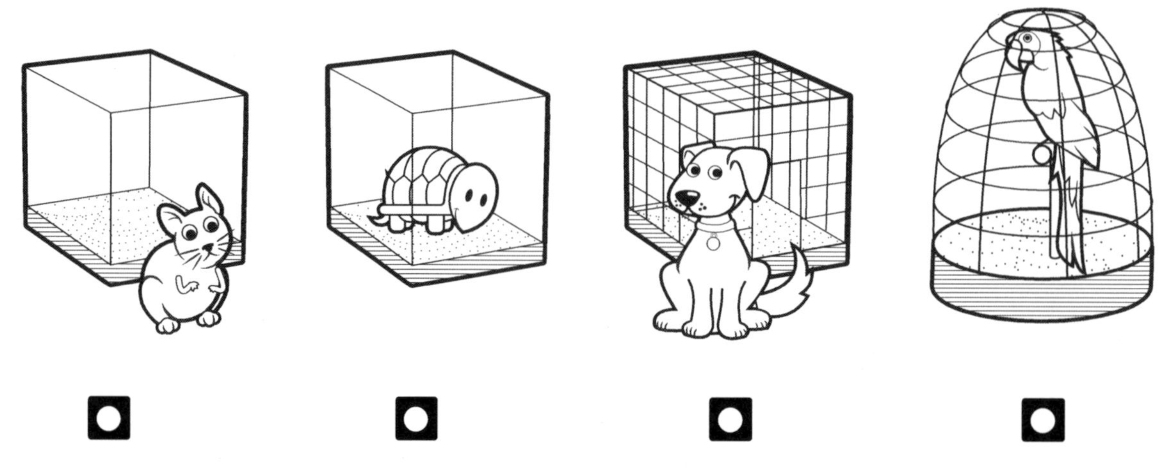

Bright Kids NYC Inc ©

7. Mark the toys that are off of the table.

8. Mark the animal that is in its cage.

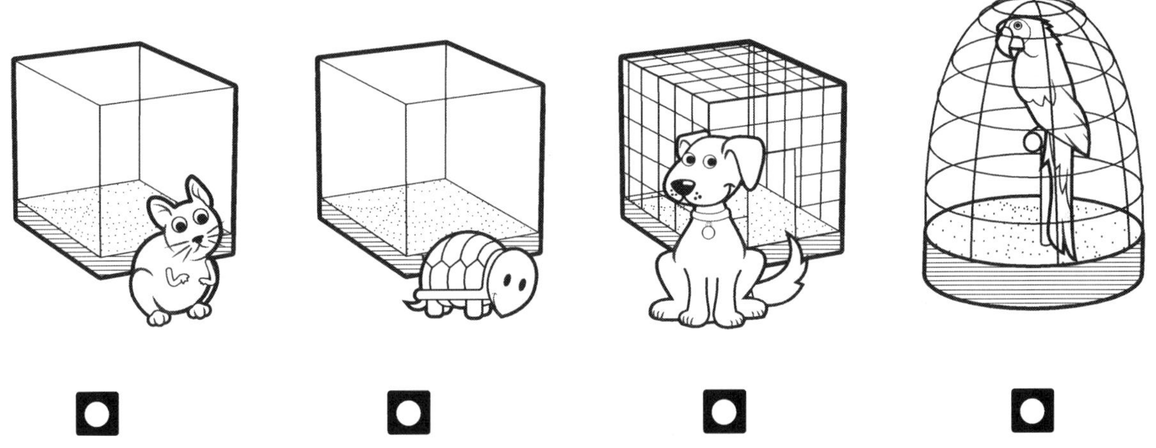

9. Mark the stamp that is on the envelope.

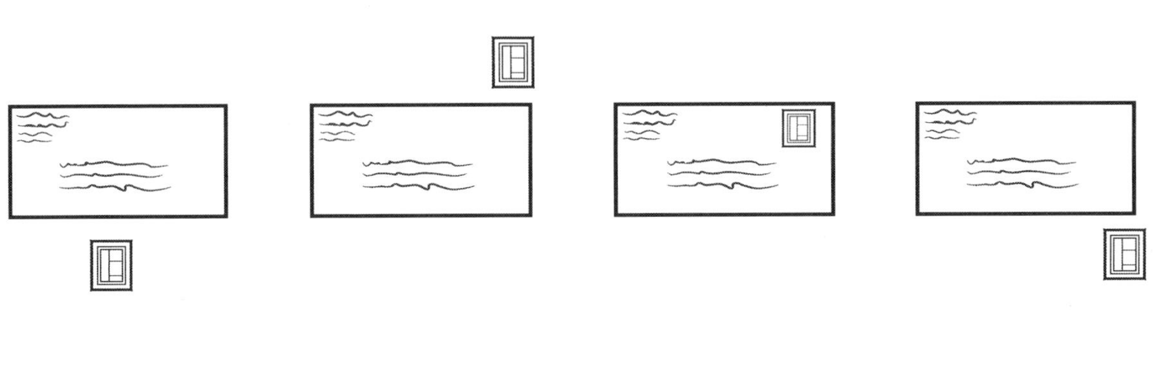

10. Mark the ball that is over the goal.

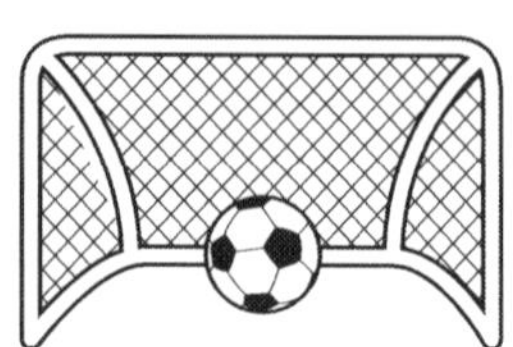

11. Mark the girl who is under the water.

12. Mark the girl who has a bracelet around her wrist.

13. Mark the knife that is cutting through the cake.

14. Mark the dog that is jumping over the fence.

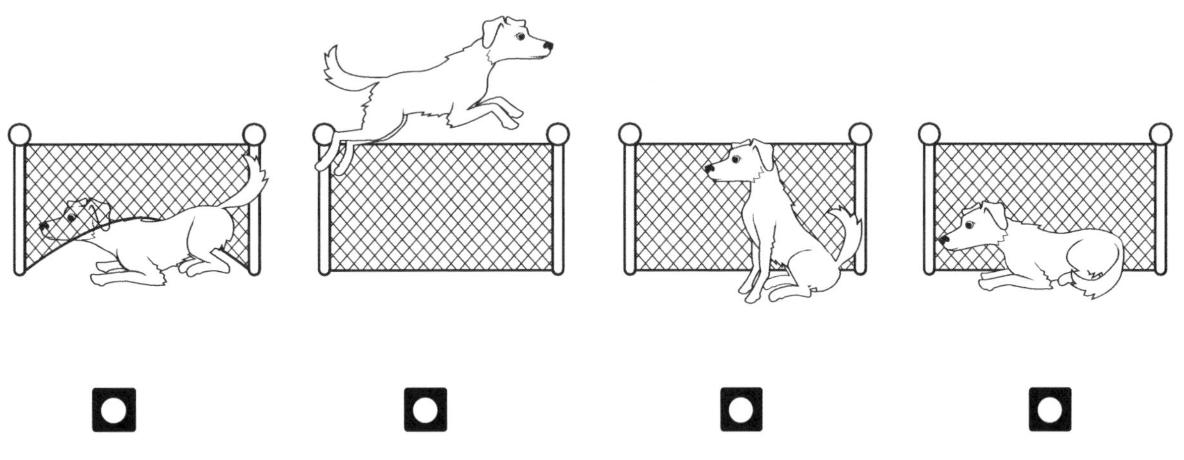

15. Mark the bird that is under the cage.

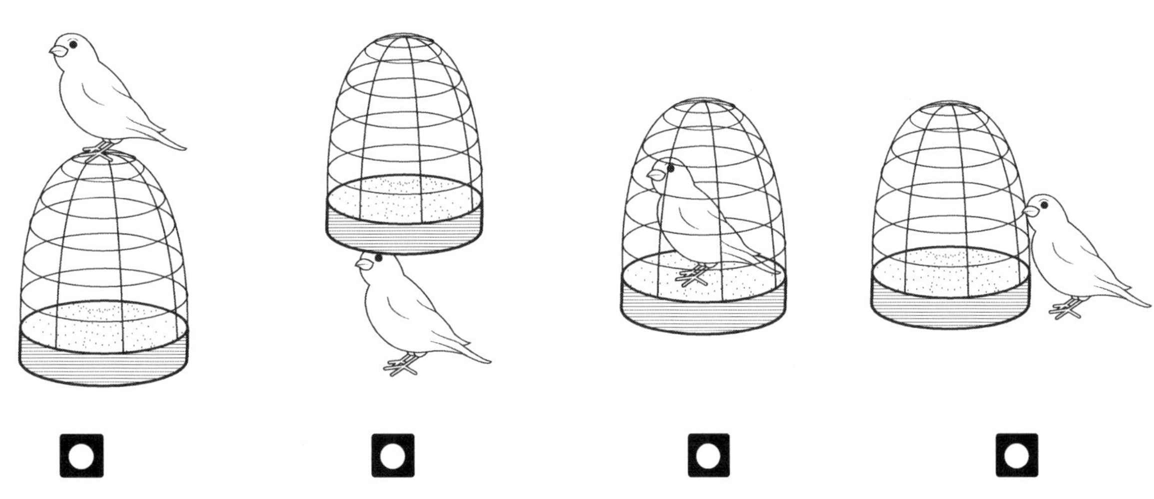

16. Mark the picture that shows water around the bird.

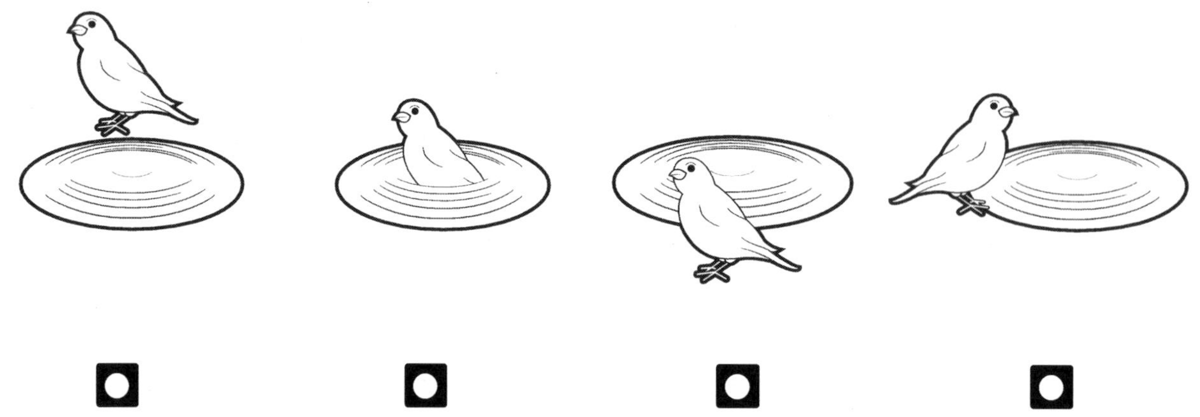

17. Mark the picture that shows the top of the alligator.

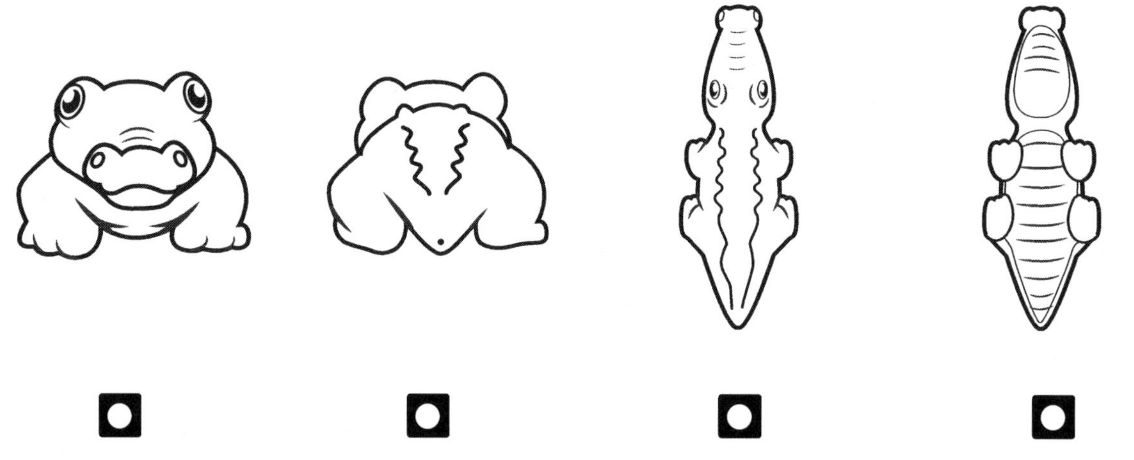

18. Mark the picture that shows the front of the pumpkin.

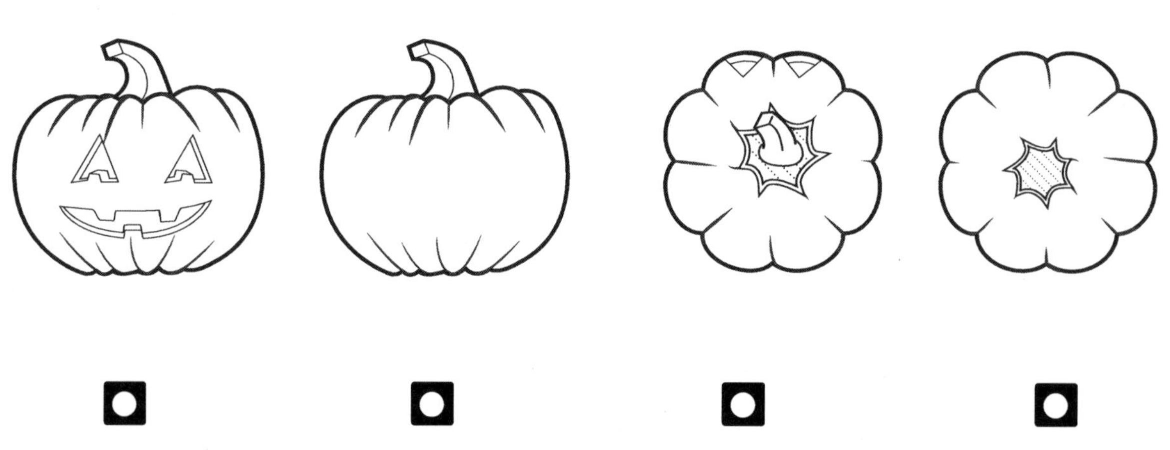

 Bright Kids NYC Inc ©

19. Mark the picture that shows the back of the cat.

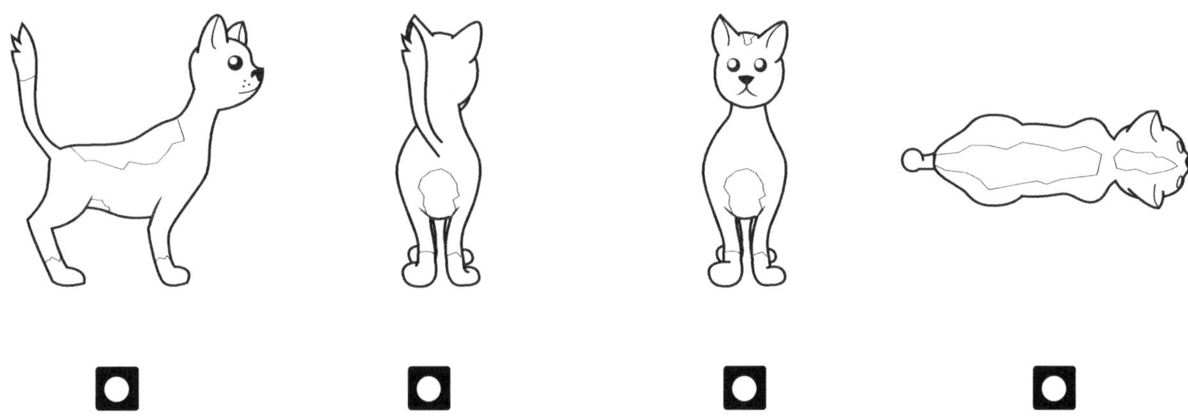

20. Mark the child sitting in the front seat.

21. Mark the child sitting in the back seat.

22. Mark the bottom of the foot.

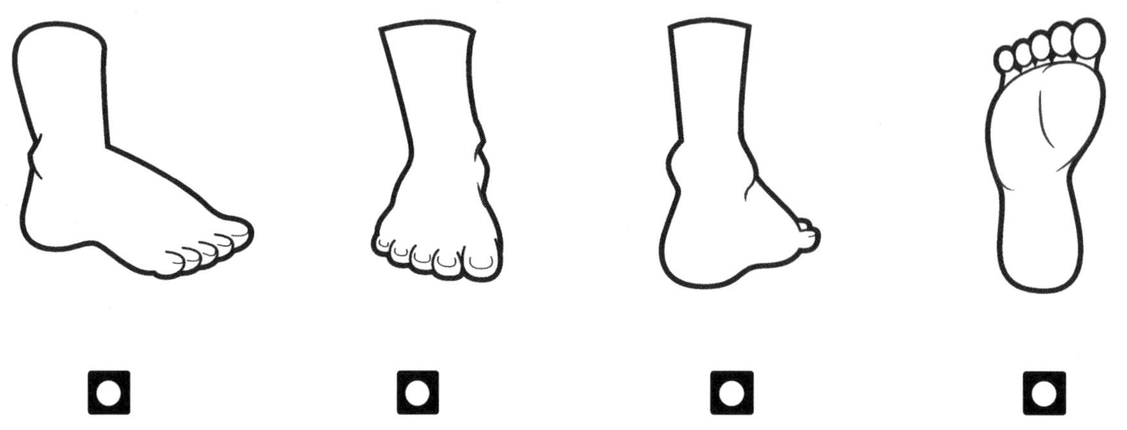

23. Mark the children who are apart.

24. Mark the circle that is outside the triangle.

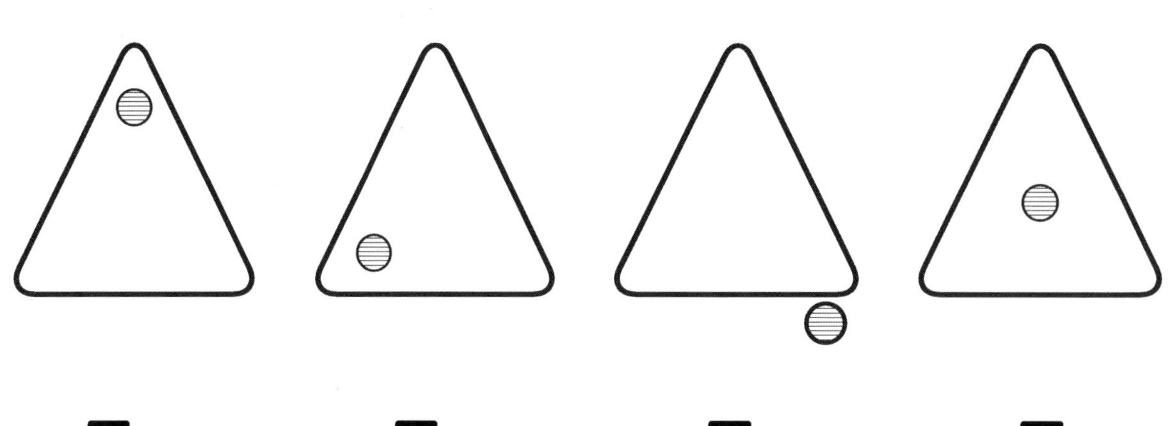

25. Mark the shovel that is inside the bucket.

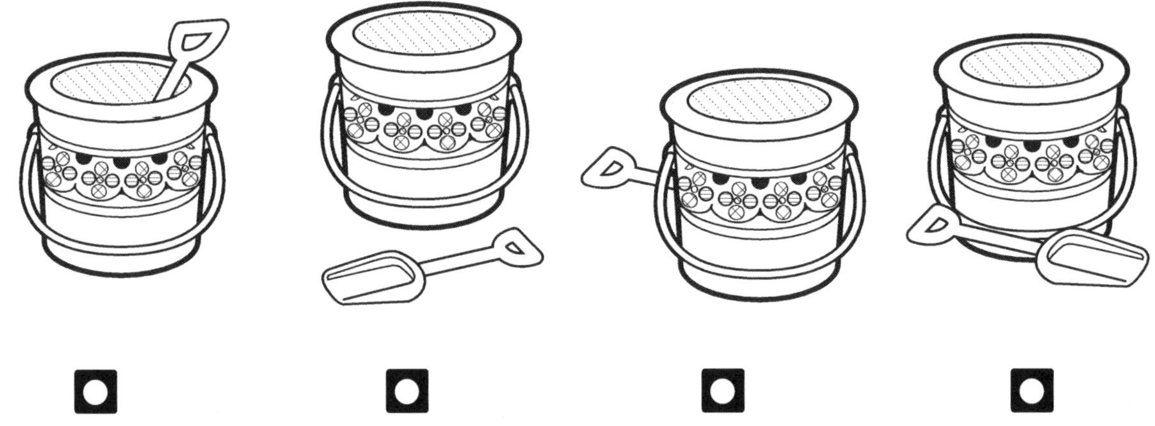

26. Mark the flowers that are together.

27. Mark the animals that are inside their cages.

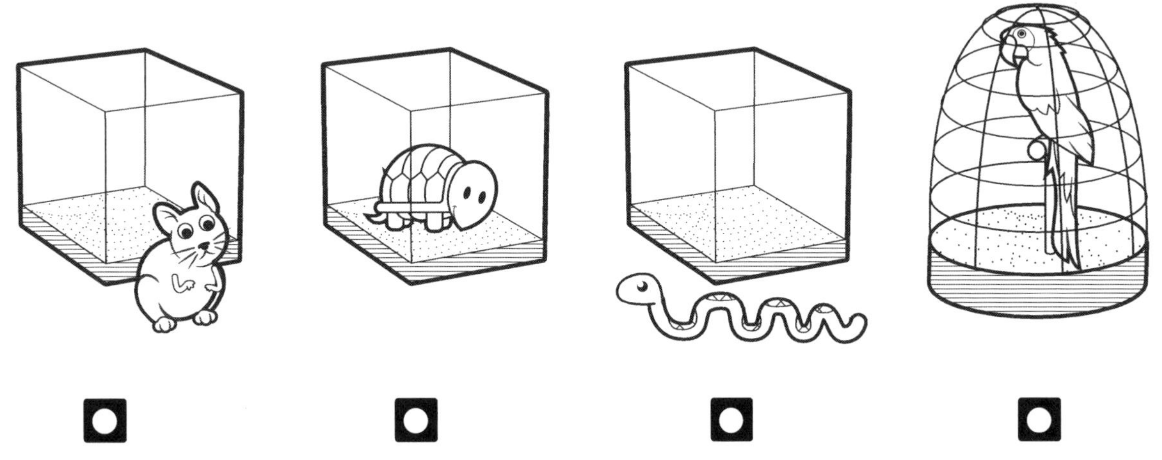

28. Mark the flag that is still.

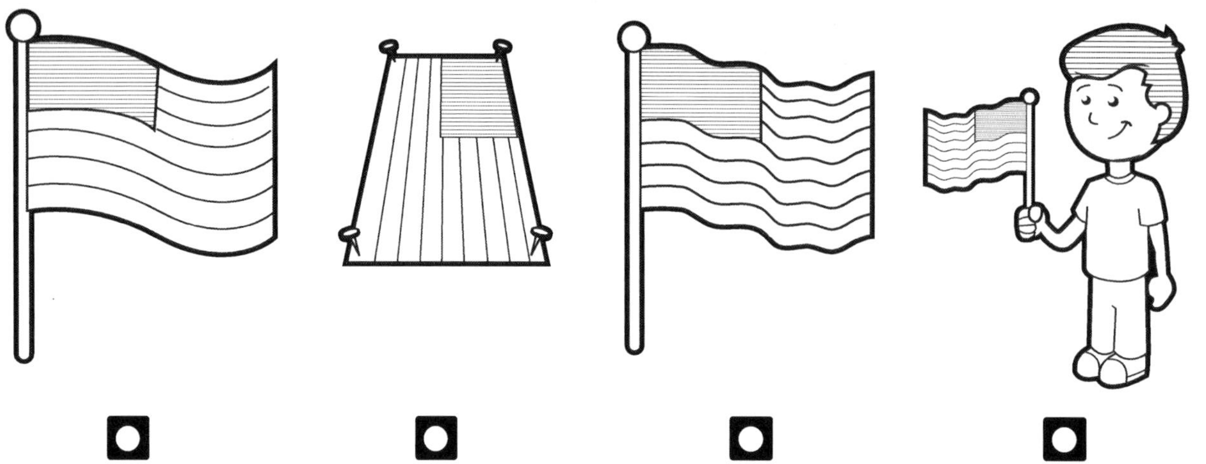

29. Mark the girl who is on top of the stairs.

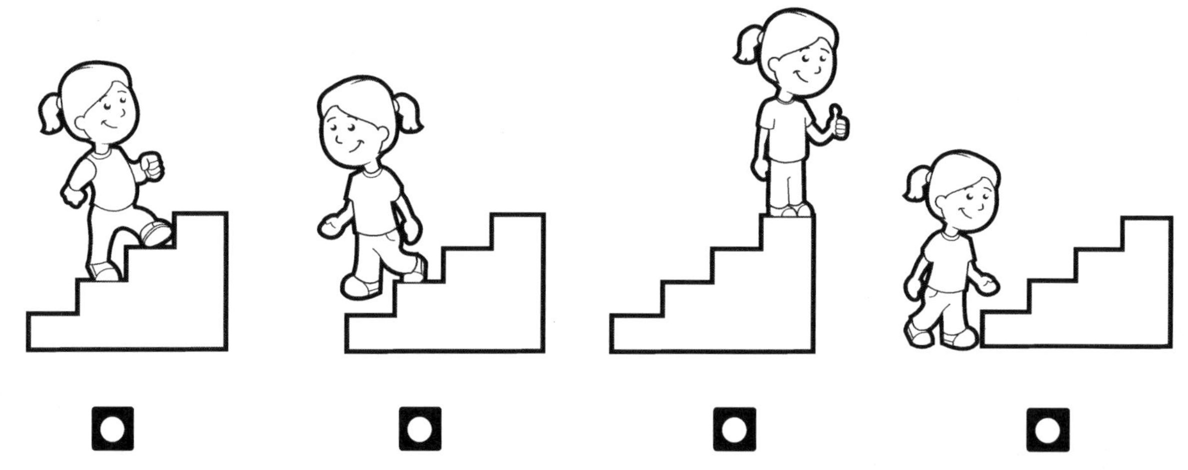

30. Mark the dog that is in the middle.

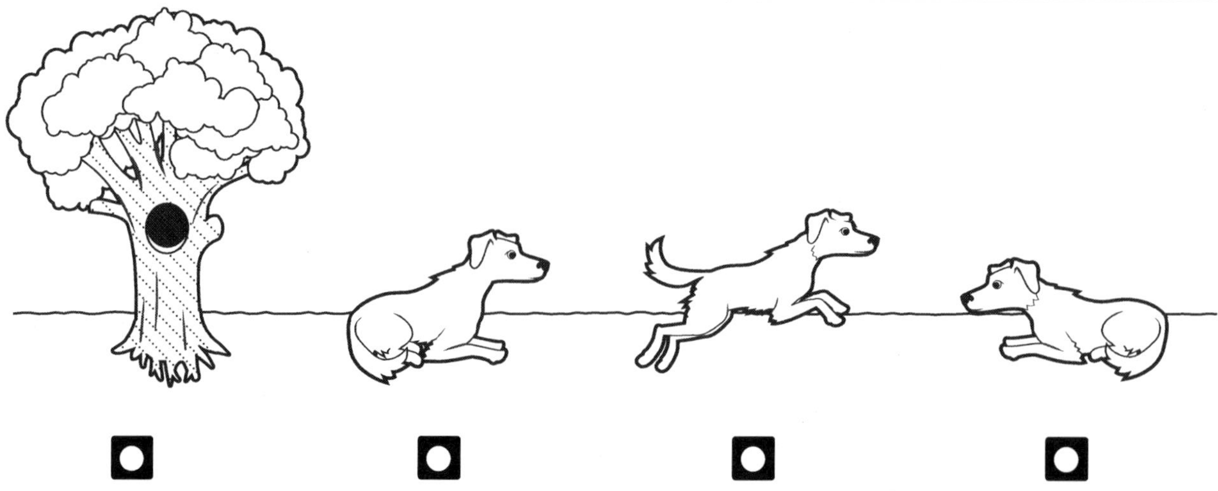

31. Mark the child who is still.

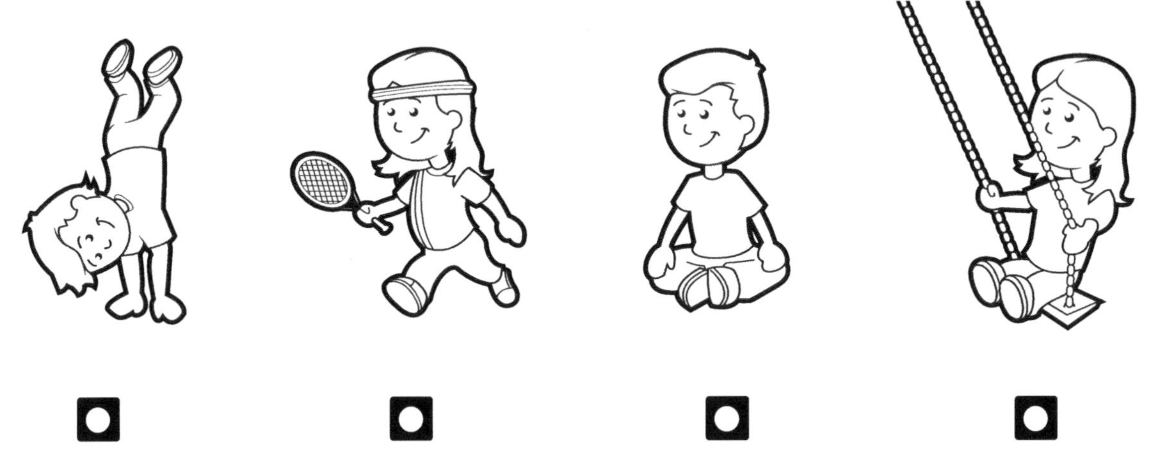

32. Mark the arrow that is going up.

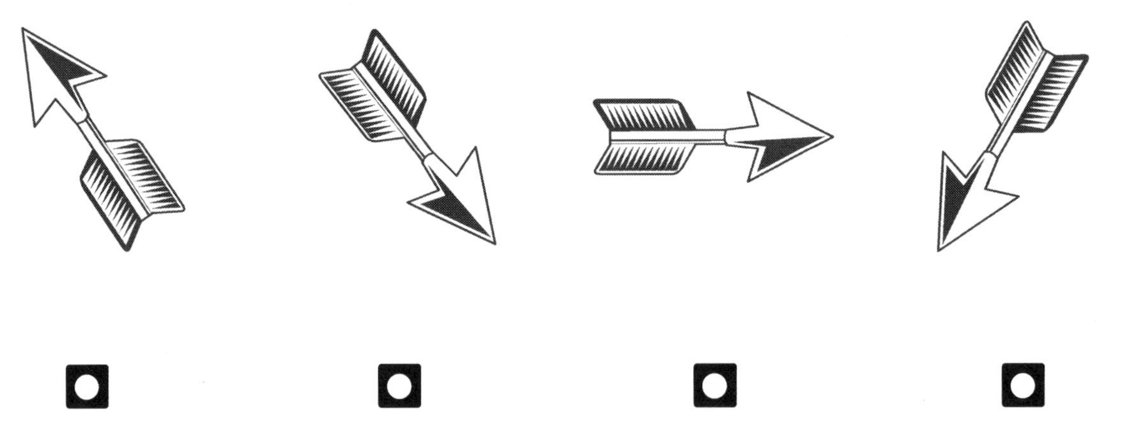

33. Mark the child going down the slide.

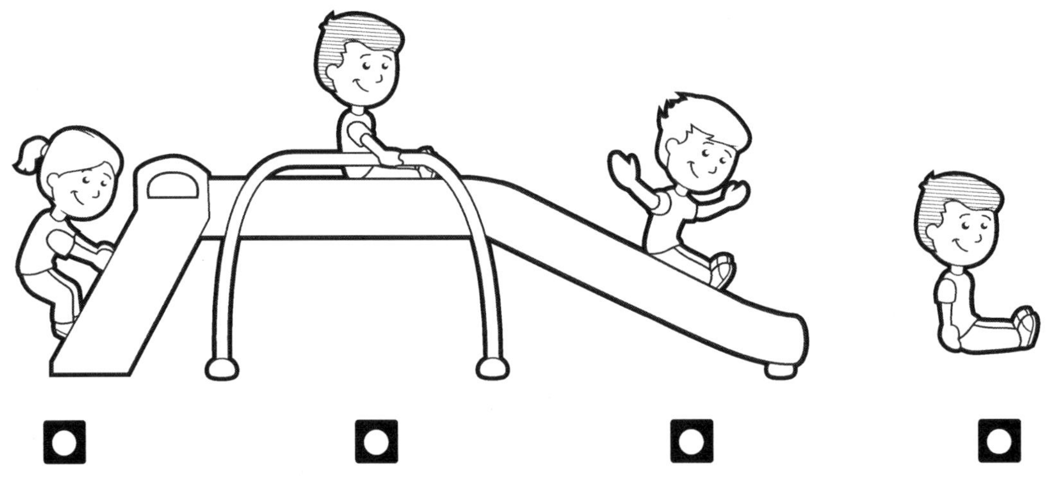

34. Mark the cat that is in front of the tree.

35. Mark the hand that is behind the ruler.

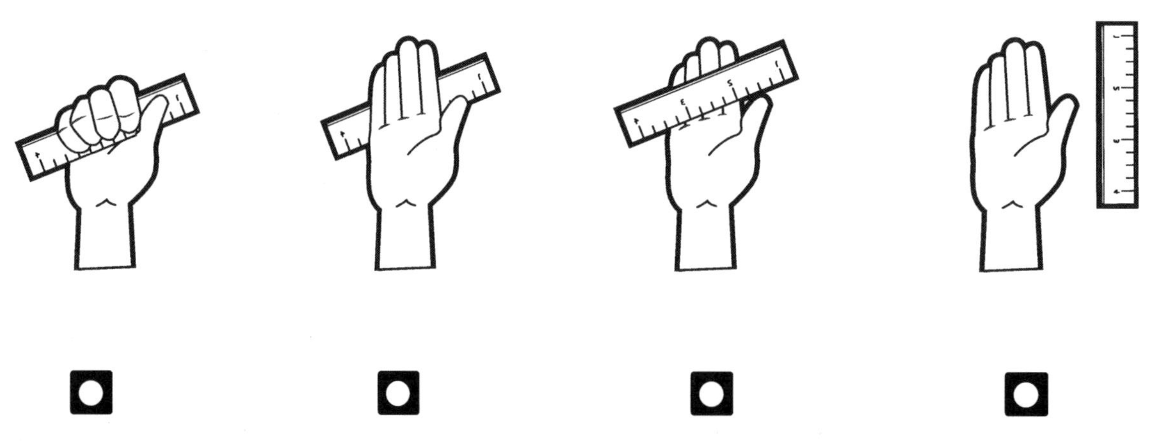

36. Mark the dog that is in between the cats.

37. Mark the child who is next to the table.

38. Mark the teddy bear that is in front of the chair.

39. Mark the cow that is behind the tree.

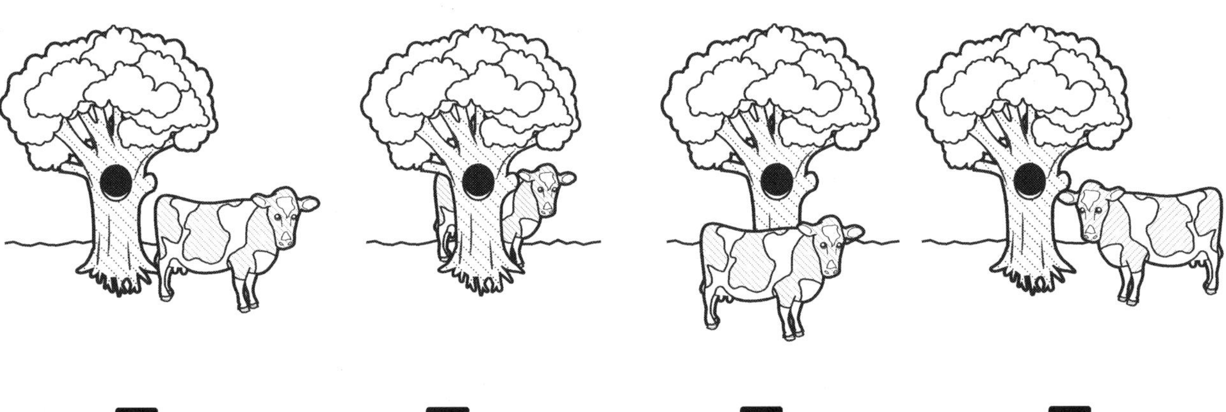

40. Mark the cheese that is in between the sandwich.

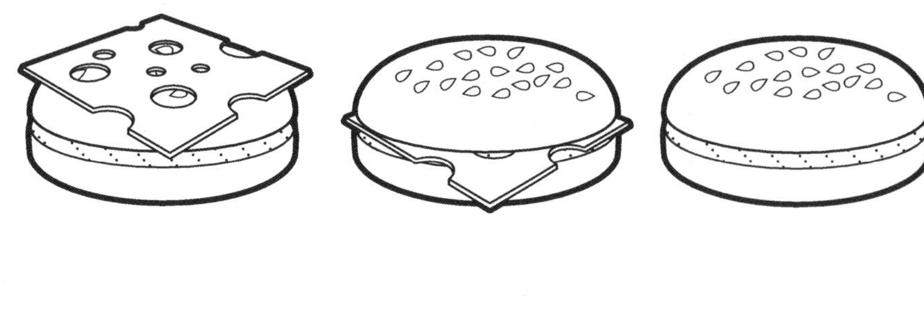

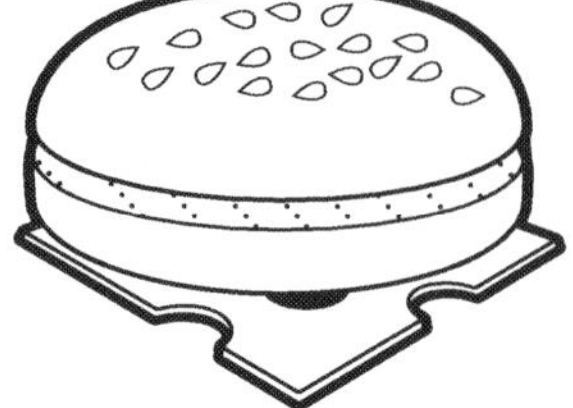

41. Mark the helicopter that is high.

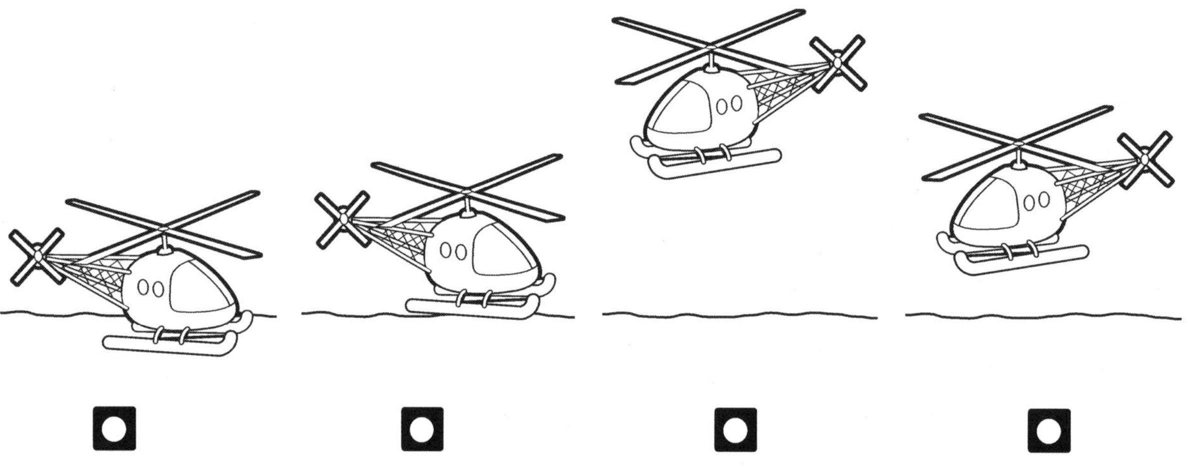

42. Mark the train that is near the child.

43. Mark the car that is far away.

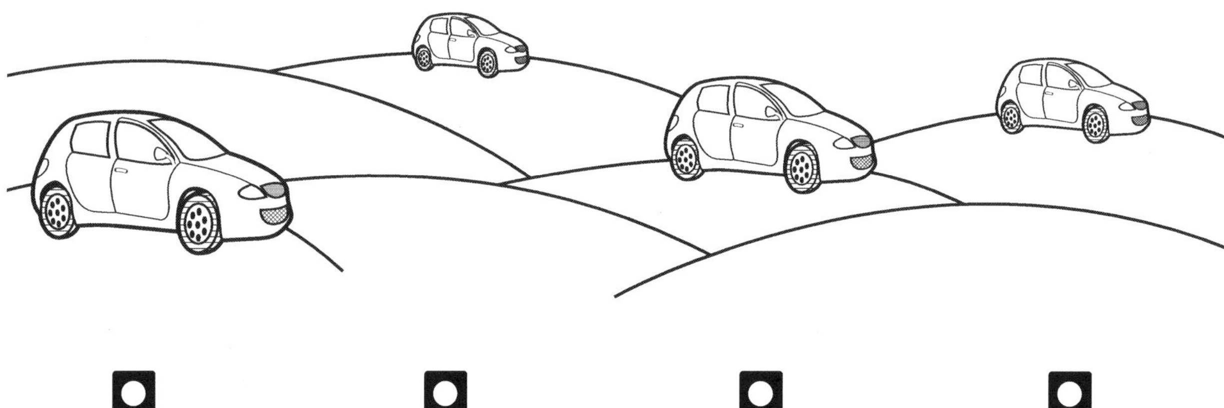

44. Mark the low-flying airplane.

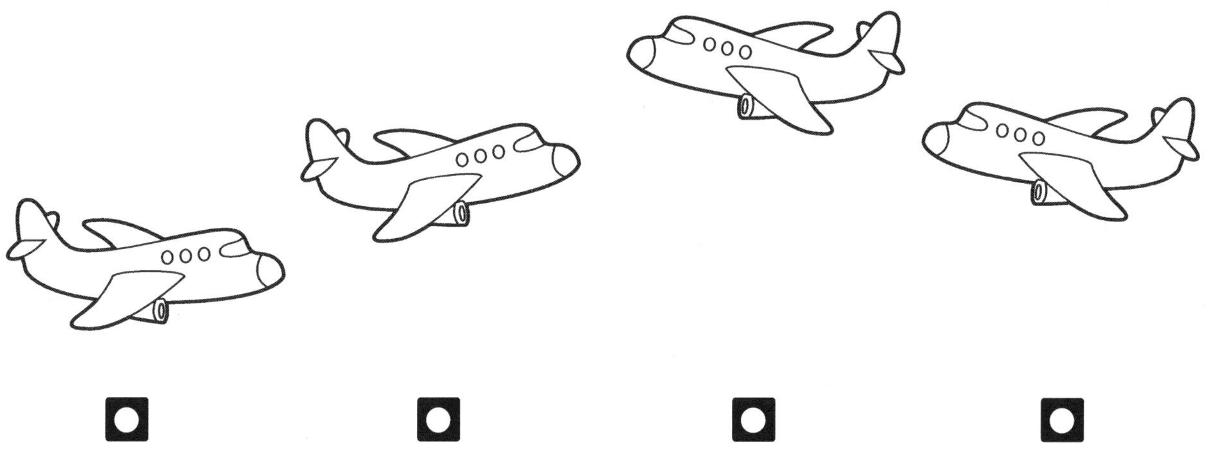

45. Mark the vase that is high.

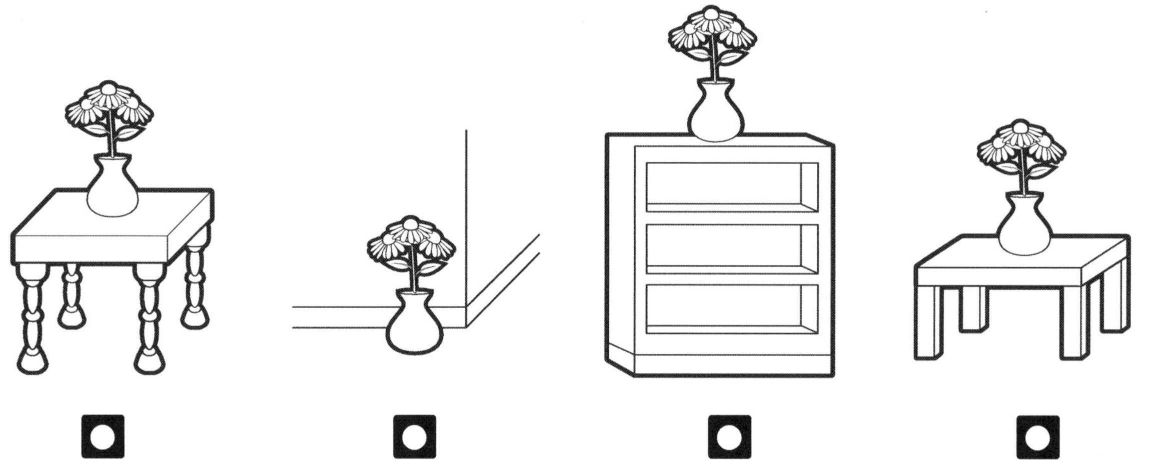

46. Mark the house that is near.

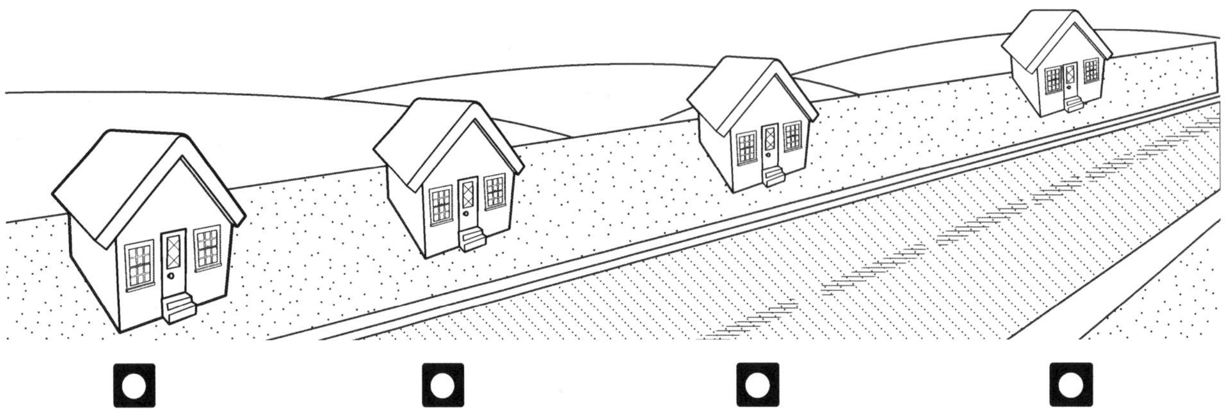

47. Mark the bowl that is upside down.

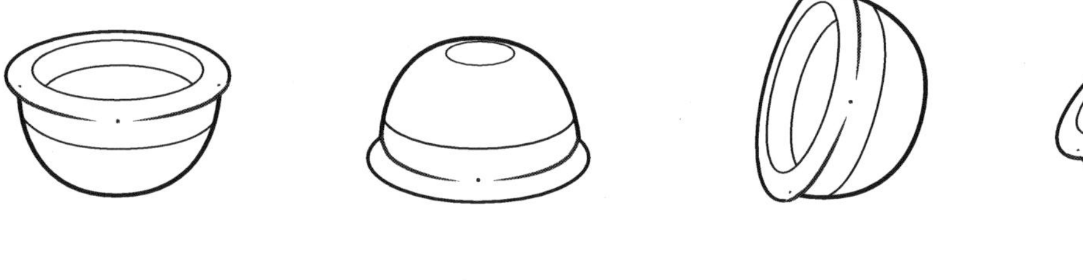

48. Mark the dress that is upside down.

49. Mark the umbrella that is inside out.

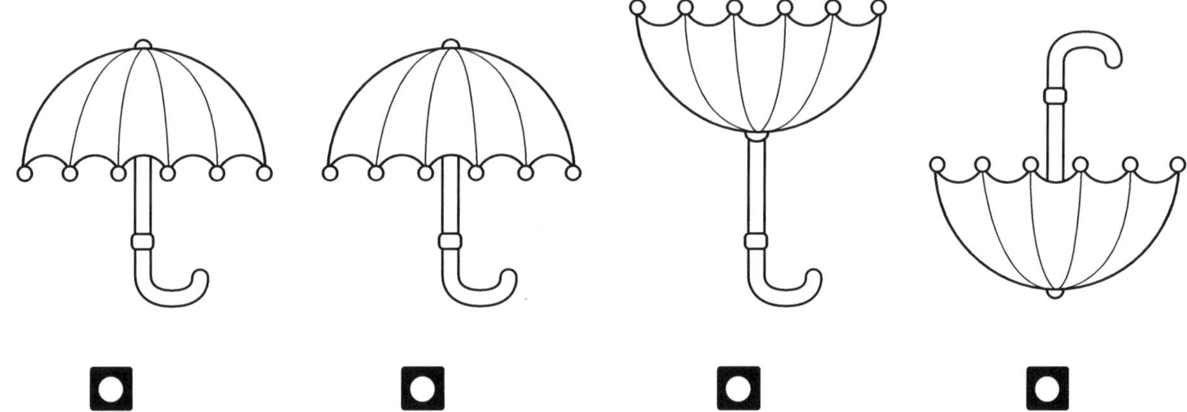

50. Mark the chair that is upside down.

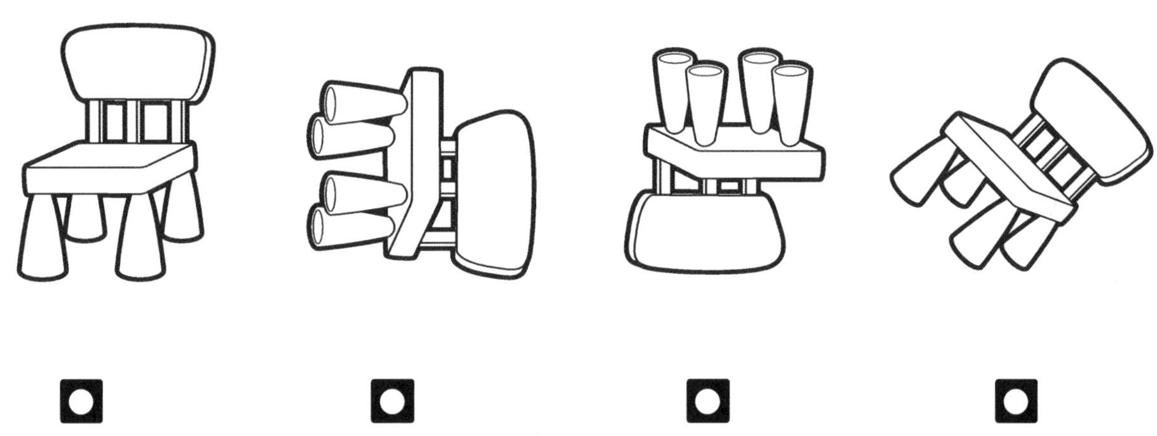

51. Mark the child who is at the end of the seesaw.

52. Mark the teddy bear that is at the edge of the table.

53. Mark the mouse that is in the corner.

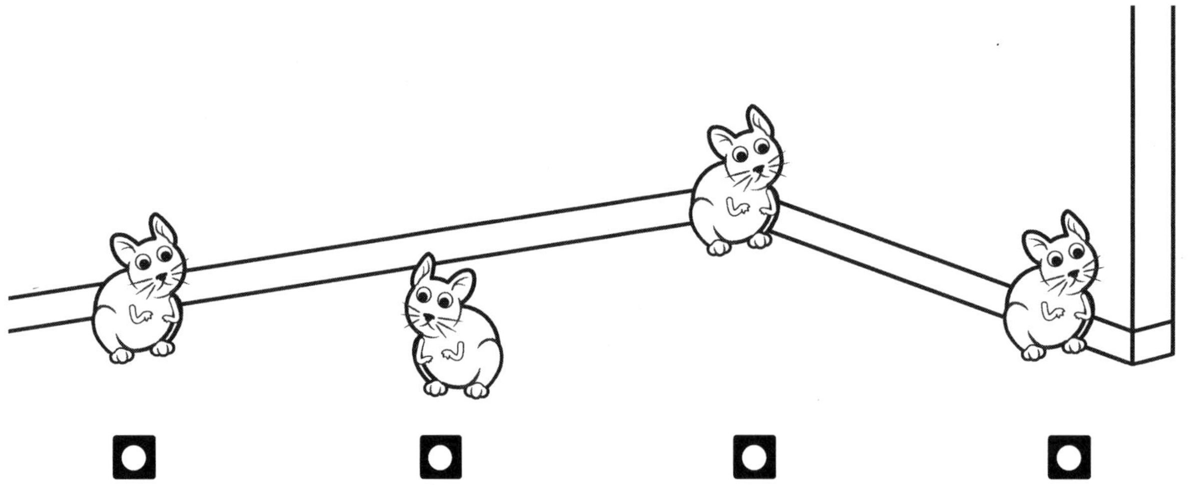

54. Mark the child who is holding the end of the rope.

 Bright Kids NYC Inc ©

55. Mark the animal that is in the corner of the picture.

56. Mark the child who is walking towards the clown.

57. Mark the dog that is moving away from the child.

58. Mark the cat facing front.

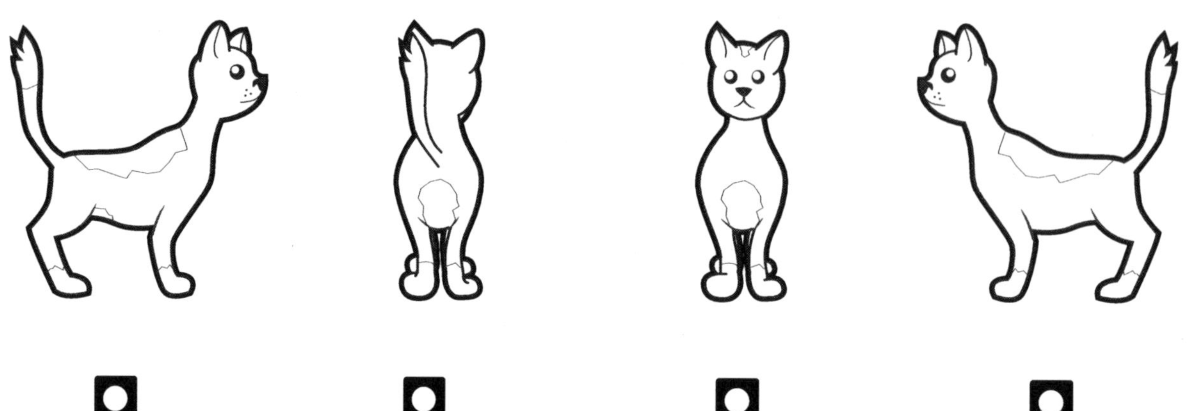

59. Mark the child who is walking away from the tree.

60. Mark the child who is stepping backwards.

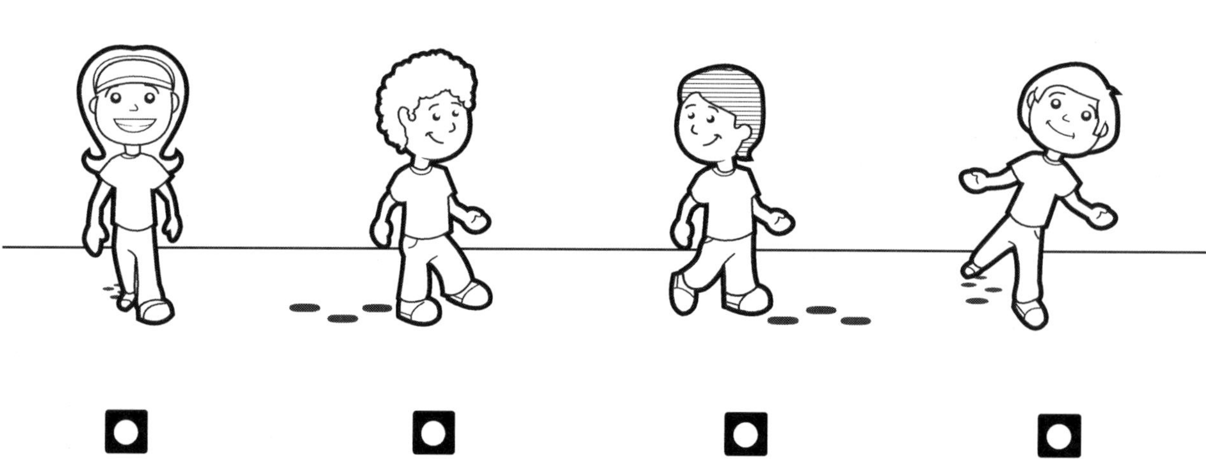

Bright Kids NYC Inc ©

61. Mark the chicken walking sideways.

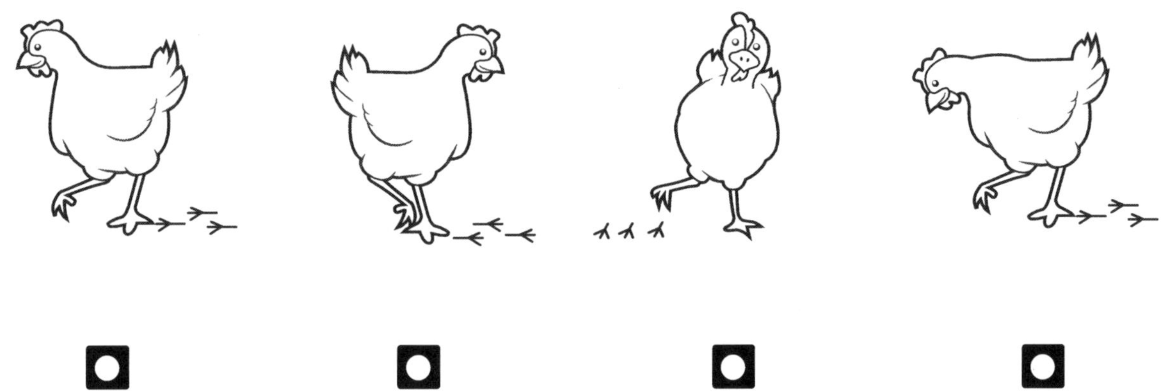

62. Mark the girl who is sitting across from the boy.

63. Mark the child swimming backwards.

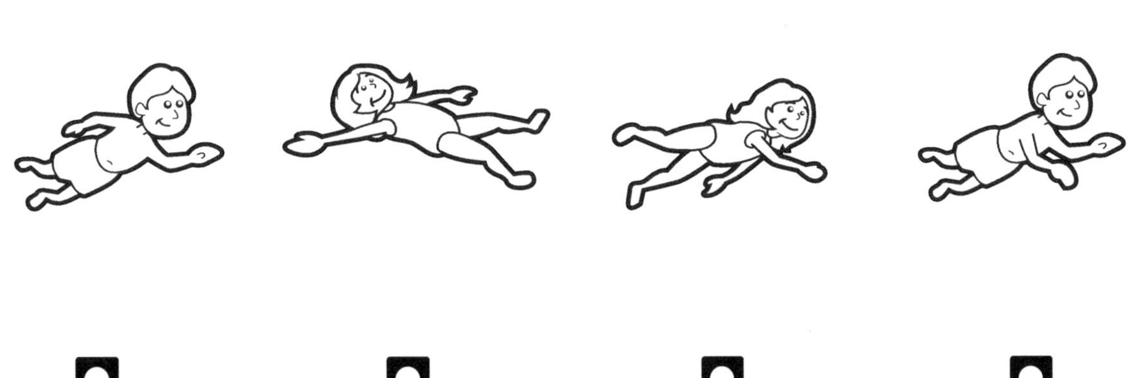

64. Mark the child skating forward.

65. Mark the child who is sitting in front of the cat.

66. Mark the smoke that is above the chimney.

 Bright Kids NYC Inc ©

67. Mark the squirrel below the table.

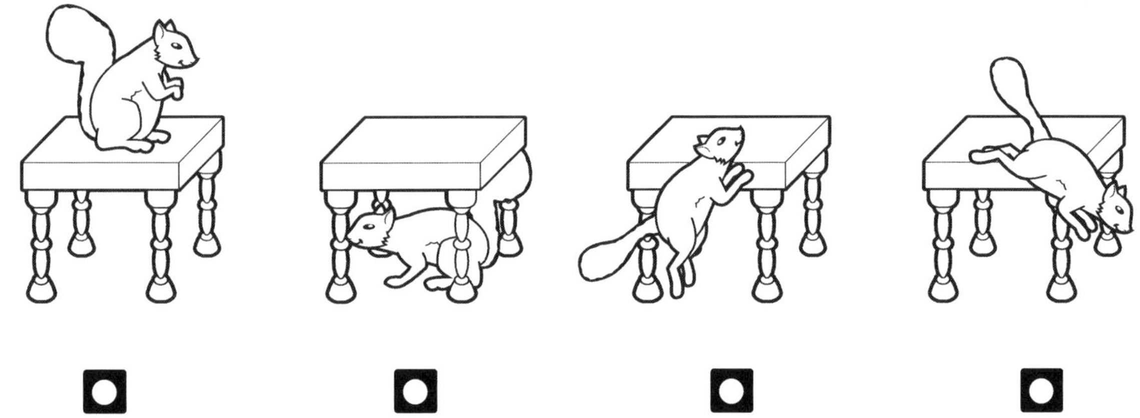

68. Mark the child who is upside down.

69. Mark the sun that is below the clouds.

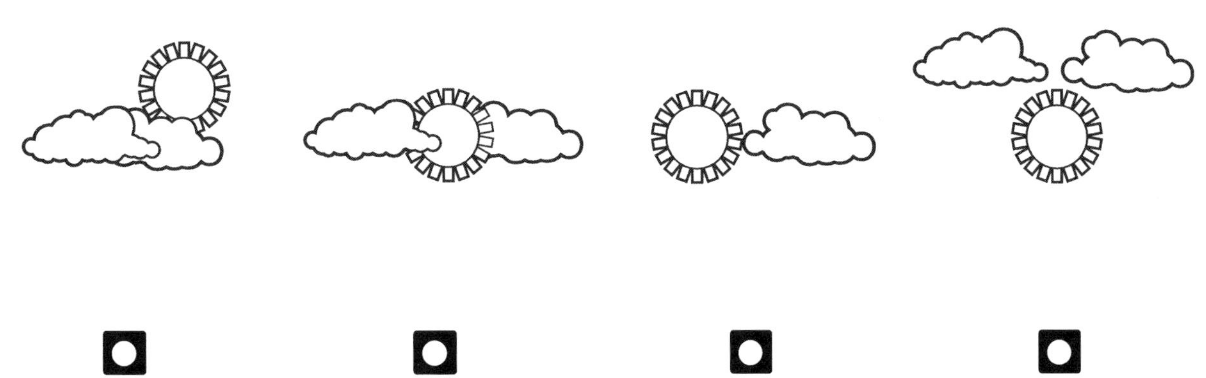

70. Mark the turtles that are facing in opposite directions.

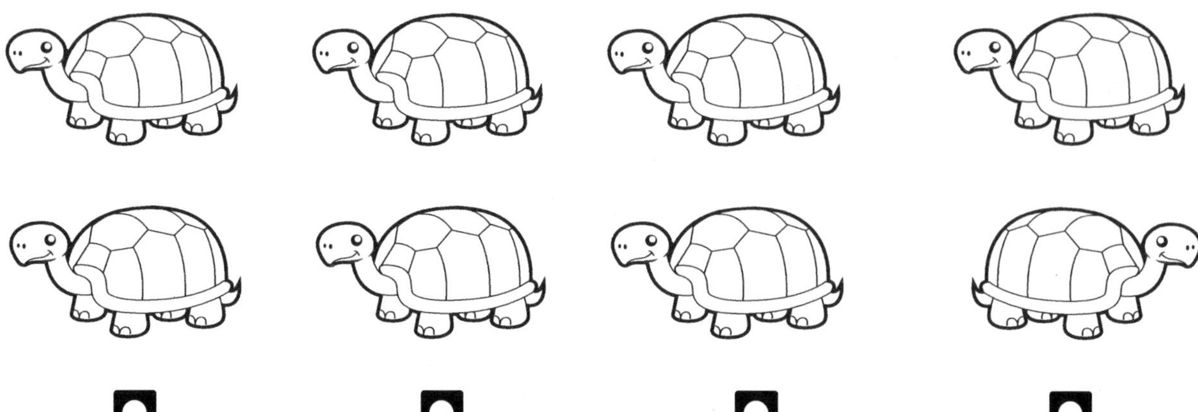

71. Mark the dish that is level.

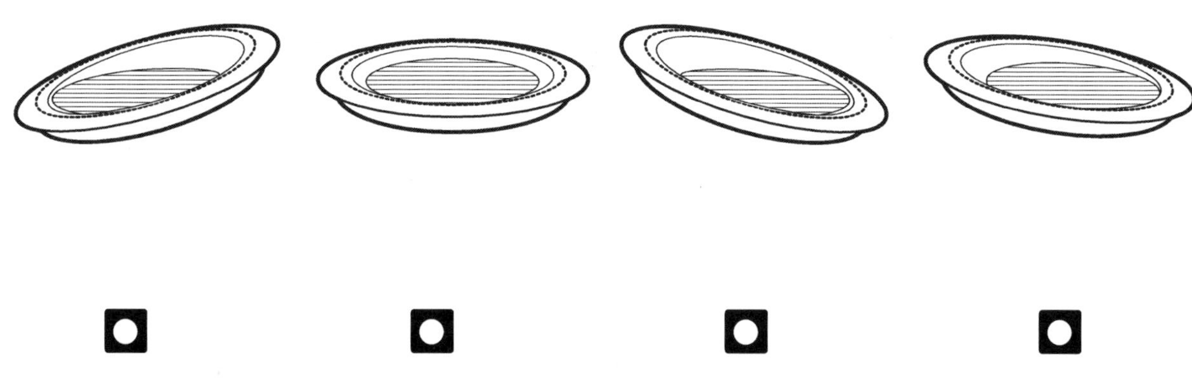

72. Mark the picture that shows the side of the refrigerator.

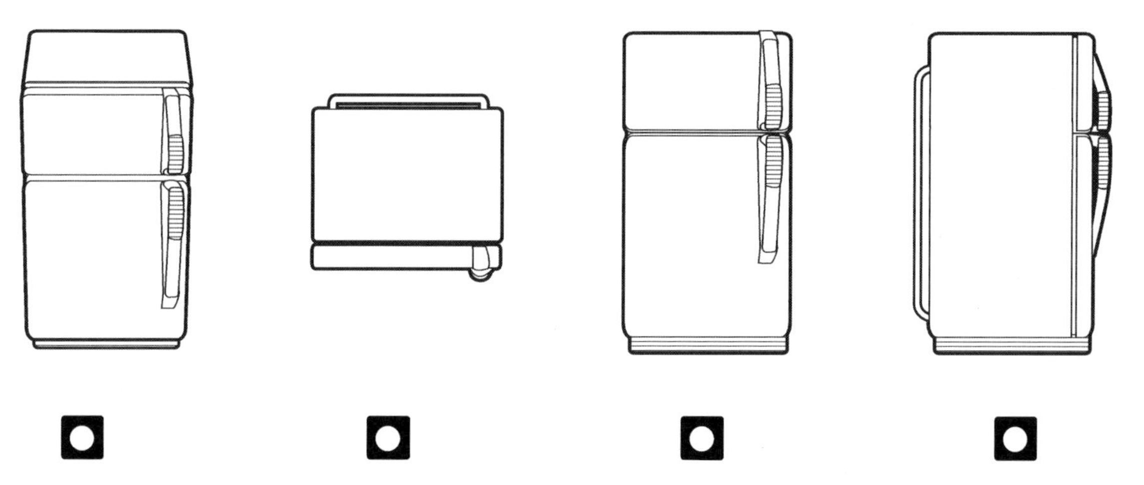

 Bright Kids NYC Inc ©

73. Mark the hands that are in opposite directions.

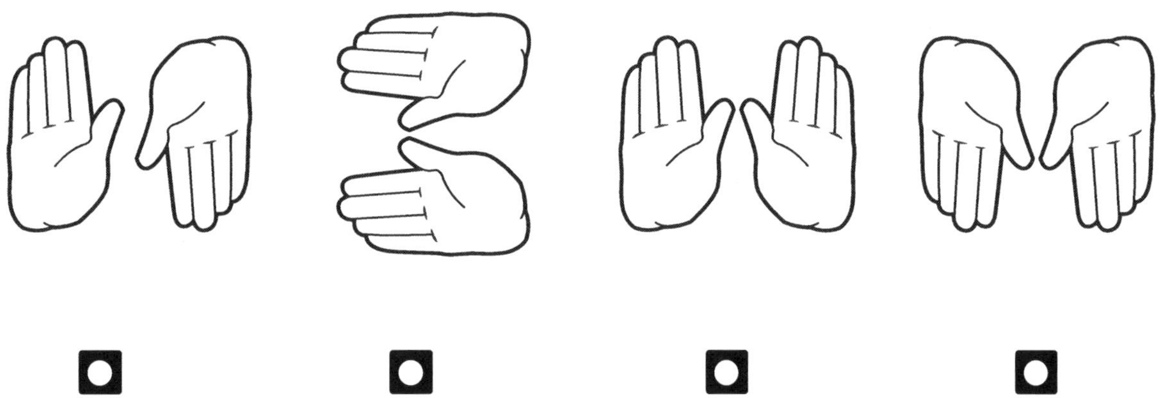

74. Mark the dog that is beside the bed.

75. Mark the picture that is in the center of the table.

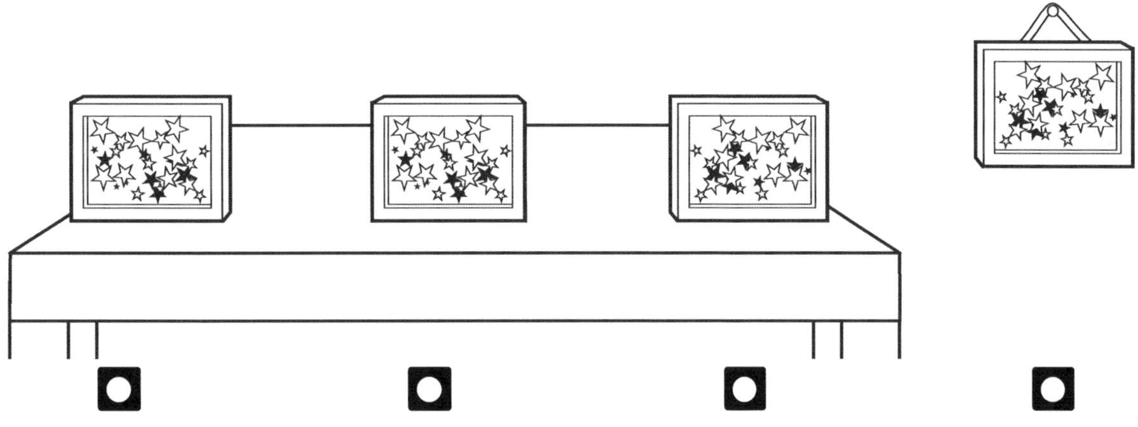

76. Mark the cup that is to the right of the saucer.

77. Mark the spoon that is beside the plate.

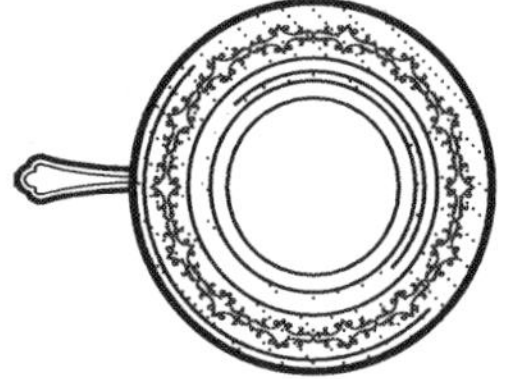

78. Mark the child who is jumping into the water.

 Bright Kids NYC Inc ©

79. Mark the child who has the ball in her right hand.

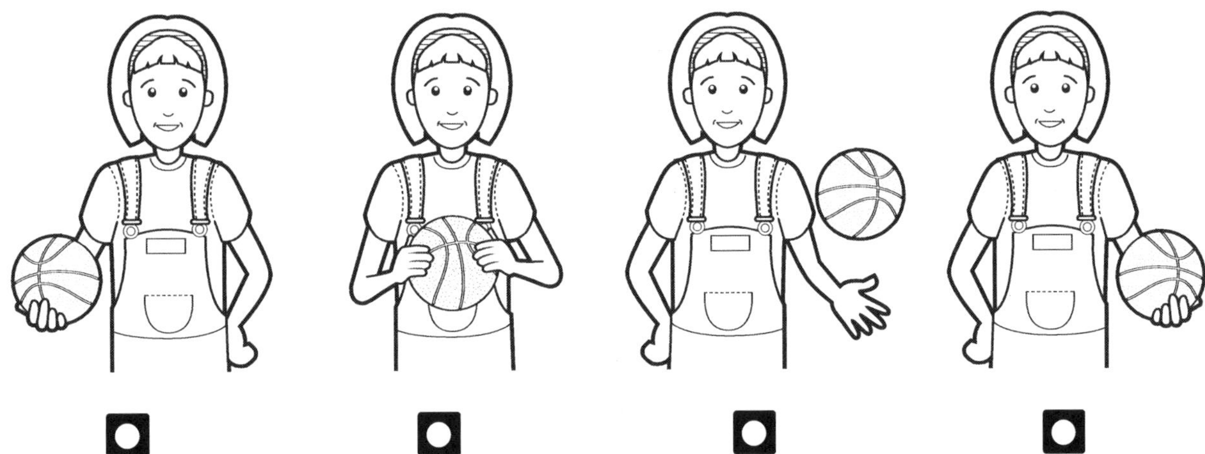

80. Mark the child who has flowers in her left hand.

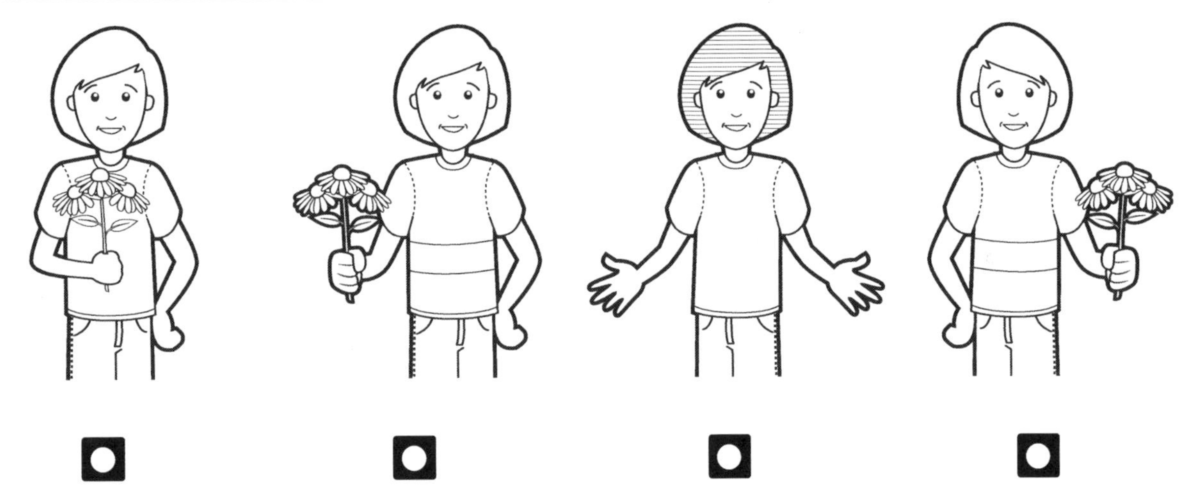

81. Mark the child turning left.

82. Mark the child turning right.

83. Mark the child who is closest to the car.

84. Mark the child who is furthest away from the house.

 Bright Kids NYC Inc ©

85. Mark the cat that is furthest away from his food.

86. Mark the children who are apart.

87. Mark the straight ribbon.

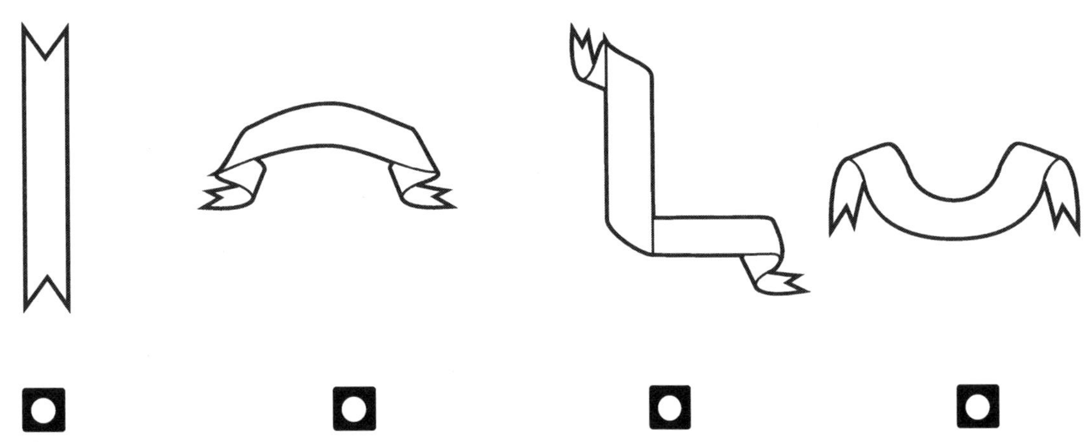

 Bright kids NYC Inc ©

ANSWER KEY

1.	Picture 2/3/4	-	Box, suitcase and mailbox
2.	Picture 1	-	First cat
3.	Picture 1/3/4	-	Coffee cup, window and mailbox
4.	Picture 2/4	-	Suitcase and house
5.	Picture 2/3/4	-	Glass, kitten and turtle
6.	Picture 1/3	-	Mouse and dog
7.	Picture 2/3	-	Second and third teddy bear
8.	Picture 4	-	Parrot in cage
9.	Picture 3	-	Third envelope
10.	Picture 3	-	Third soccer ball and net
11.	Picture 1	-	First swimmer
12.	Picture 3	-	Third girl
13.	Picture 3	-	Third cake
14.	Picture 2	-	Second dog
15.	Picture 2	-	Second bird
16.	Picture 2	-	Second bird
17.	Picture 3	-	Third alligator
18.	Picture 1	-	First pumpkin
19.	Picture 2	-	Second cat
20.	Picture 1	-	First child
21.	Picture 4	-	Fourth child
22.	Picture 4	-	Bottom of the foot
23.	Picture 3	-	Boy and girl standing apart
24.	Picture 3	-	Circle outside of triangle
25.	Picture 1	-	First bucket and shovel
26.	Picture 3	-	Third pair of flowers
27.	Picture 2/4	-	Mouse and snake
28.	Picture 2	-	Second flag
29.	Picture 3	-	Girl at top of stairs
30.	Picture 3	-	Second dog from tree
31.	Picture 3	-	Sitting child
32.	Picture 1	-	First arrow
33.	Picture 3	-	Third child
34.	Picture 1	-	First cat
35.	Picture 3	-	Third hand
36.	Picture 3	-	Dog between two cats
37	Picture 4	-	Girl standing next to table
38.	Picture 3	-	Teddy bear in front of chair
39.	Picture 2	-	Second cow
40.	Picture 2	-	Second sandwich

41.	Picture 3	-	Third helicopter
42.	Picture 2	-	Child behind the train
43	Picture 2	-	Second car
44.	Picture 1	-	First plane
45.	Picture 3	-	Vase on the bookshelf
46.	Picture 1	-	First house
47.	Picture 2	-	Upside down bowl
48.	Picture 1	-	Upside down dress
49.	Picture 3	-	Inside out umbrella
50.	Picture 3	-	Upside down chair
51.	Picture 4	-	Fourth child
52.	Picture 2	-	Second teddy bear
53.	Picture 3	-	Third mouse
54.	Picture 1	-	First child
55.	Picture 1	-	Tiger
56.	Picture 1	-	First child
57.	Picture 2	-	Second dog
58.	Picture 3	-	Third cat
59.	Picture 1	-	First child
60.	Picture 4	-	Fourth child
61.	Picture 3	-	Third chicken
62.	Picture 4	-	Fourth child
63.	Picture 2	-	Second swimmer
64.	Picture 3	-	Third child
65.	Picture 1	-	First child
66.	Picture 2	-	Second chimney
67.	Picture 2	-	Squirrel under table
68.	Picture 1	-	Upside down boy
69.	Picture 4	-	Sun under clouds
70.	Picture 4	-	Fourth pair of turtles
71.	Picture 2	-	Second dish
72.	Picture 4	-	Fourth refrigerator
73.	Picture 1	-	First pair of hands
74.	Picture 3	-	Third dog
75.	Picture 2	-	Second picture
76.	Picture 4	-	Fourth cup and saucer
77.	Picture 3	-	Third plate and spoon
78.	Picture 1	-	First child
79.	Picture 1	-	First girl
80.	Picture 4	-	Fourth girl

81.	Picture 1	-	First child
82.	Picture 2	-	Second child
83.	Picture 2	-	Second child
84.	Picture 1	-	First child
85.	Picture 3	-	Third cat
86.	Picture 3	-	Boy and girl standing apart
87.	Picture 1	-	First ribbon

Bright kids NYC Inc ©

123
ABC

SECTION SEVEN:
SOCIAL AWARENESS

1. Mark the person who is crying.

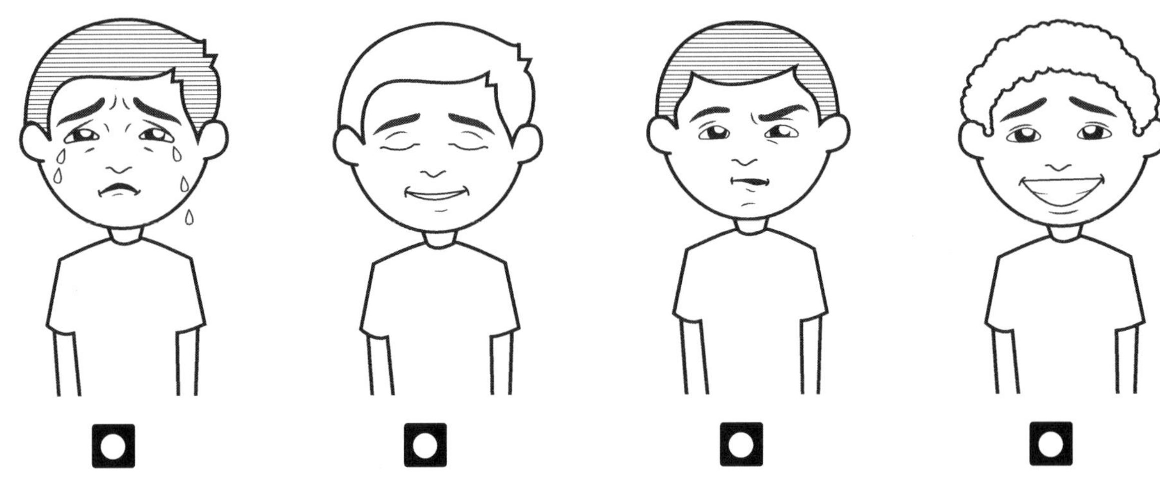

2. Mark the sleepy dog.

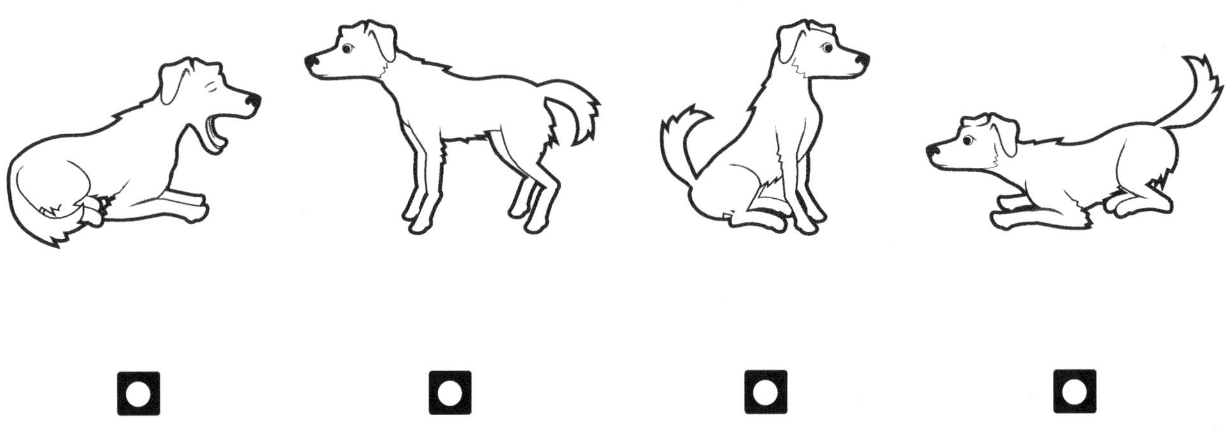

3. Mark the child who is resting.

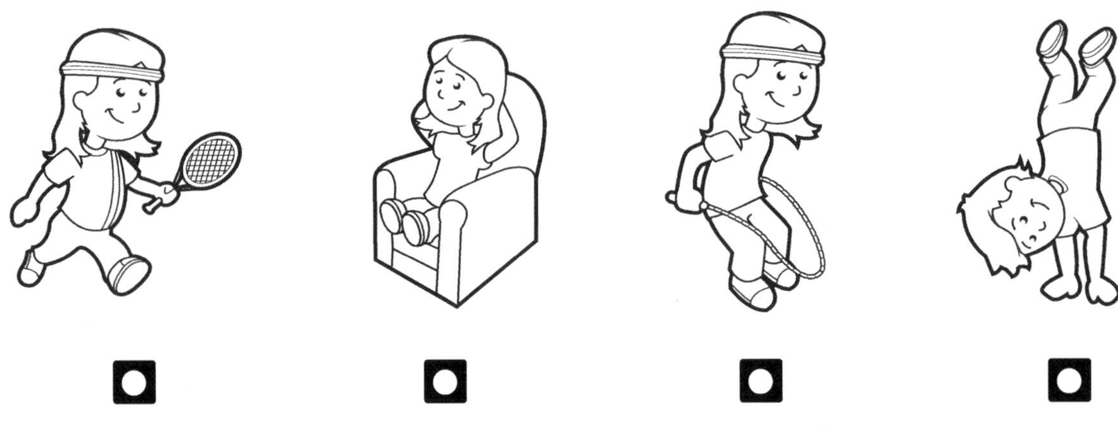

4. Mark the picture that is wrong.

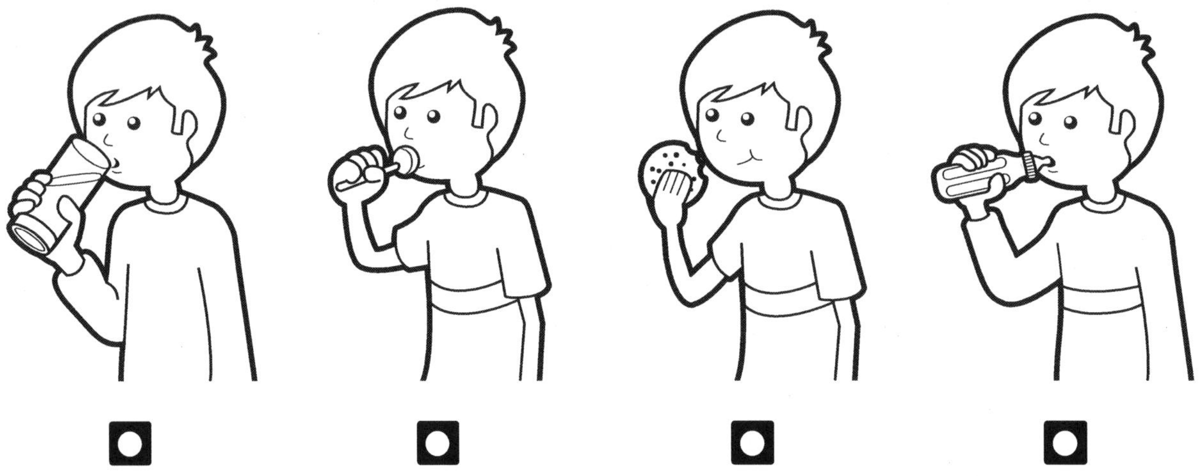

5. Mark the child who is happy.

6. Mark the child who is sad.

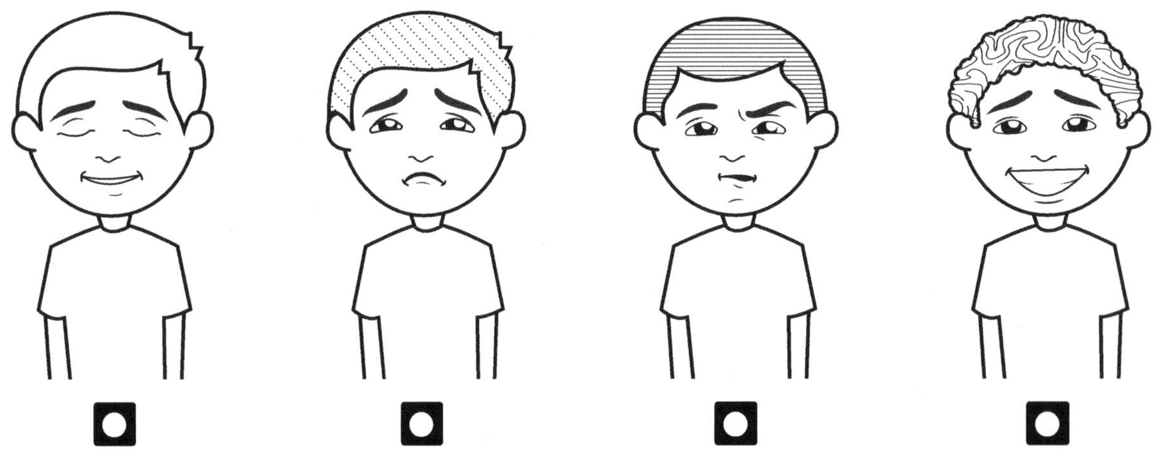

7. Mark the picture that is wrong.

8. Mark the picture that is right.

9. Mark the child who is disappointed.

10. Mark the child who is angry.

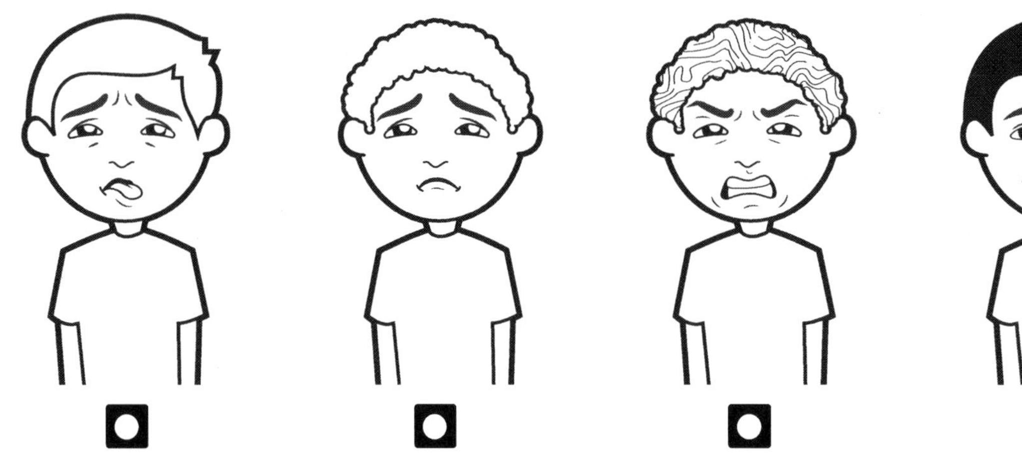

11. Mark the child who is excited.

12. Mark the child who is doing something difficult.

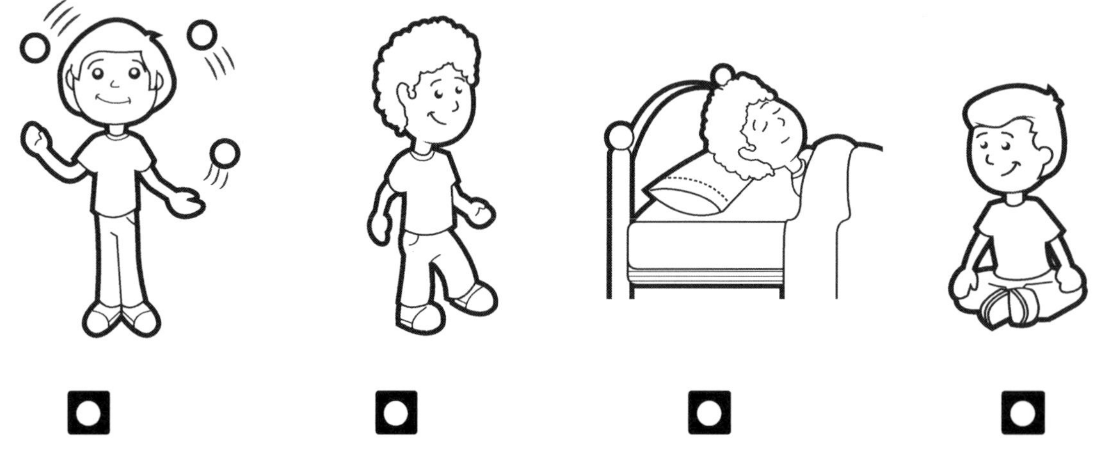

13. Mark the young kittens.

14. Mark the old person.

15. Mark the item that is easy to carry.

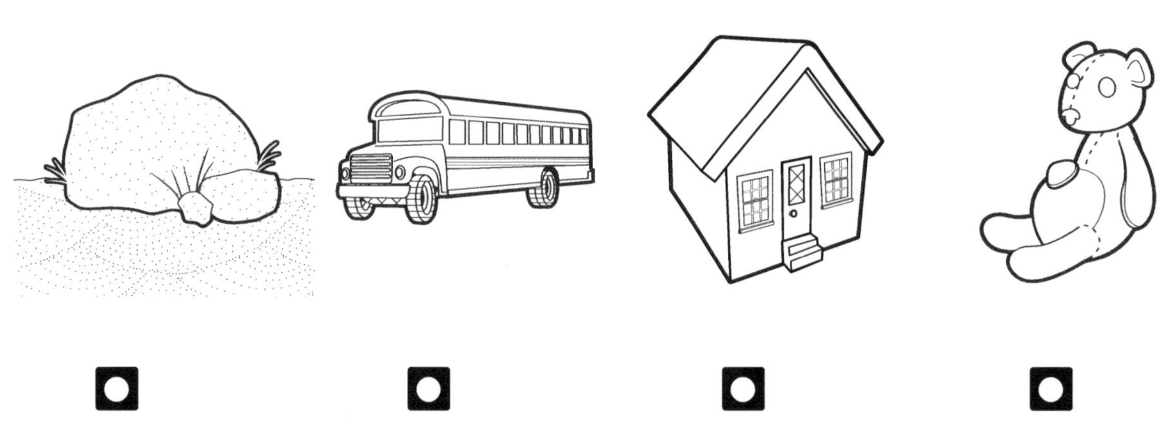

16. Mark the child who is doing something difficult.

17. Mark the child who is sick.

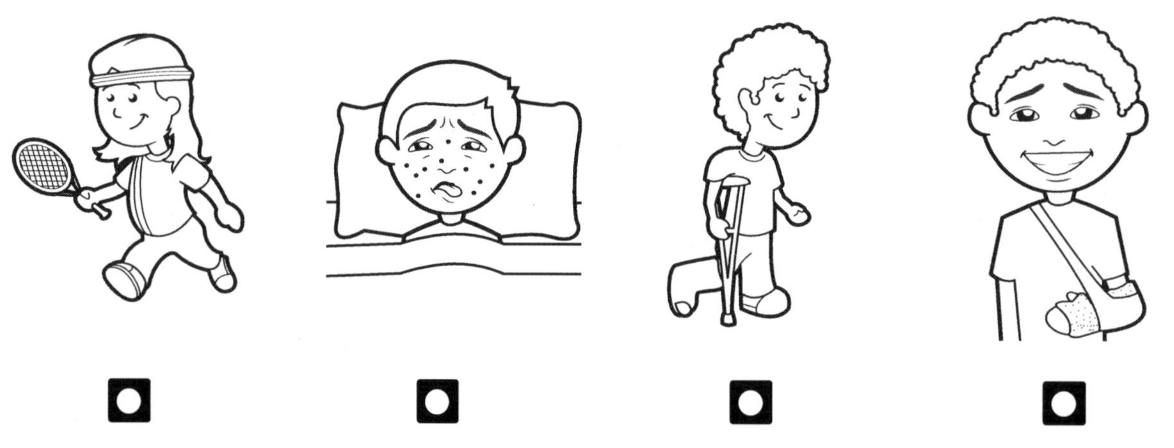

18. Mark the child who is healthy.

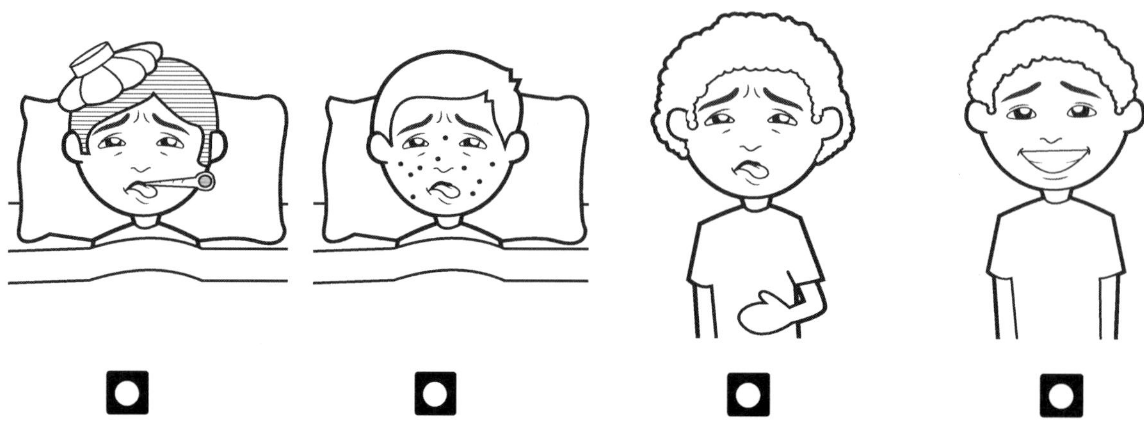

19. Mark the person who is friendly.

20. Mark the person who is relaxing.

21. Mark the child who is sick.

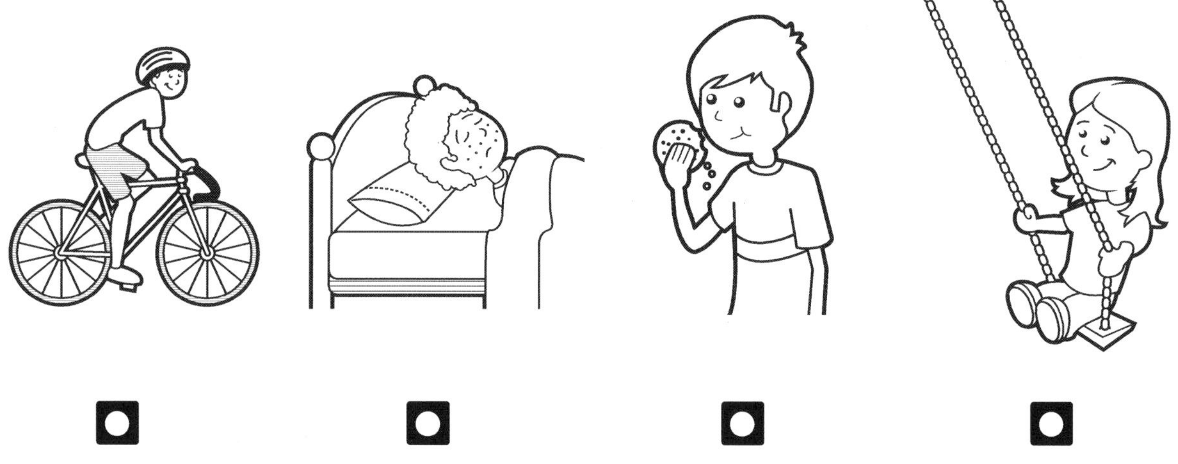

22. Mark the child who is healthy.

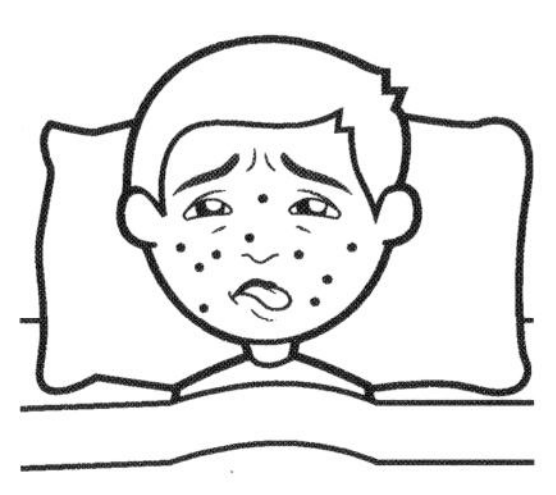

23. Mark the girl who is friendly.

24. Mark the cat that is curious.

25. Mark the child who is afraid.

26. Mark the cat that is tired.

27. Mark the person who is exhausted.

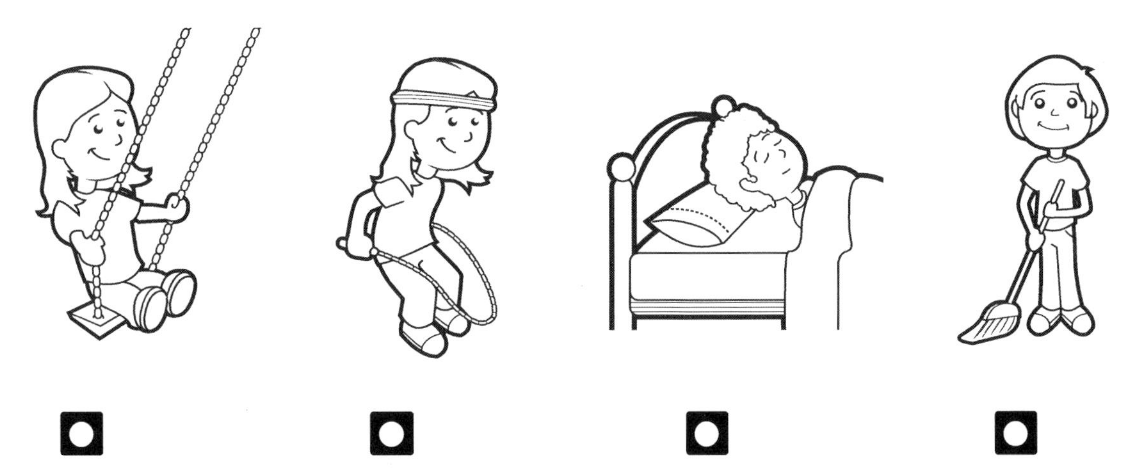

28. Mark the child who is curious.

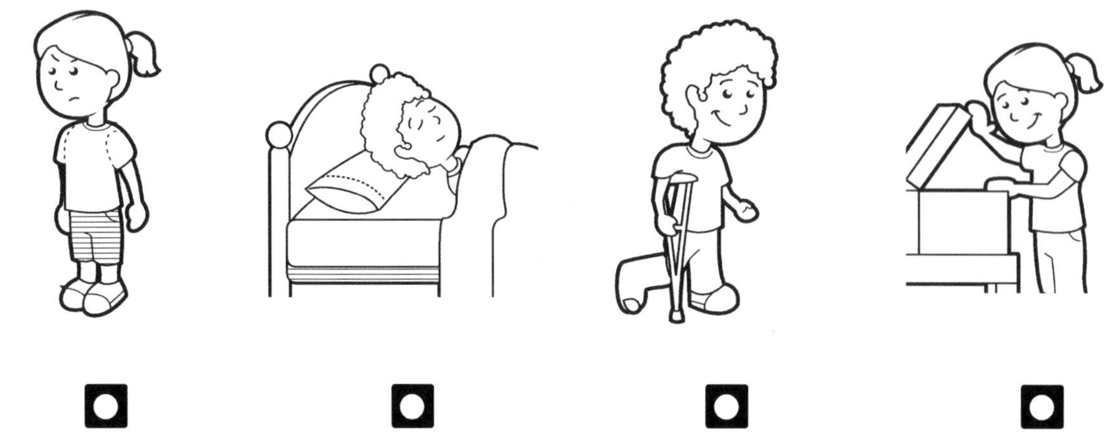

29. Mark the person who is afraid.

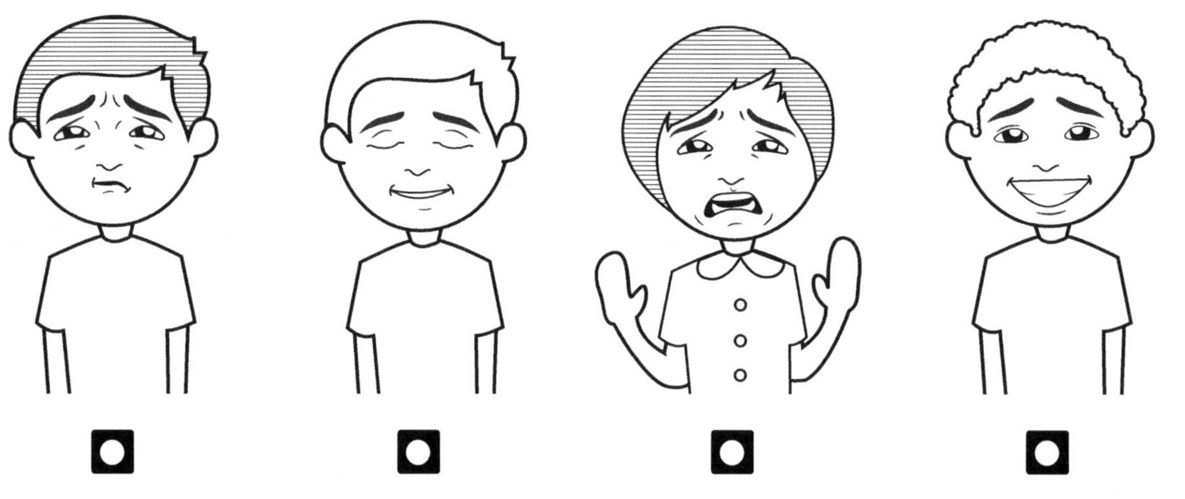

30. Mark the person who is tired.

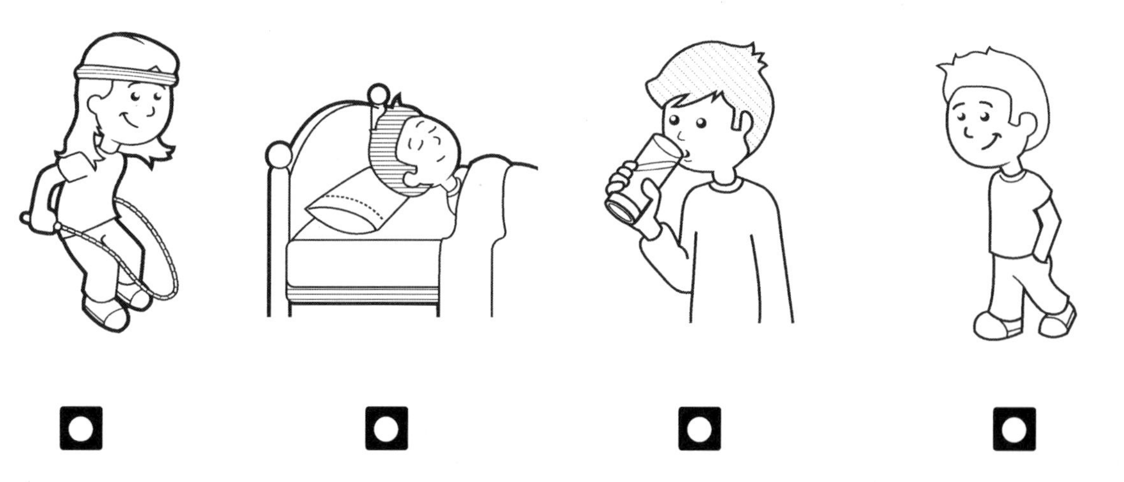

Bright Kids NYC Inc ©

31. Mark the person who is angry.

32. Mark the person who is excited.

33. Mark the person who is sad.

34. Mark the child who is worried.

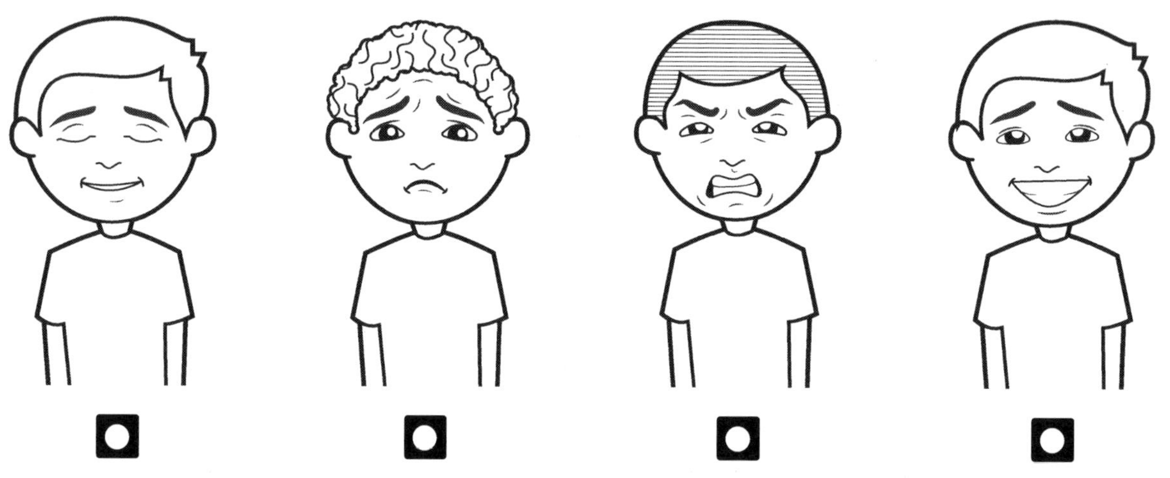

35. Mark the child who is laughing.

36. Mark the person who is frowning.

 Bright Kids NYC Inc ©

ANSWER KEY

1.	Picture 1	-	First boy
2.	Picture 1	-	Yawning dog
3.	Picture 2	-	Girl sitting in the chair
4.	Picture 4	-	Boy drinking from a baby bottle
5.	Picture 4	-	Smiling boy
6.	Picture 2	-	Frowning boy
7.	Picture 1	-	Upside down bird
8.	Picture 3	-	Kitten playing with yarn
9.	Picture 3	-	Upset child
10.	Picture 3	-	Angry boy
11.	Picture 1	-	Excited boy
12.	Picture 1	-	Juggling boy
13.	Picture 4	-	Two kittens
14.	Picture 3	-	Bald man with wrinkles
15.	Picture 4	-	Teddy bear
16.	Picture 1	-	Balancing boy
17.	Picture 2	-	Boy in bed
18.	Picture 4	-	Smiling boy
19.	Picture 3	-	Waving boy
20.	Picture 3	-	Girl sitting on chair
21.	Picture 2	-	Child in bed
22.	Picture 1	-	Girl with tennis racquet
23.	Picture 1	-	Girl petting the cat
24.	Picture 2	-	Cat peeking in a bowl
25.	Picture 3	-	Scared boy
26.	Picture 3	-	Sleeping cat
27.	Picture 3	-	Child sleeping in bed
28.	Picture 4	-	Girl peeking into box
29.	Picture 3	-	Scared girl
30.	Picture 2	-	Boy sleeping in bed
31.	Picture 4	-	Angry boy
32.	Picture 1	-	Excited girl
33.	Picture 1	-	Frowning boy
34.	Picture 2	-	Worried boy
35.	Picture 1	-	Laughing girl
36.	Picture 2	-	Frowning boy

SECTION EIGHT:
TEXTURE/MATERIAL

1. Mark something dull.

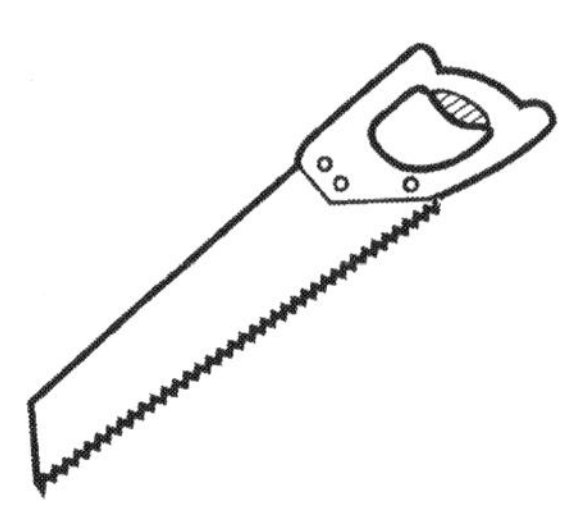
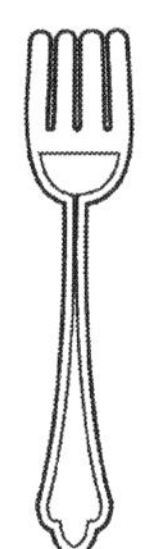

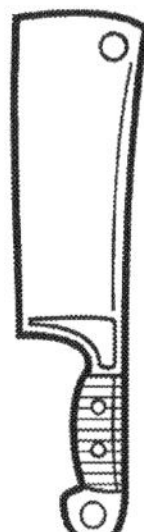

2. Mark something hard.

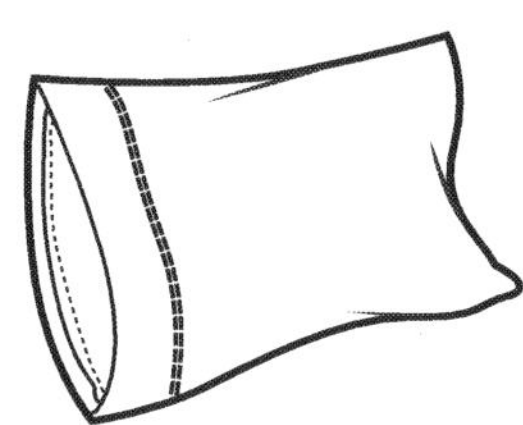

3. Mark something soft.

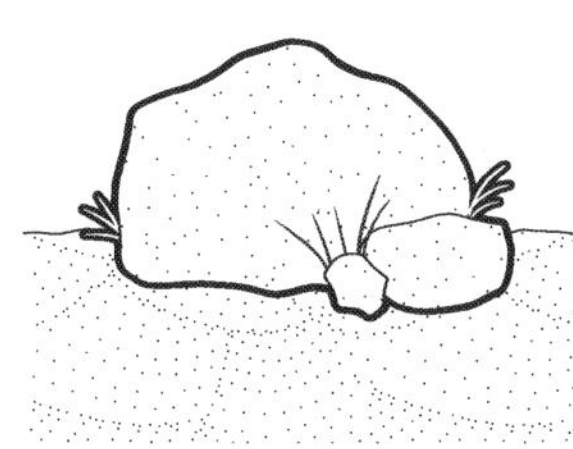
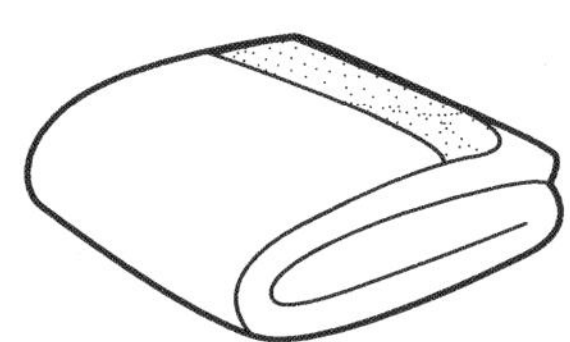
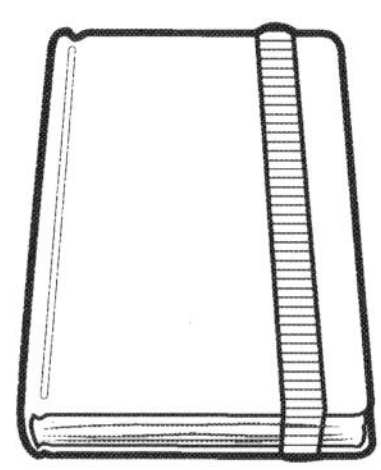

4. **Mark something sharp.**

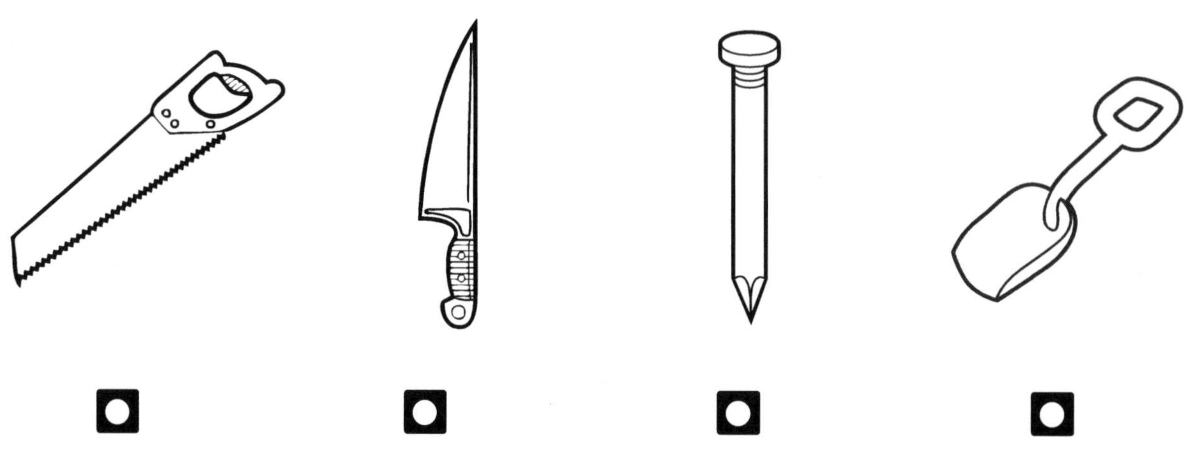

5. **Mark something dull.**

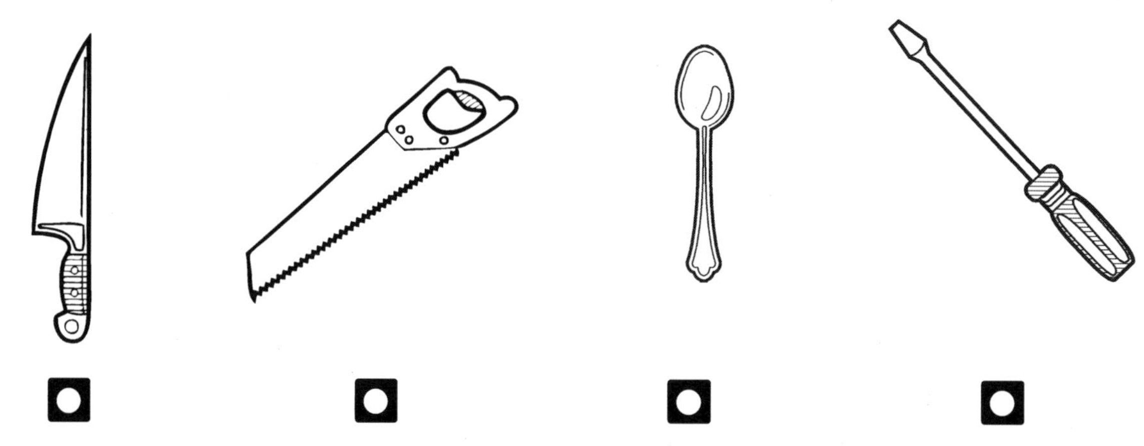

6. **Mark something cold.**

 Bright Kids NYC Inc ©

7. Mark something hot.

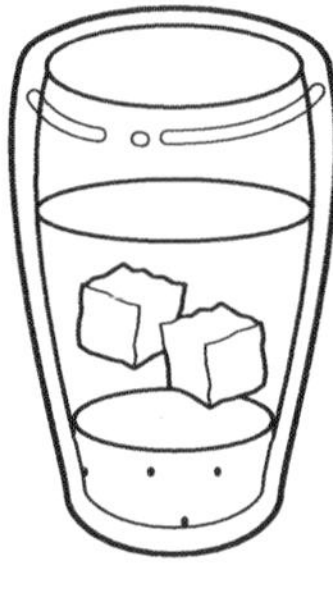

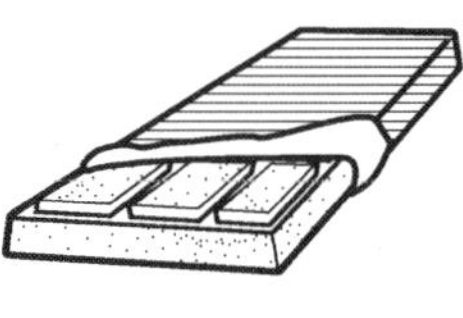

8. Mark something warm.

9. Mark something cold.

10. Mark something hot.

11. Mark something made of cloth.

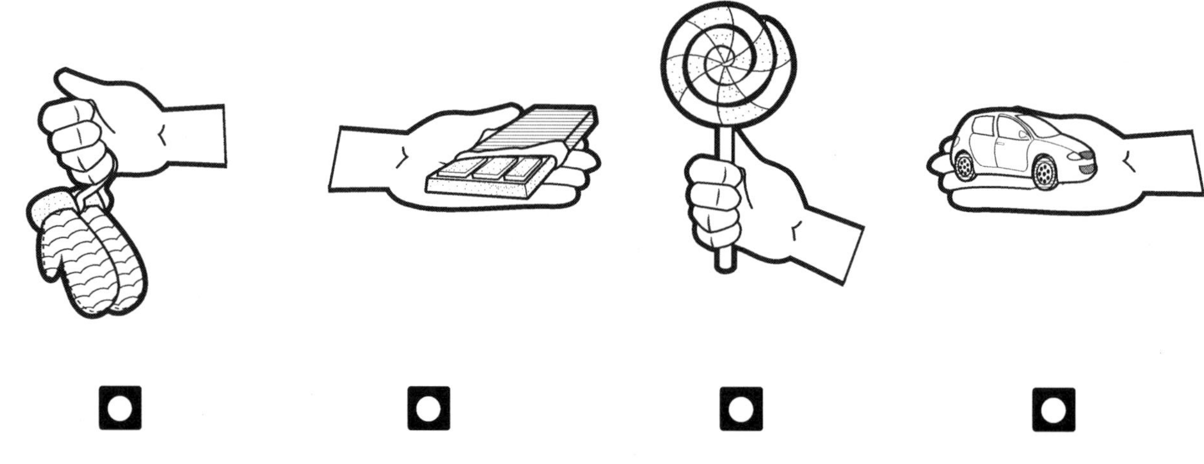

12. Mark something made of glass.

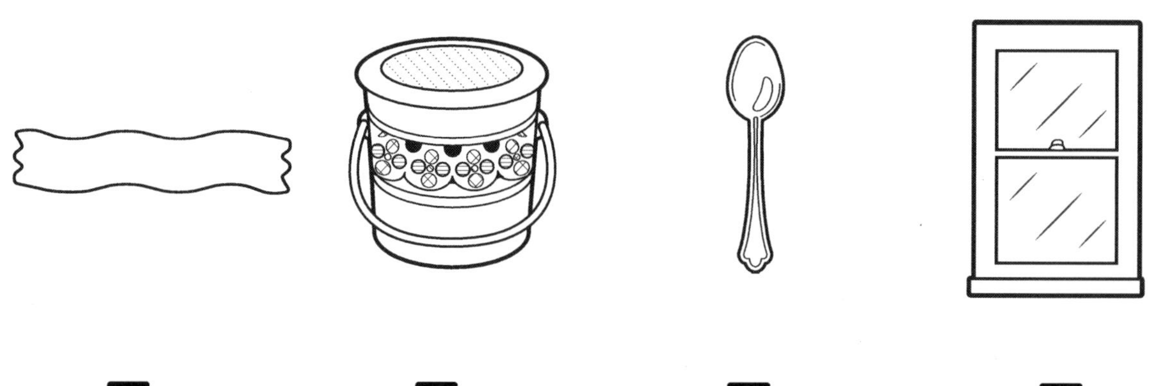

Bright Kids NYC Inc ©

13. Mark something made of metal.

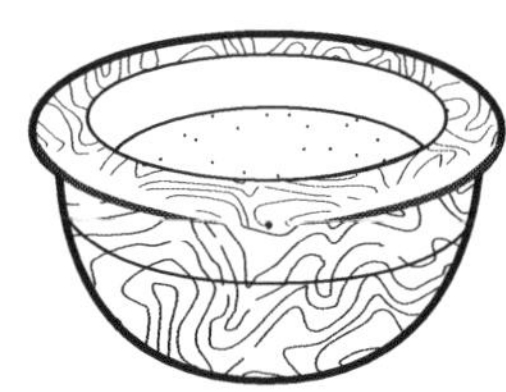
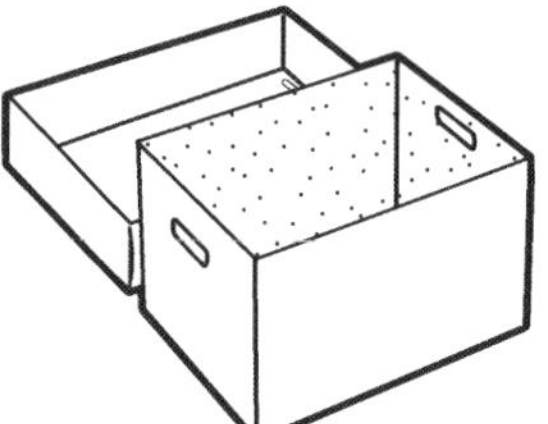

14. Mark something made of wood.

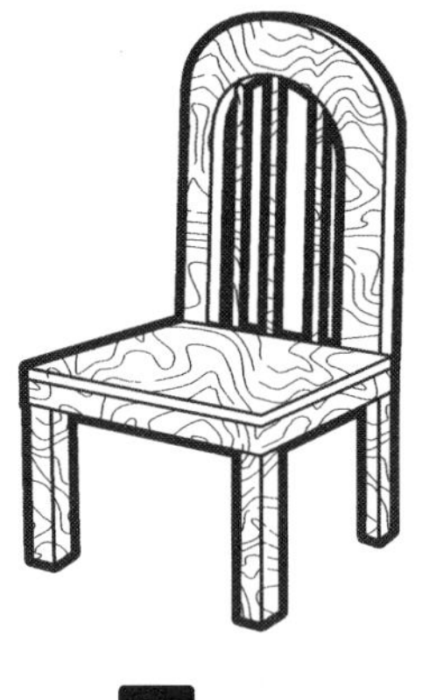

15. Mark something made of glass.

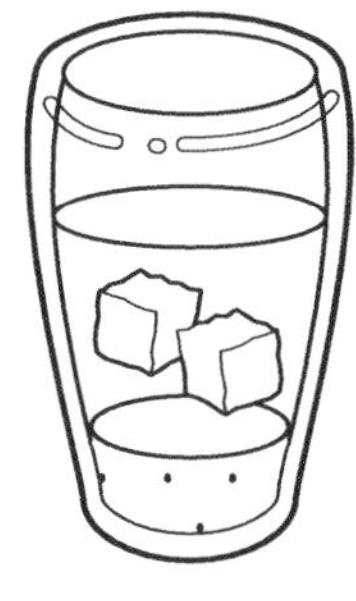
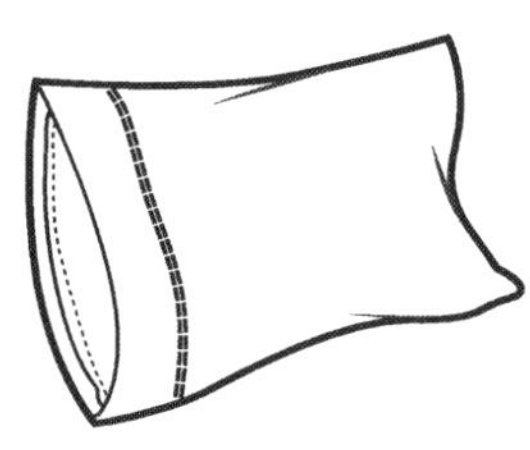

16. Mark the object that is metal.

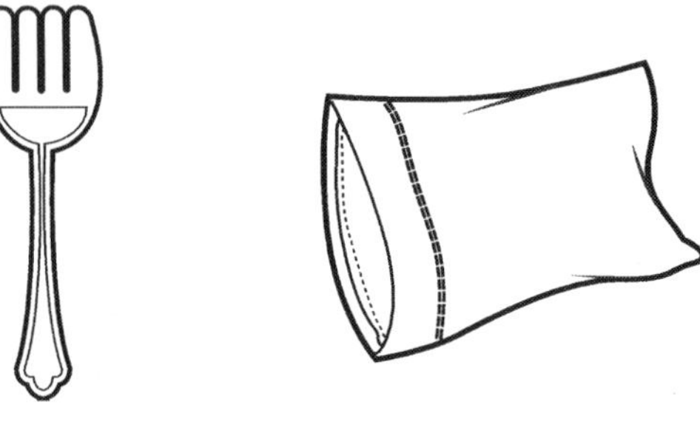

17. Mark the object that would feel rough.

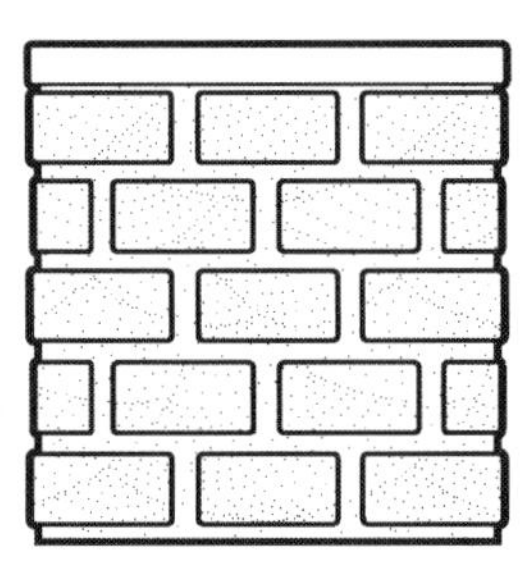
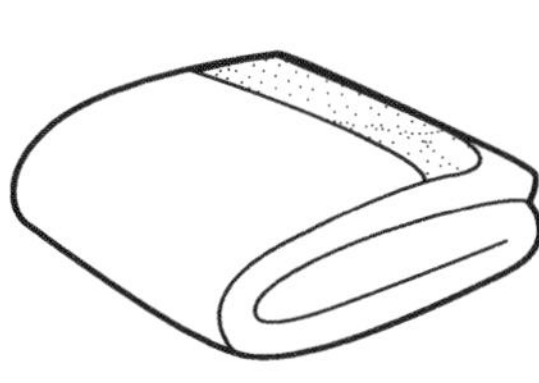

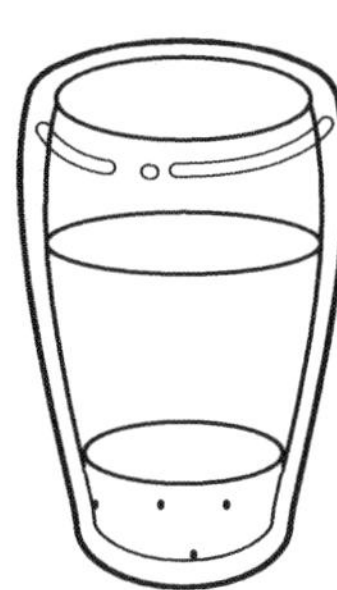

18. Mark the rock that is smooth.

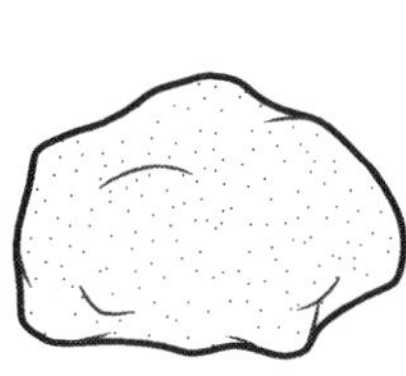

19. Mark the road that is rough.

20. Mark the clear cup.

21. Mark the shiny ball.

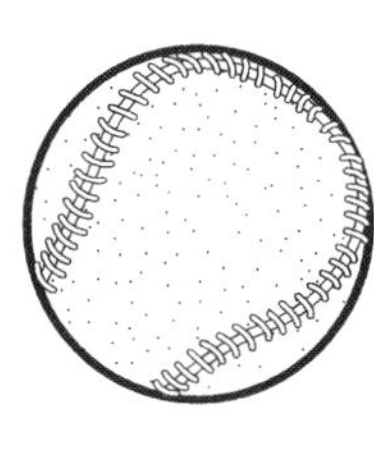

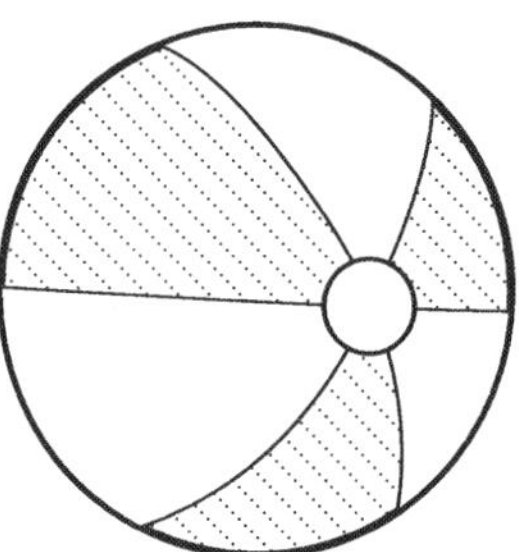

22. Mark the light that is bright.

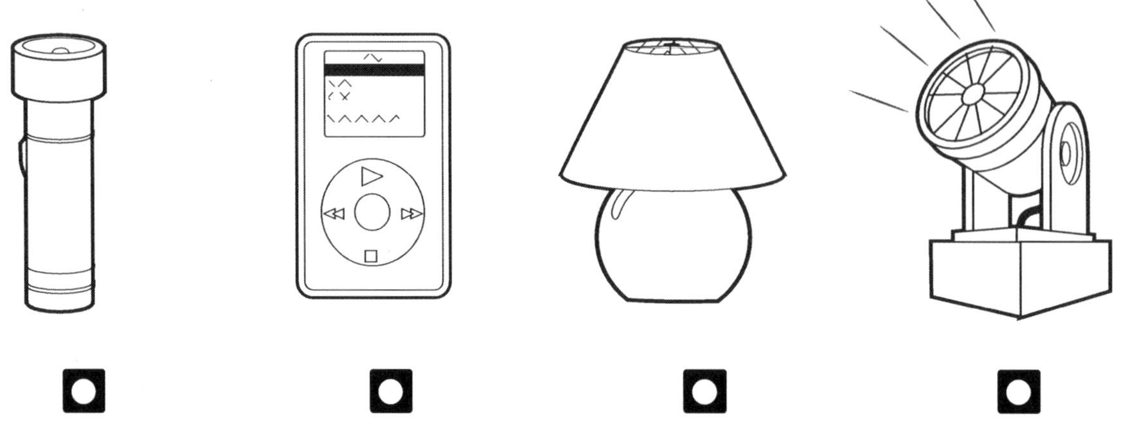

23. Mark the clear vase.

24. Mark the shoes that are shiny.

25. Mark the carpet that is flat.

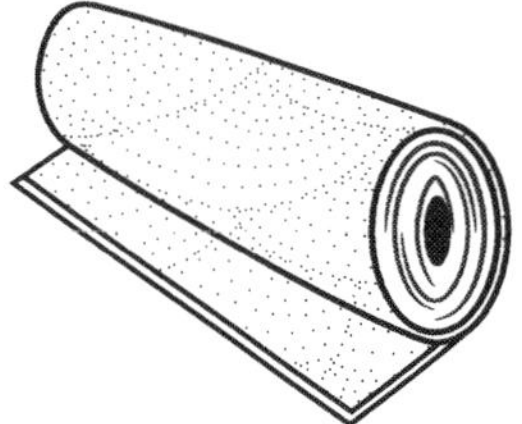 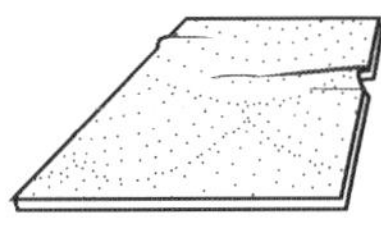 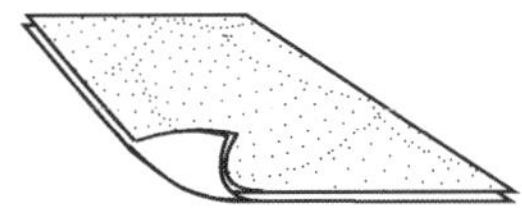 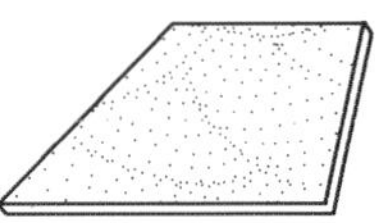

26. Mark something loud.

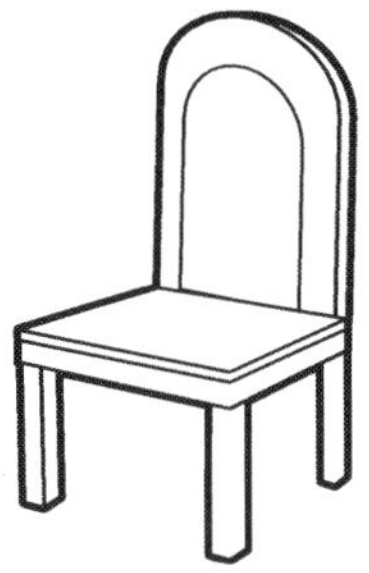 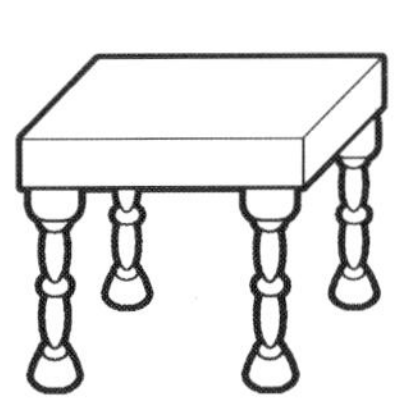  

27. Mark the child with dark hair.

28. Mark the picture that is light.

   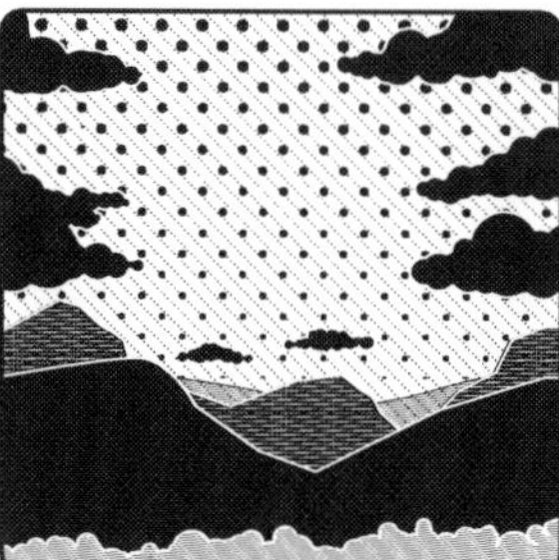

29. Mark the animal that is quiet.

30. Mark the animal that is loud.

31. Mark the loose rope.

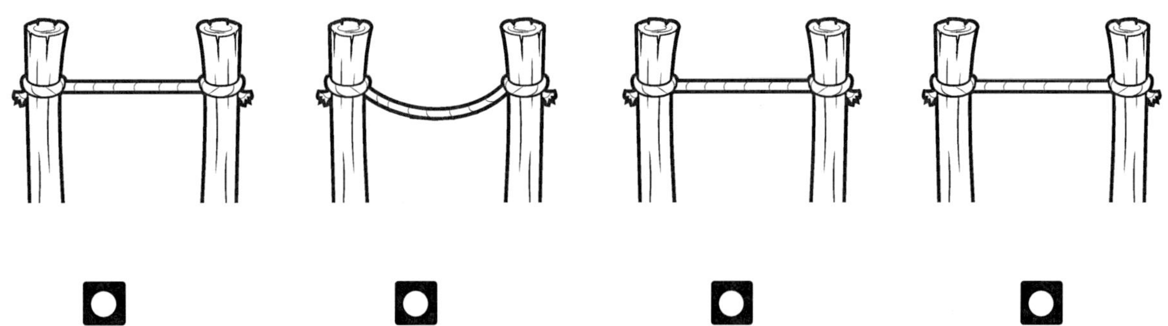

32. Mark the tight rope.

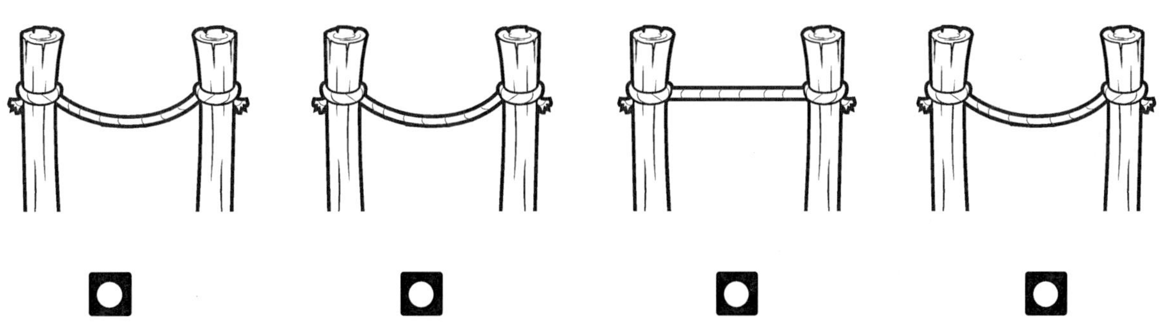

33. Mark the flat rug.

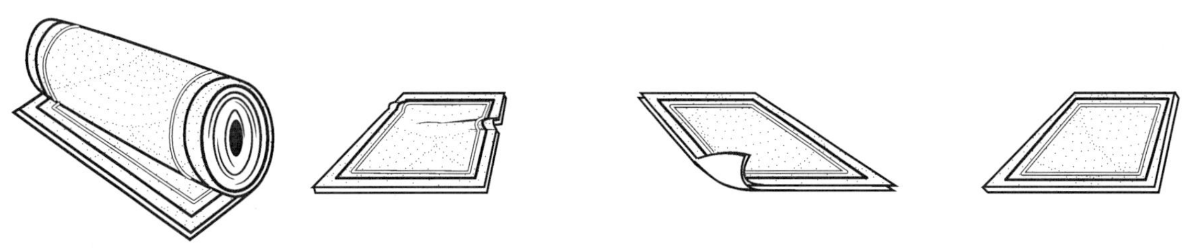

34. Mark the smooth table.

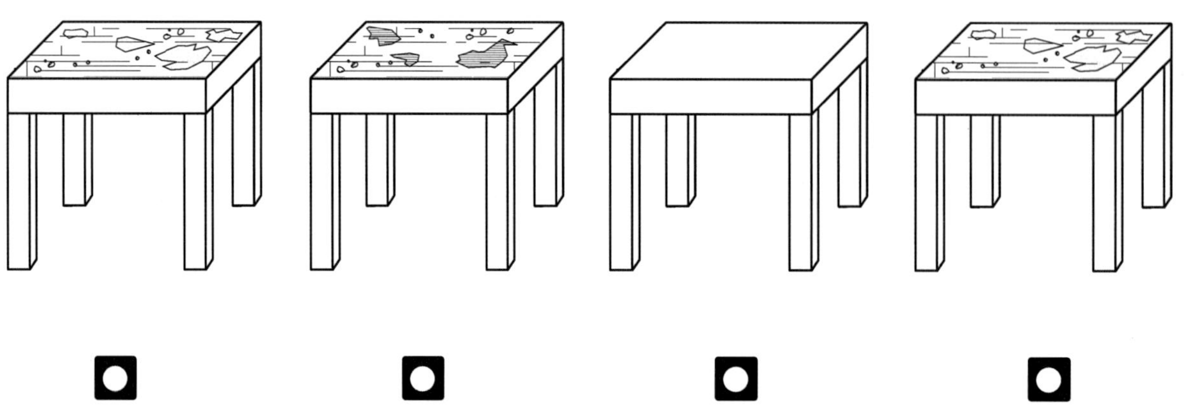

35. Mark the rough surface.

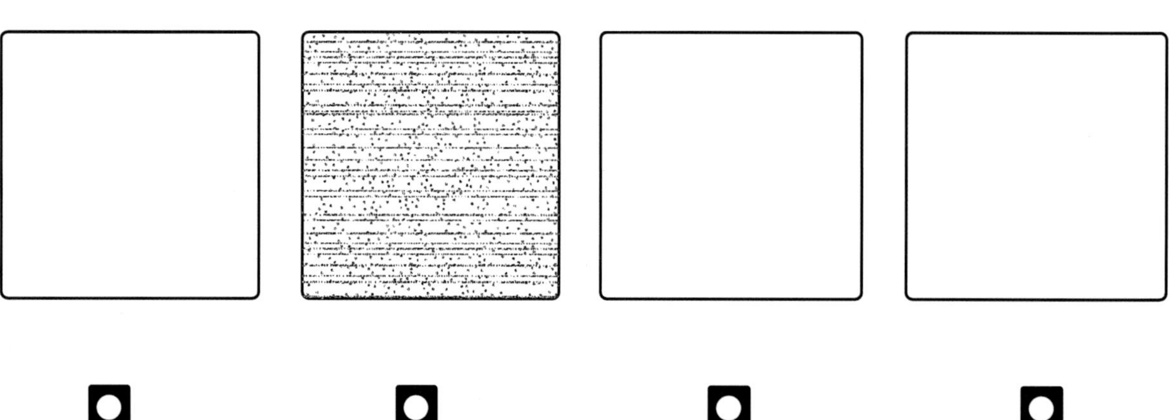

36. Mark the dark color.

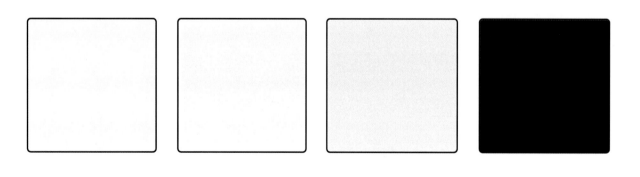

 Bright Kids NYC Inc ©

37. Mark something warm.

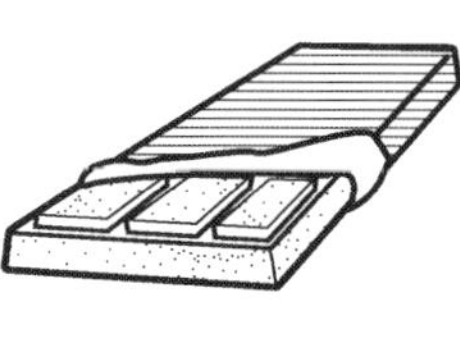

38. Mark the dry jacket.

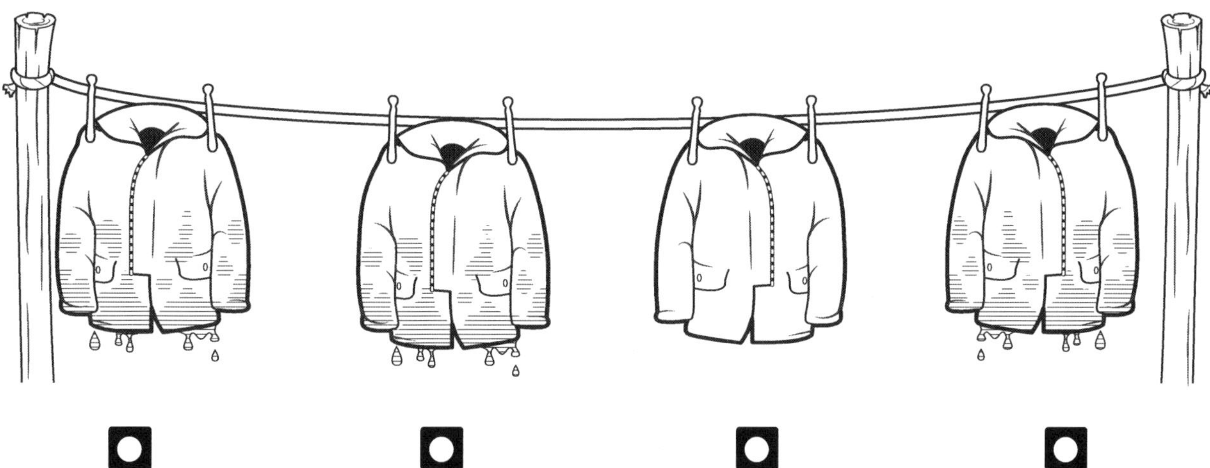

39. Mark the wet child.

ANSWER KEY

 Bright kids NYC Inc ©

1.	Picture 2	-	Fork
2.	Picture 2	-	Lollipop
3.	Picture 2	-	Blanket
4.	Picture 1/2/3	-	Saw, knife and nail
5.	Picture 3	-	Spoon
6.	Picture 1	-	Ice cream cone
7.	Picture 2	-	Steaming bowl of soup
8.	Picture 4	-	Steaming cookie
9.	Picture 1	-	Popsicle
10.	Picture 1	-	Sun
11.	Picture 1	-	Hand holding mittens
12.	Picture 4	-	Window
13.	Picture 1	-	Coins
14.	Picture 1	-	Wooden chair
15.	Picture 2	-	Glass
16.	Picture 1	-	Fork
17.	Picture 1	-	Brick wall
18.	Picture 3	-	Third rock
19.	Picture 2	-	Second car on the road
20.	Picture 4	-	Fourth cup
21.	Picture 1	-	First ball
22.	Picture 4	-	Spotlight
23.	Picture 3	-	Third vase
24.	Picture 2	-	High heeled shoes
25.	Picture 4	-	Fourth rug
26.	Picture 4	-	Snare drum
27.	Picture 3	-	Third child
28.	Picture 3	-	Third picture
29.	Picture 3	-	Turtle
30.	Picture 4	-	Lion
31.	Picture 2	-	Second rope
32.	Picture 3	-	Third rope
33.	Picture 4	-	Fourth rug
34.	Picture 3	-	Third table
35.	Picture 2	-	Second picture
36.	Picture 4	-	Dark purple
37.	Picture 1	-	Apple pie
38.	Picture 3	-	Third jacket
39.	Picture 4	-	Fourth child

123
ABC

SECTION NINE:
MATH CONCEPTS

1. Mark the full basket.

2. Mark the empty bowl.

3. Mark the picture of the whole train.

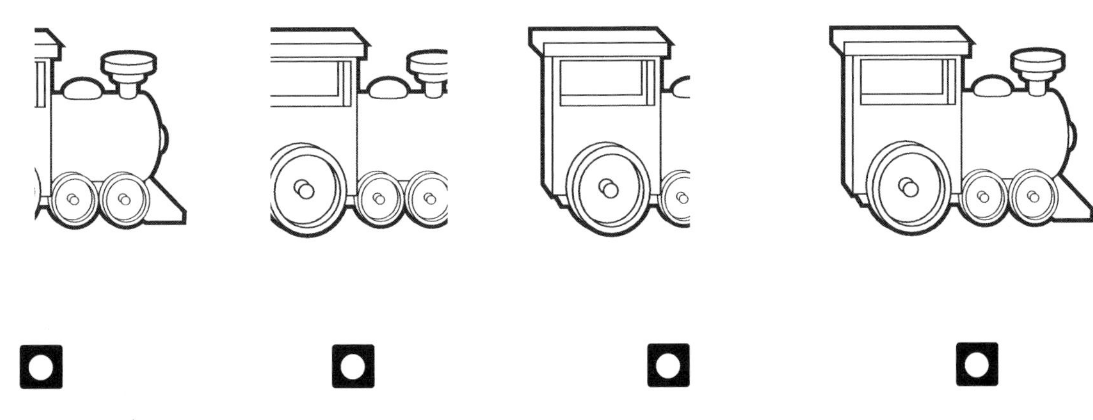

4. Mark the cookie that is cut in half.

  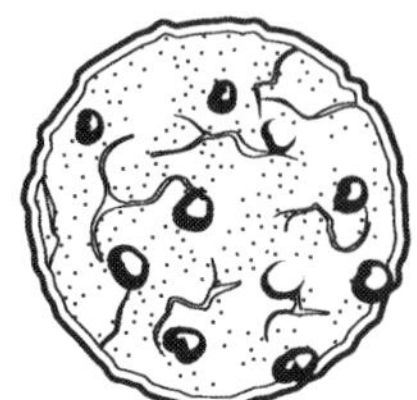 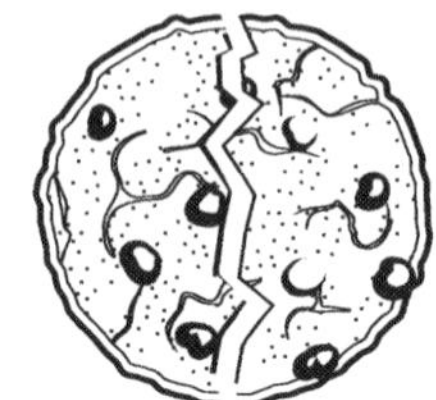

5. Mark the picture that shows a piece of a bowl.

6. Mark the picture that shows a couple of stools.

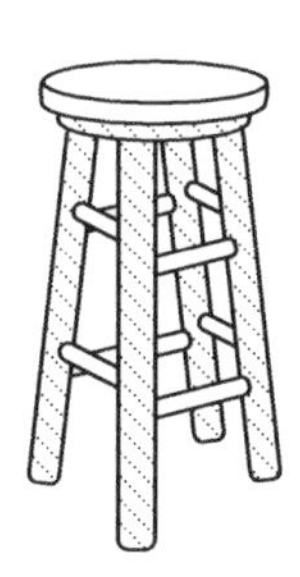   

7. Mark the single banana.

8. Mark the picture that shows a couple of crayons.

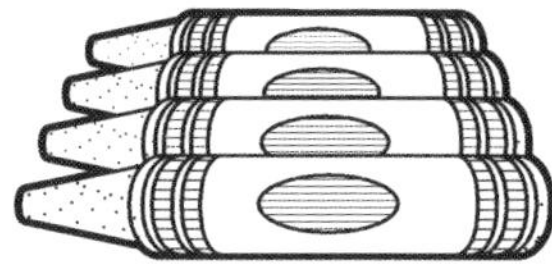 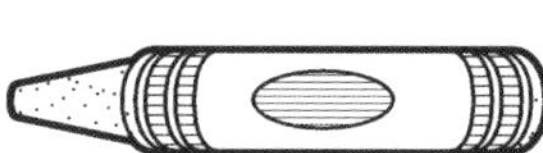 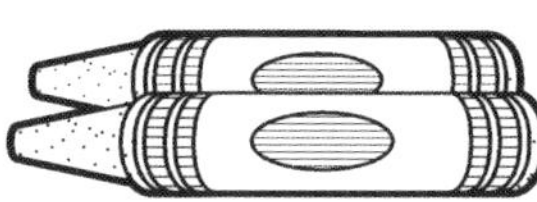 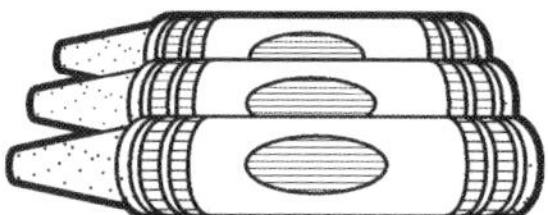

9. Mark the picture with both glasses broken.

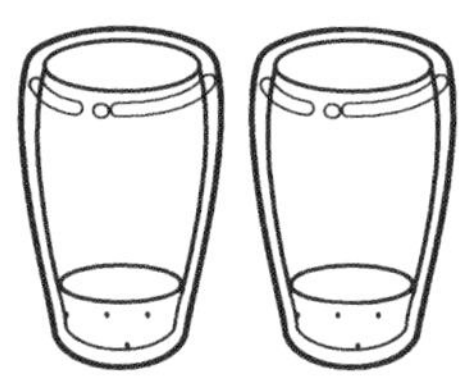 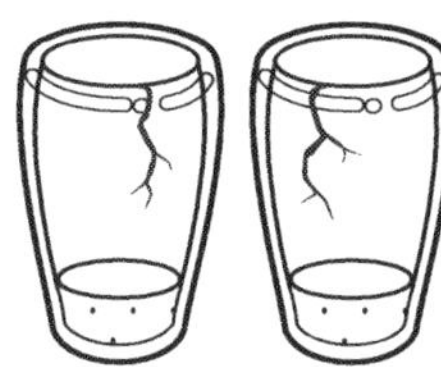 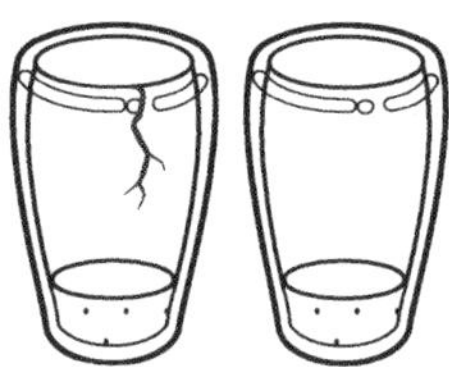 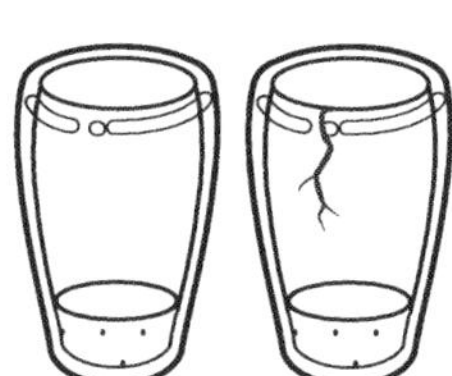

10. Mark the giraffe that is alone.

11. Mark the basket without any fruit.

12. Mark the glass with little juice.

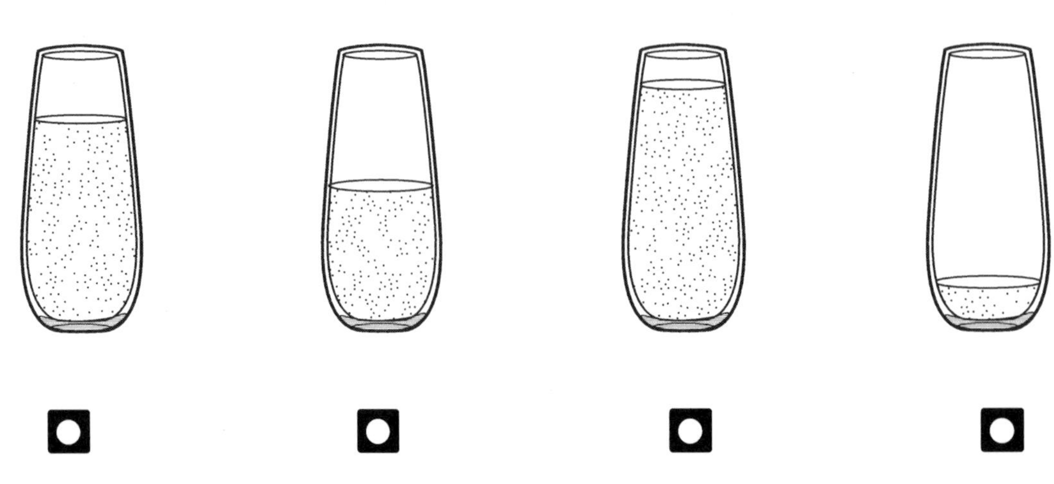

13. Mark the picture that has all the parts except the nose.

14. Mark the window without a crack.

 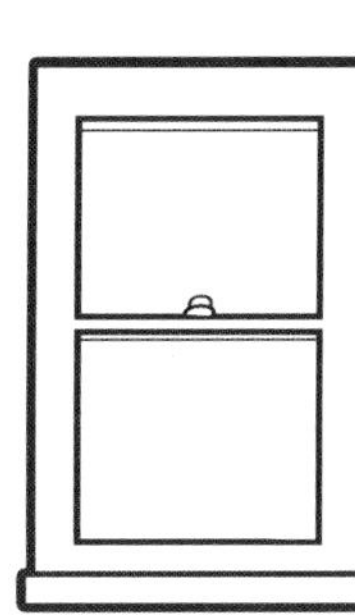 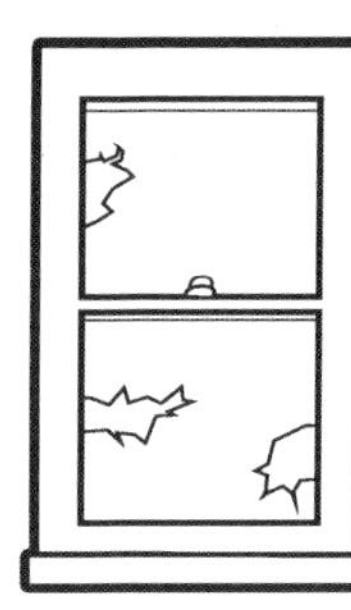 

15. Mark every child with a ball.

16. Mark the branch with the greatest number of birds.

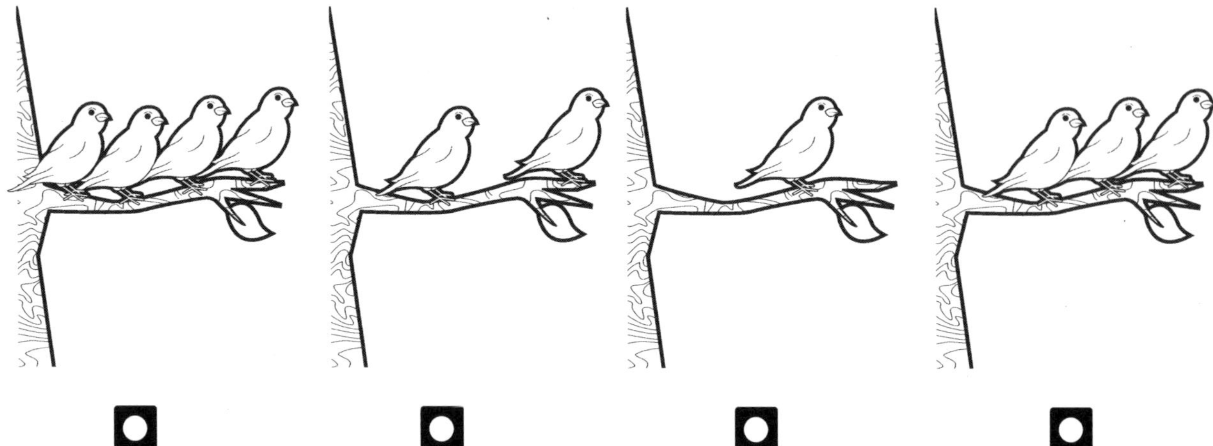

17. Mark every cat with a collar.

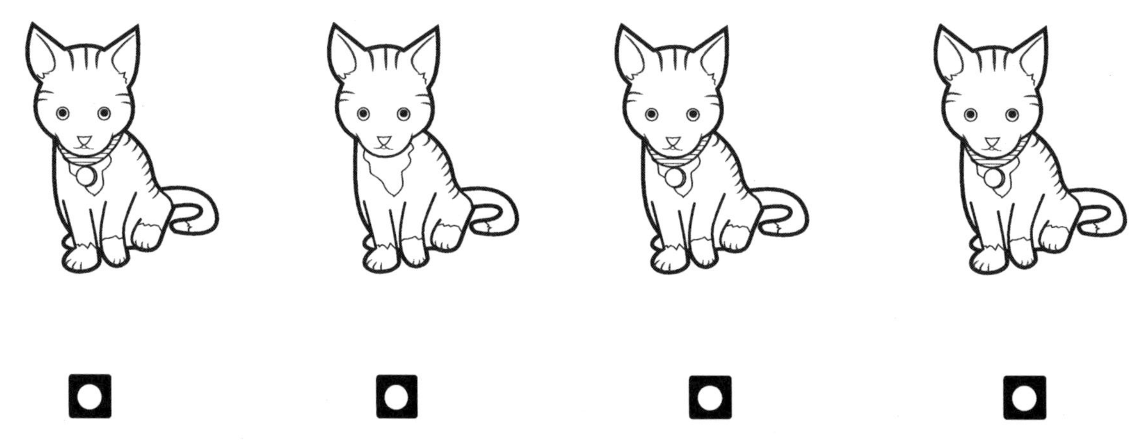

18. Mark all the children with a book.

 Bright Kids NYC Inc ©

19. Mark the tank with several fish.

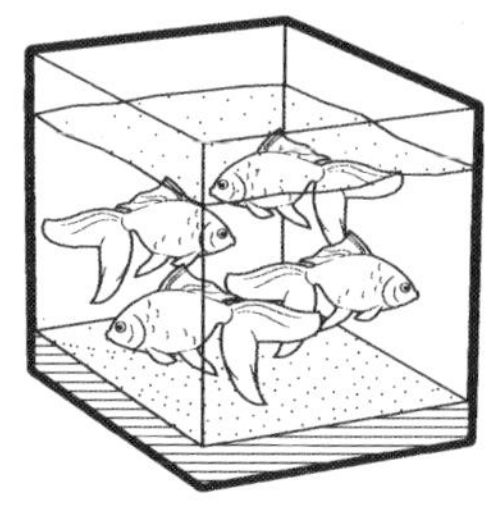 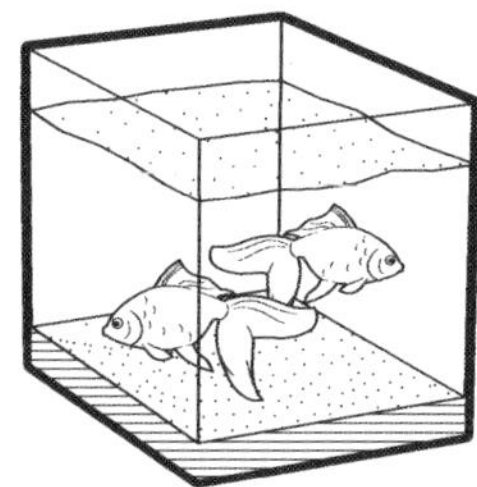 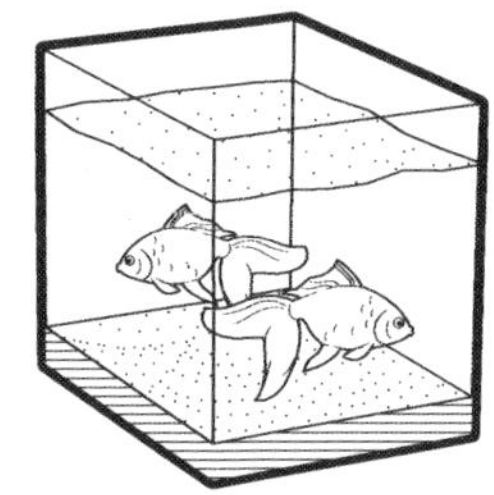 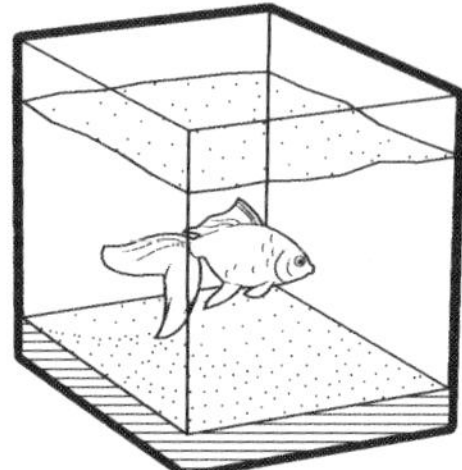

20. Mark the bowl with only apples in it.

21. Mark every alligator.

22. Mark the cat with the yarn.

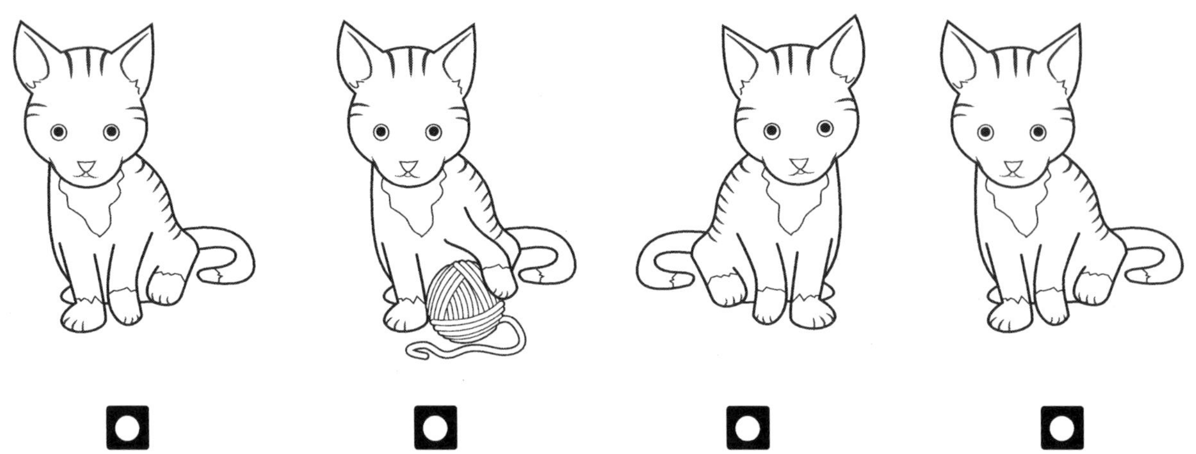

23. Mark the glass with the most juice in it.

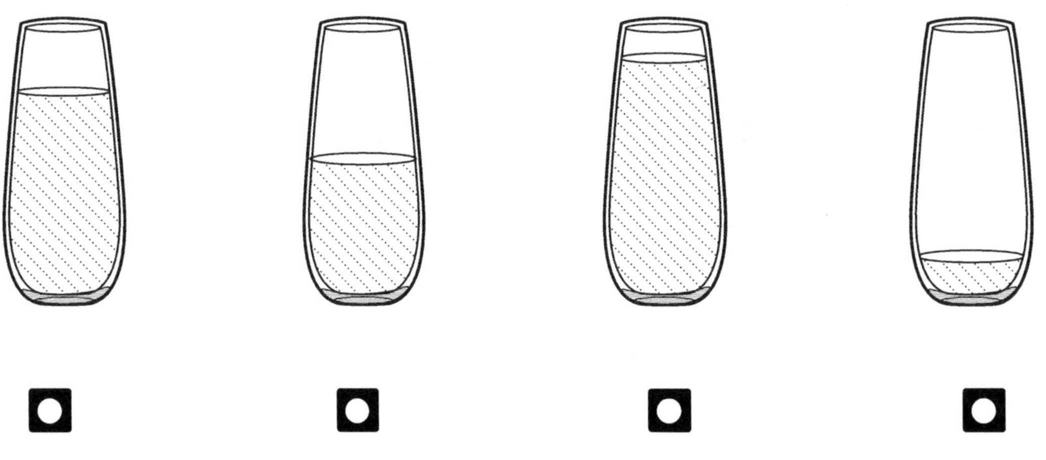

24. Mark the pair of cats.

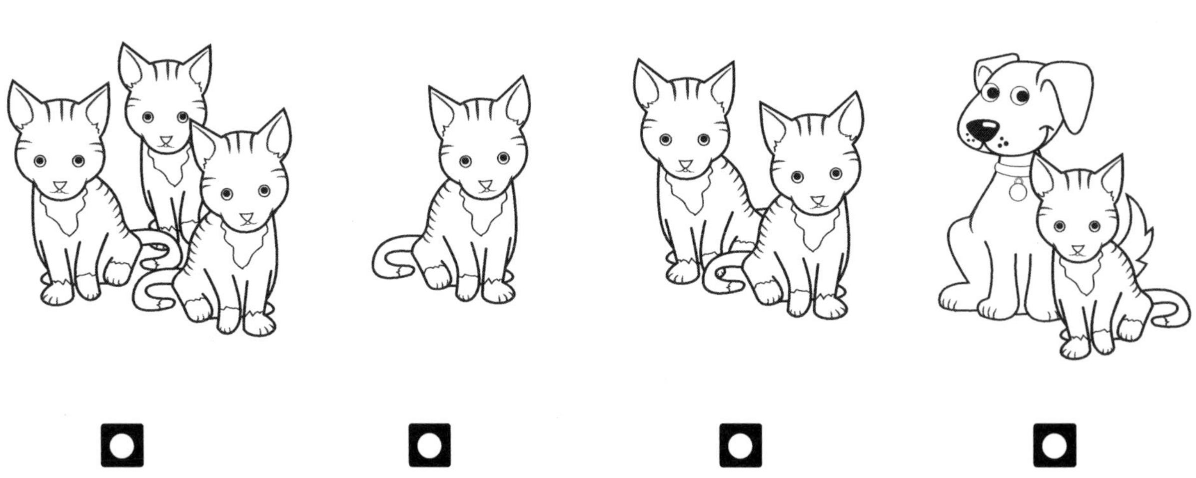

 Bright Kids NYC Inc ©

25. Mark the boy taking another apple.

26. Mark the picture in which neither child is wearing shorts.

27. Mark the glass with the most water.

28. Mark the plate with the least cake.

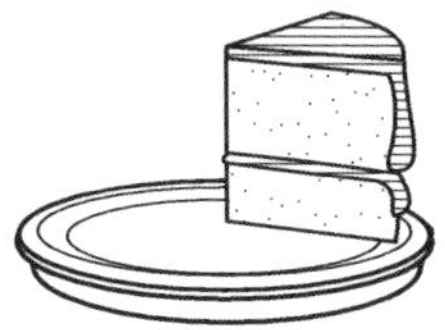 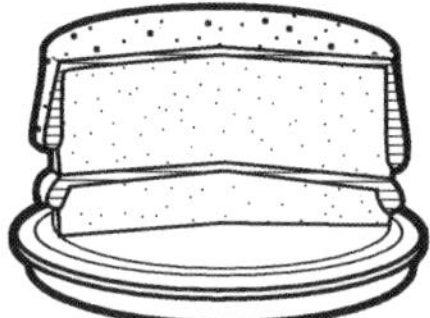  

29. Mark the pair of birds.

30. Mark the boy who is putting another apple on the table.

 Bright Kids NYC Inc ©

31. Mark the child who is the least wet.

32. Mark the glass with the least juice.

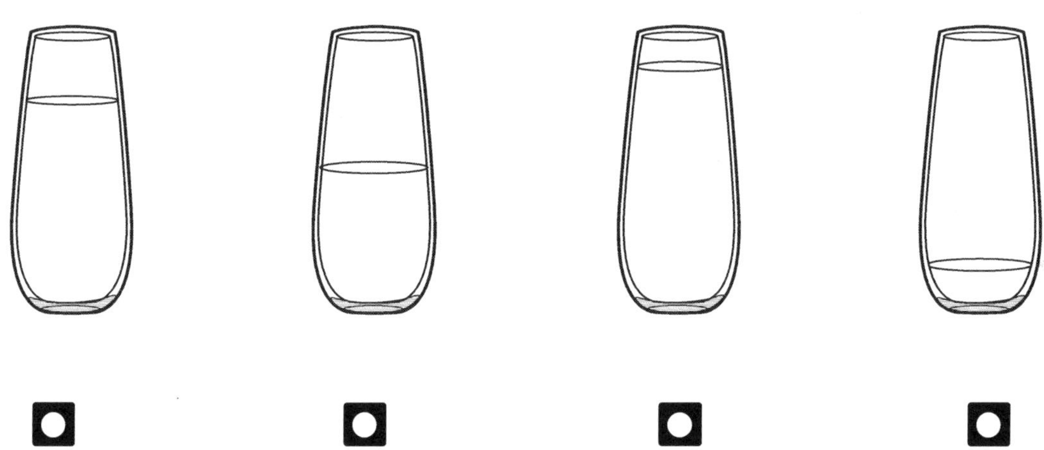

33. Mark the shoe that is the least dirty.

34. Mark the child with the most blocks.

35. Mark the mailbox with the least mail.

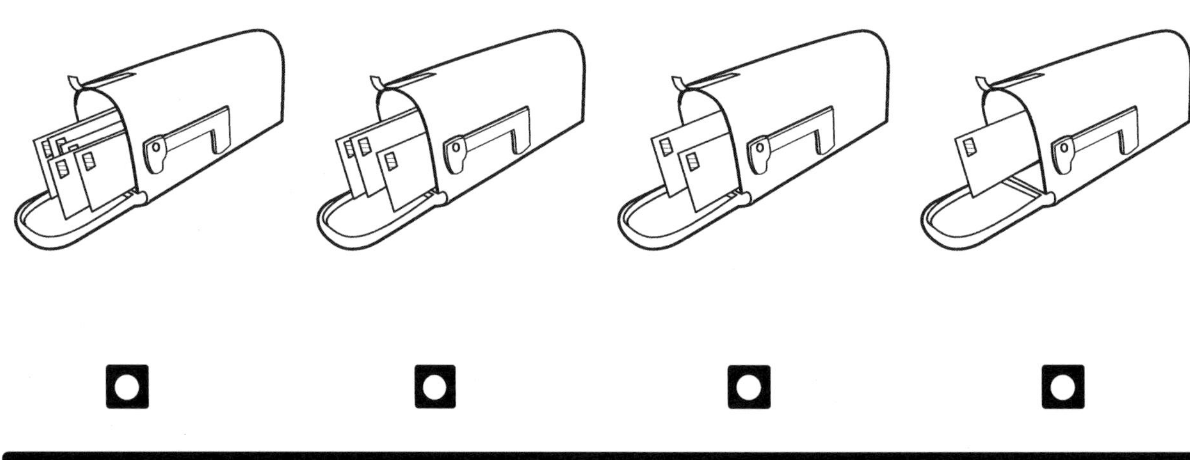

36. Mark the glass that is nearly empty.

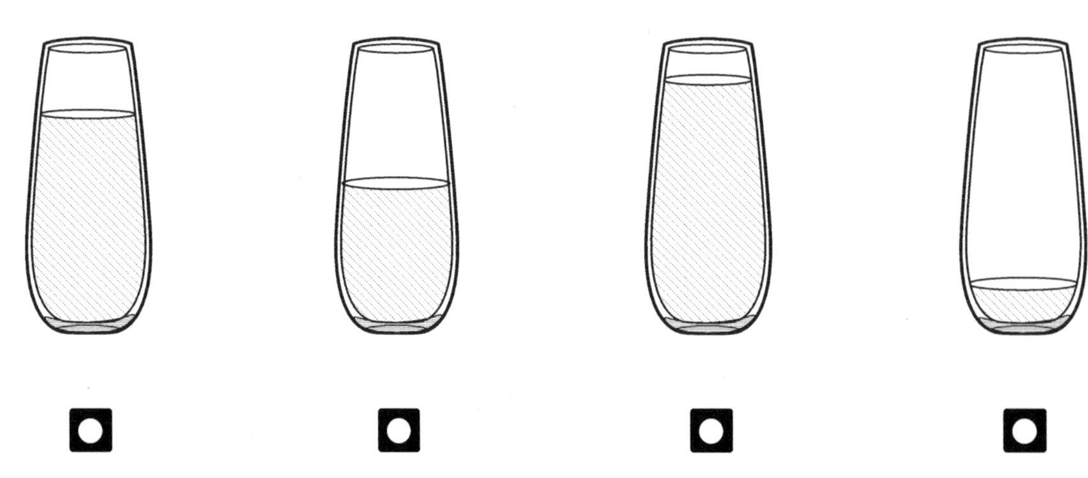

37. Mark the nest that has twice as many eggs as birds.

38. Mark the bowl that has more bananas than apples.

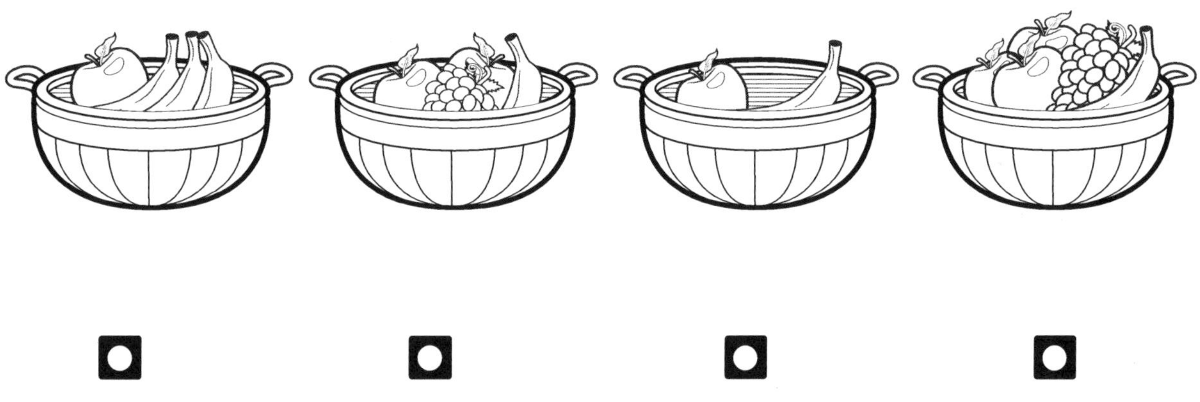

39. Mark the card with as many hearts as stars.

40. Mark the empty box.

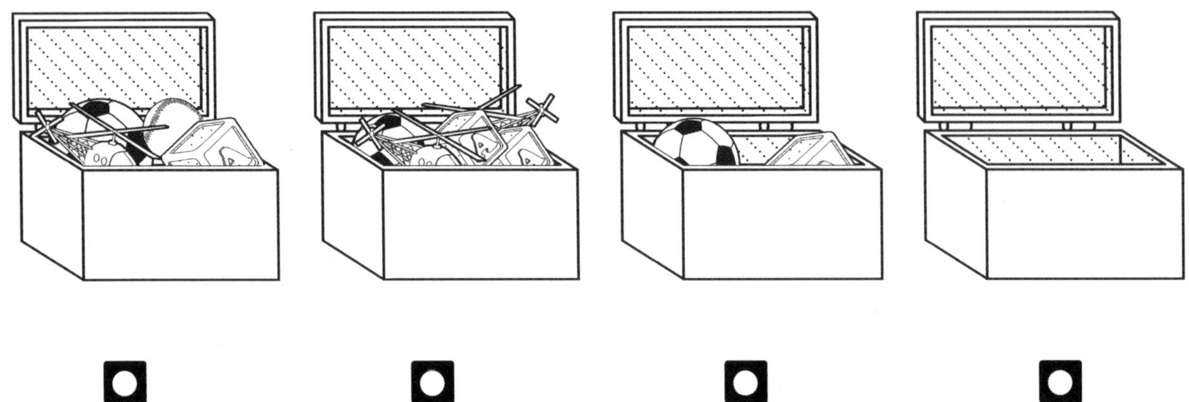

41. Mark the child who has less flowers than the others.

42. Mark the cookie that is almost all eaten.

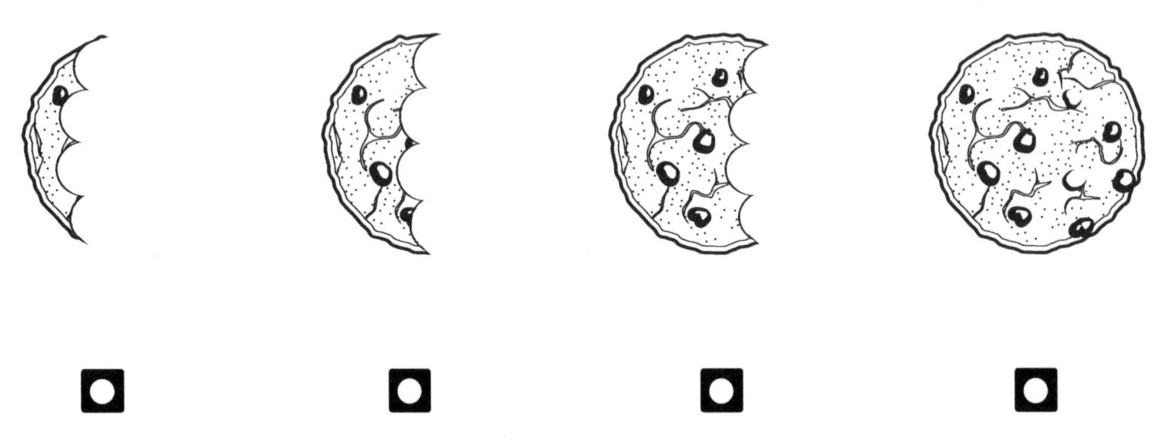

43. Mark the group that has as many hats as mittens.

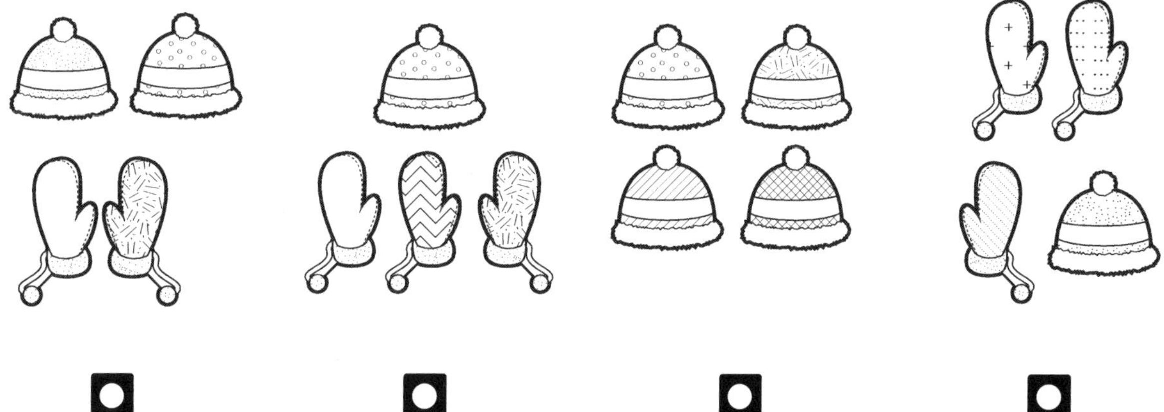

44. Mark the toothpaste with the missing cap.

45. Mark the plate that has no cake left.

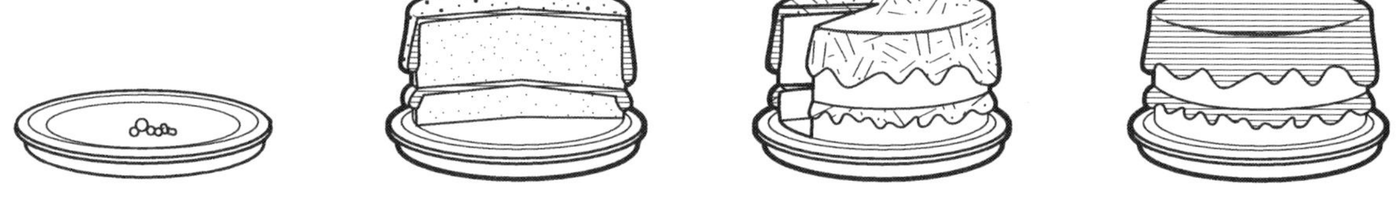

46. Mark the triple scoop of ice cream.

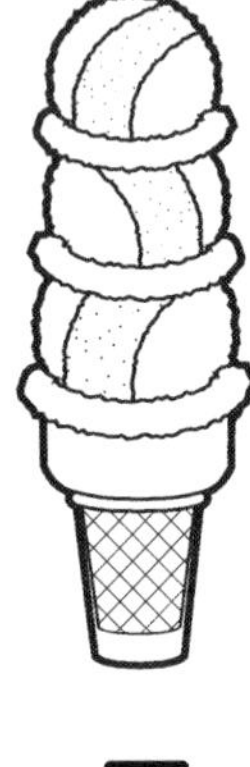   

47. Mark the child who has a double serving of cake.

48. Mark the plus sign.

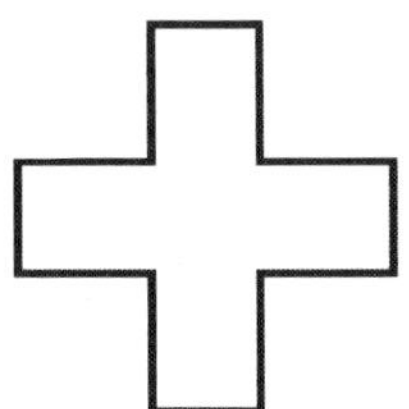 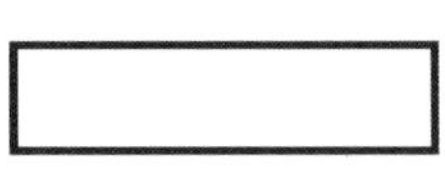 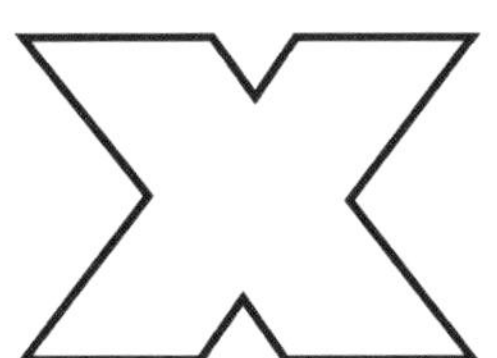 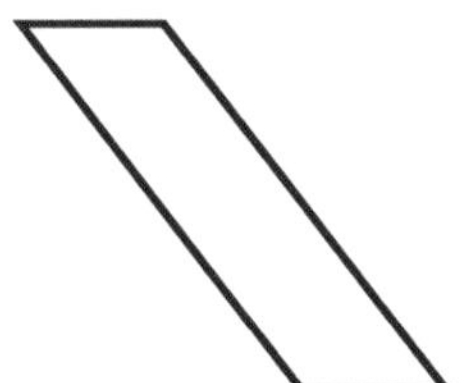

 Bright Kids NYC Inc ©

49. Mark the minus sign.

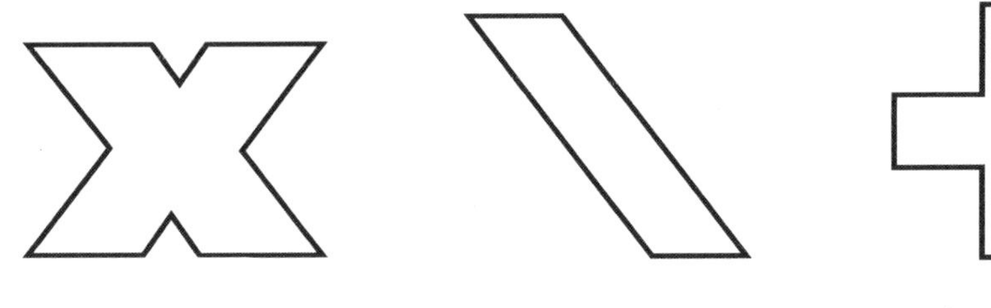

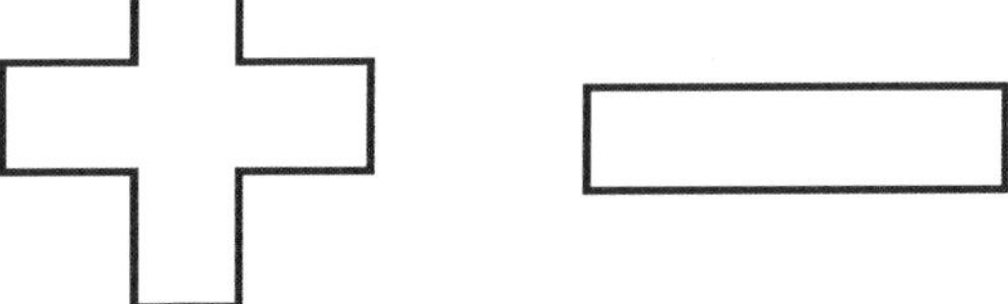

50. Mark the multiplication sign.

51. Mark the division sign.

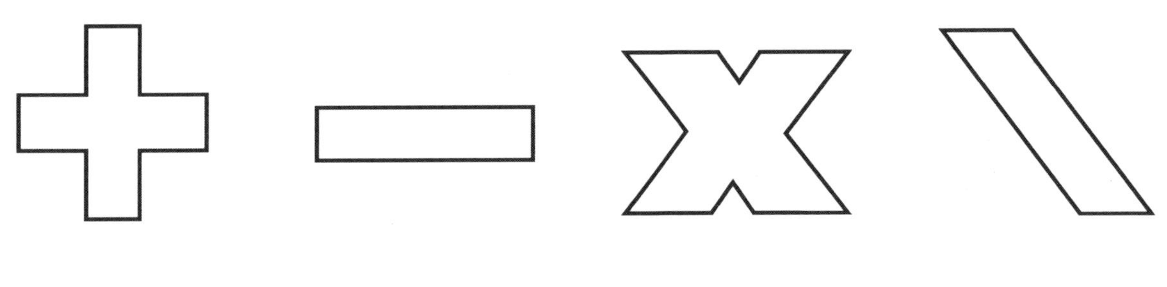

52. Mark the third of a pie.

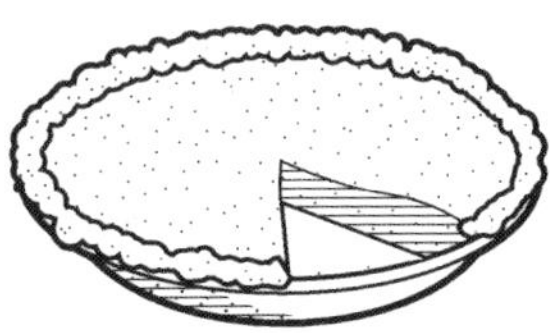 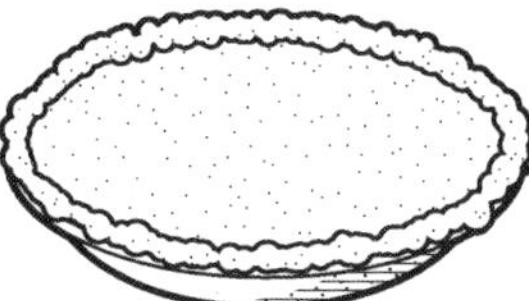 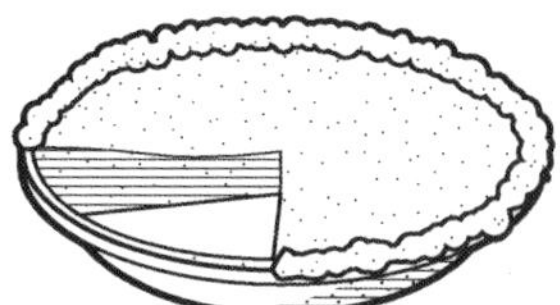 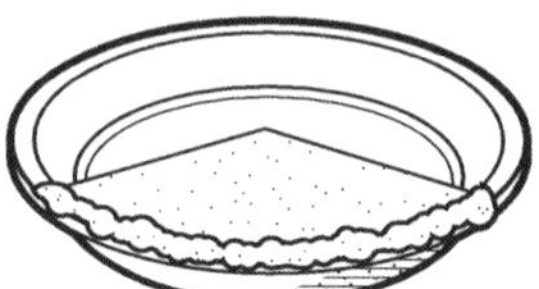

53. Mark the dozen eggs.

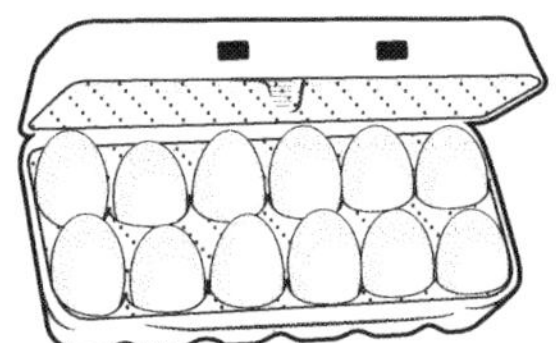 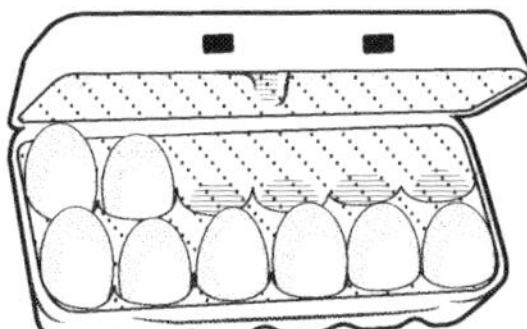 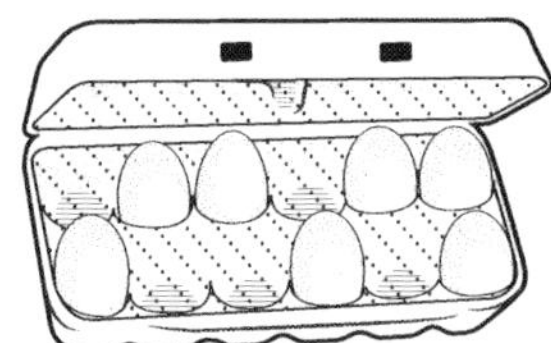 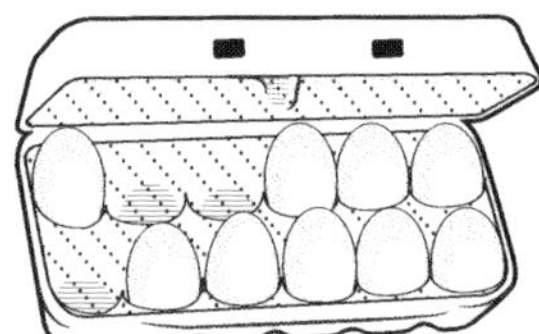

54. Mark the half dozen marbles.

  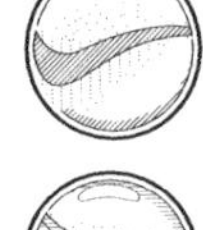 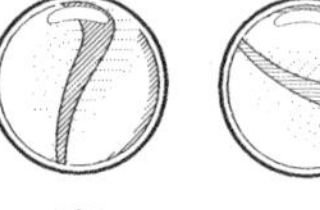 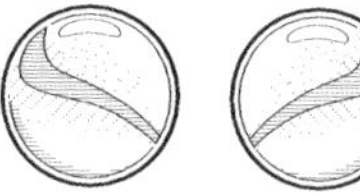

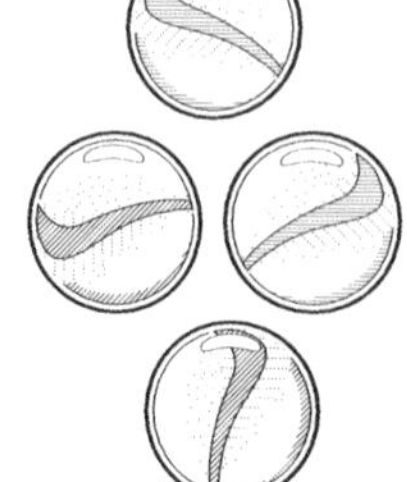

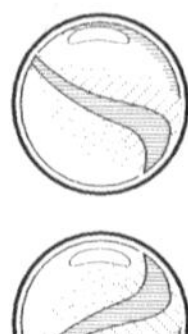 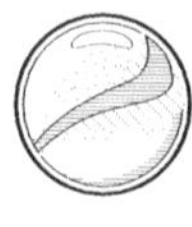

 Bright Kids NYC Inc ©

55. Mark the child who has lots of stickers.

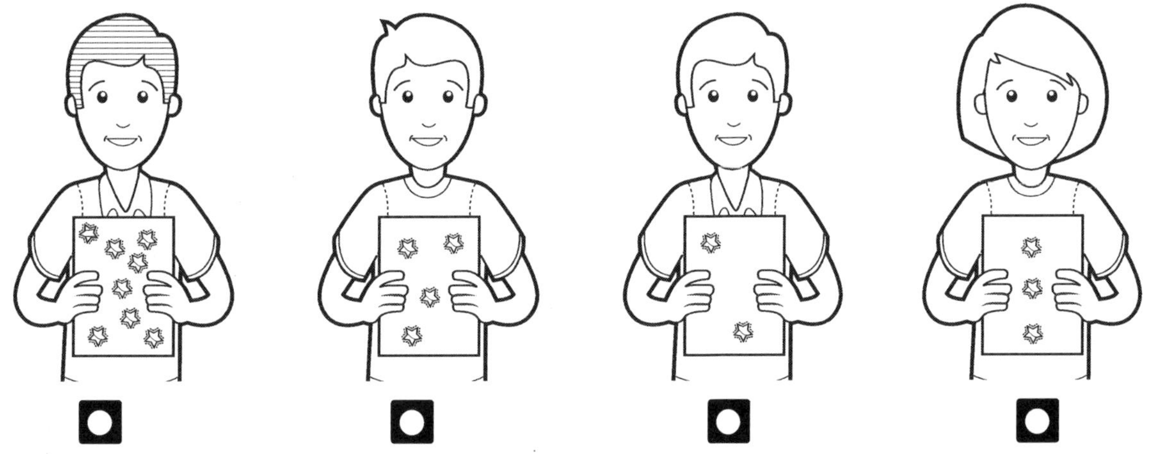

56. Mark the tank with a few fish.

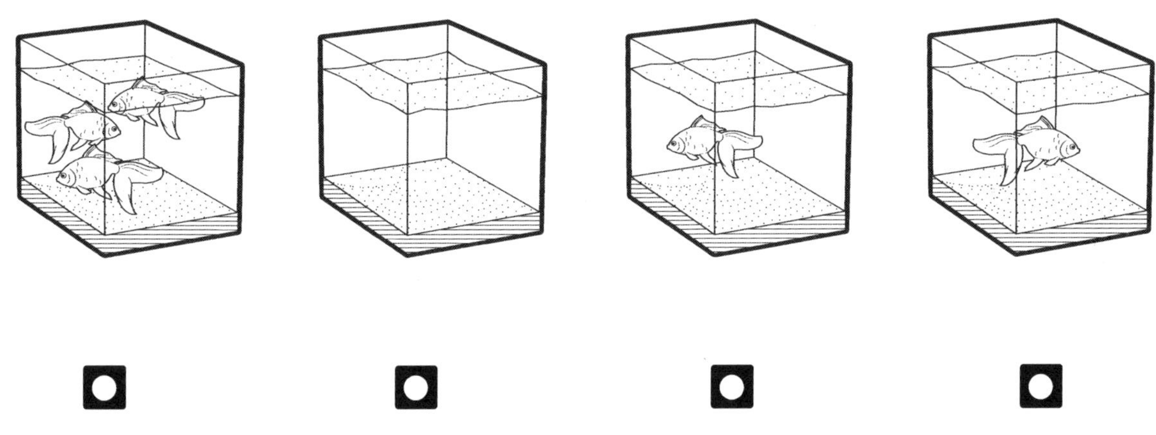

57. Mark the child who has more french fries than the others.

58. Mark the child that has all the fruit except the banana.

59. Mark the tank with a pair of fish.

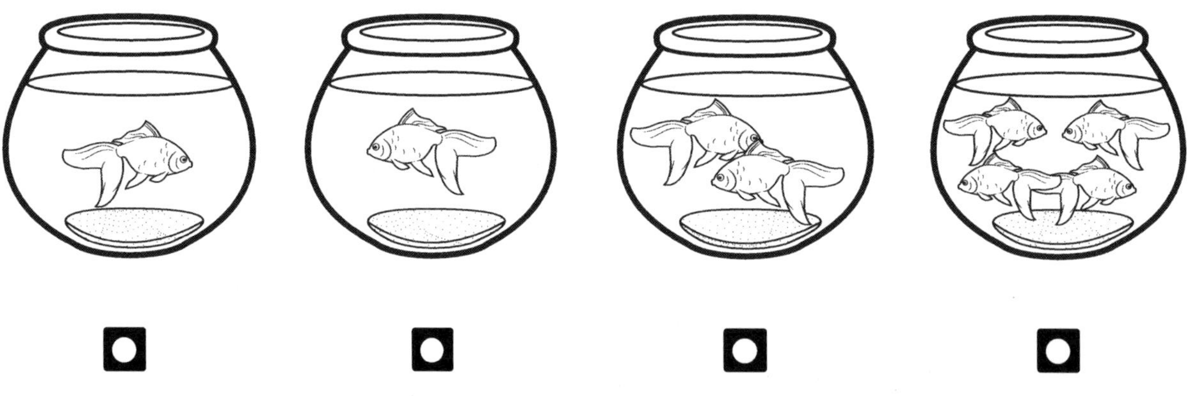

60. Mark the kid who has nothing.

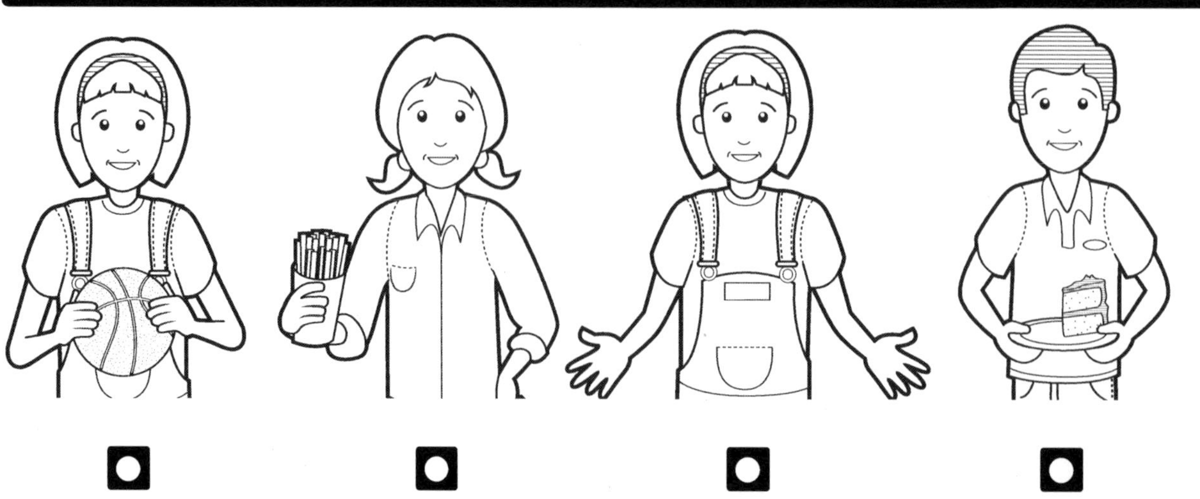

 Bright Kids NYC Inc ©

ANSWER KEY

1.	Picture 4	-	Fourth basket
2.	Picture 4	-	Fourth bowl
3.	Picture 4	-	Fourth train
4.	Picture 4	-	Cookie cut in half
5.	Picture 4	-	Broken bowl
6.	Picture 4	-	Group of two stools
7.	Picture 2	-	Single banana
8.	Picture 3	-	Two Crayons
9.	Picture 2	-	Second pair of glasses
10.	Picture 4	-	Giraffe
11.	Picture 3	-	Empty basket
12.	Picture 4	-	Fourth glass
13.	Picture 4	-	Fourth picture
14.	Picture 2	-	Second window
15.	Picture 1/2/4	-	First, second and fourth child
16.	Picture 1	-	Branch with four birds
17.	Picture 1/3/4	-	First, third and fourth kitten
18.	Picture 1/2/3	-	First, second and third child
19.	Picture 1	-	Tank with four fish
20.	Picture 1	-	First basket
21.	Picture 1/3/4	-	First, third, and fourth picture
22.	Picture 2	-	Second cat
23.	Picture 3	-	Third glass
24.	Picture 3	-	Two cats
25.	Picture 3	-	Third boy
26.	Picture 4	-	Fourth pair of children
27.	Picture 2	-	Second glass
28.	Picture 1	-	First plate
29.	Picture 1	-	Two birds
30.	Picture 3	-	Third boy
31.	Picture 3	-	Third girl
32.	Picture 4	-	Fourth glass
33.	Picture 3	-	Third shoe
34.	Picture 1	-	First boy
35.	Picture 4	-	Fourth mailbox
36	Picture 4	-	Fourth glass
37.	Picture 3	-	Third picture
38.	Picture 1	-	First bowl
39	Picture 3	-	Third card
40.	Picture 4	-	Fourth toy box

41.	Picture 3	-	Third boy
42.	Picture 1	-	First cookie
43.	Picture 1	-	First set of hats and mittens
44.	Picture 2	-	Second tube of toothpaste
45.	Picture 1	-	Plate with no cake
46.	Picture 1	-	First ice cream cone
47.	Picture 2	-	Second person
48.	Picture 1	-	Plus sign
49.	Picture 4	-	Minus sign
50.	Picture 2	-	Multiplication sign
51.	Picture 4	-	Division sign
52.	Picture 4	-	Fourth pie tin
53.	Picture 1	-	Full carton of eggs
54.	Picture 1	-	Six marbles
55.	Picture 1	-	First child
56.	Picture 1	-	Tank with three fish
57.	Picture 2	-	Second child
58.	Picture 1	-	First child
59.	Picture 3	-	Third bowl
60.	Picture 3	-	Third child
61.	Picture 2	-	Two fish
62.	Picture 2	-	Four stars
63.	Picture 4	-	Three balls
64.	Picture 4	-	Six ladybugs
65.	Picture 3	-	Five marbles
66.	Picture 2	-	Eight marbles
67.	Picture 4	-	Seven cupcakes
68.	Picture 1	-	Ten birds
69.	Picture 2	-	Nine birds

123
ABC

SECTION TEN:
TIME/ORDER

1. Mark the child who is late to school.

2. Mark the child who is early to class.

3. Mark the child next in line to buy ice cream.

4. Mark the first turtle in line.

5. Mark the second duck in the row.

6. Mark the third child holding an apple.

7. Mark the first pear from the branch.

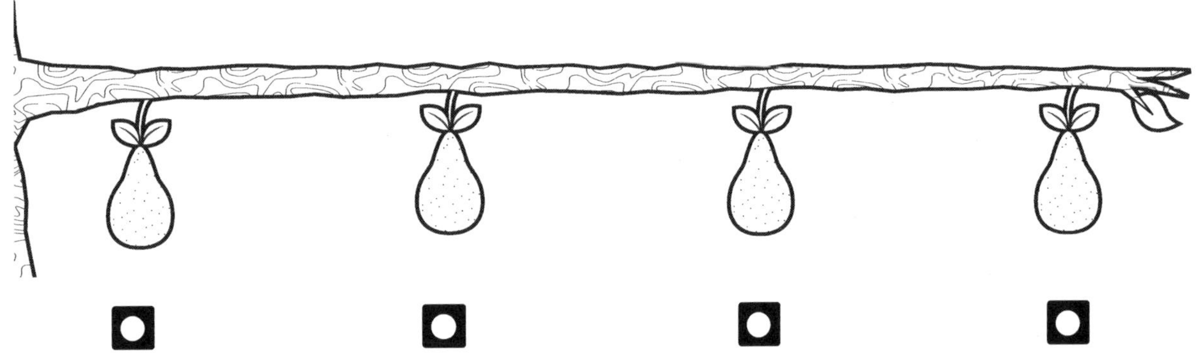

8. Mark the second turtle.

9. Mark the third child holding the rope.

10. Mark the fourth plane.

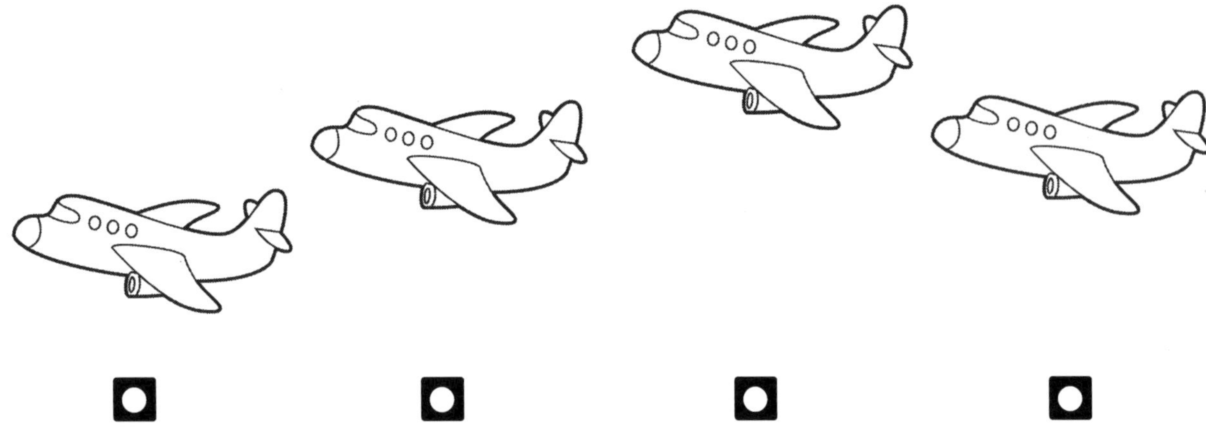

11. Mark the child who will be first to get ice cream.

12. Mark the child who will be the last to get cake.

13. Mark the child who is going fast.

14. Mark the child who will be the last to go outside.

15. Mark the animal that is slow.

16. Mark the child who will be the first to turn in the paper.

17. Mark the picture that shows after the party.

18. Mark what you would use after a bath.

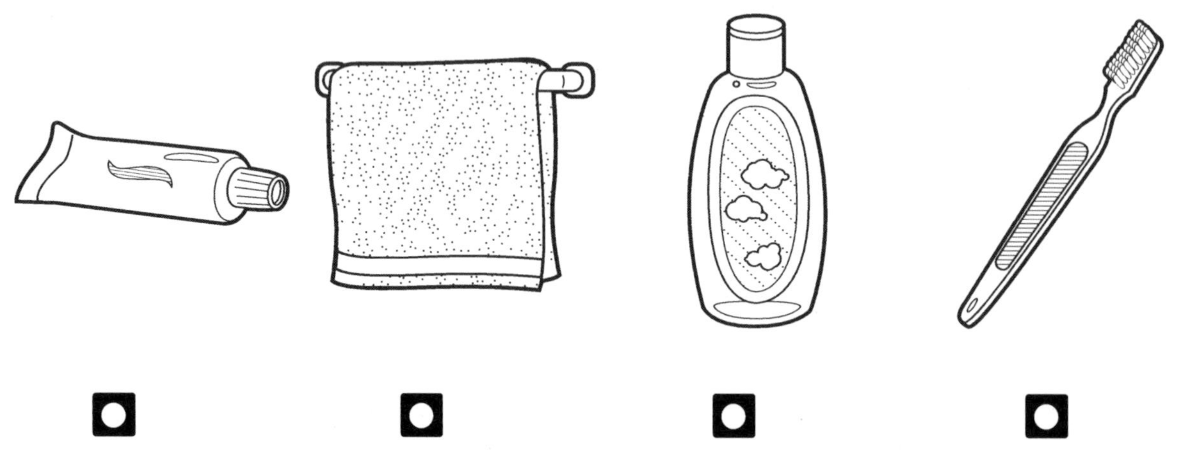

 Bright Kids NYC Inc ©

19. Mark the boy who is before the girl.

20. Mark the picture that shows winter.

21. Mark the picture that shows spring.

22. Mark the picture that shows winter.

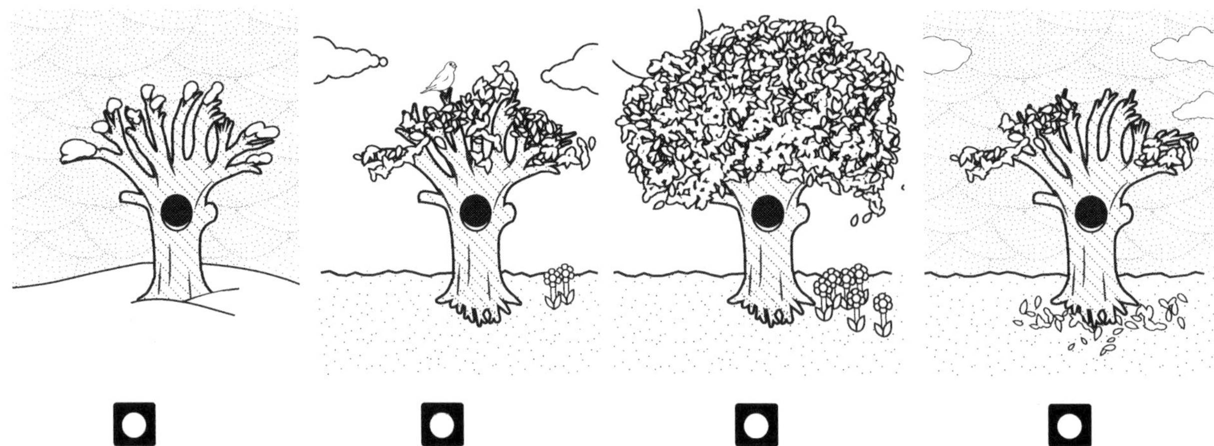

23. Mark the picture that shows summer.

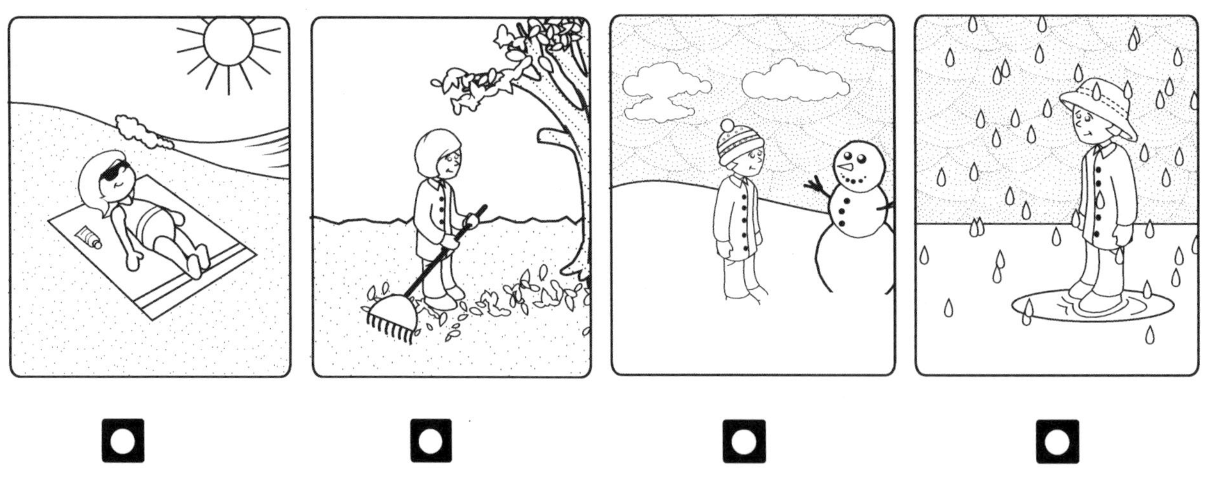

24. Mark the picture that shows fall.

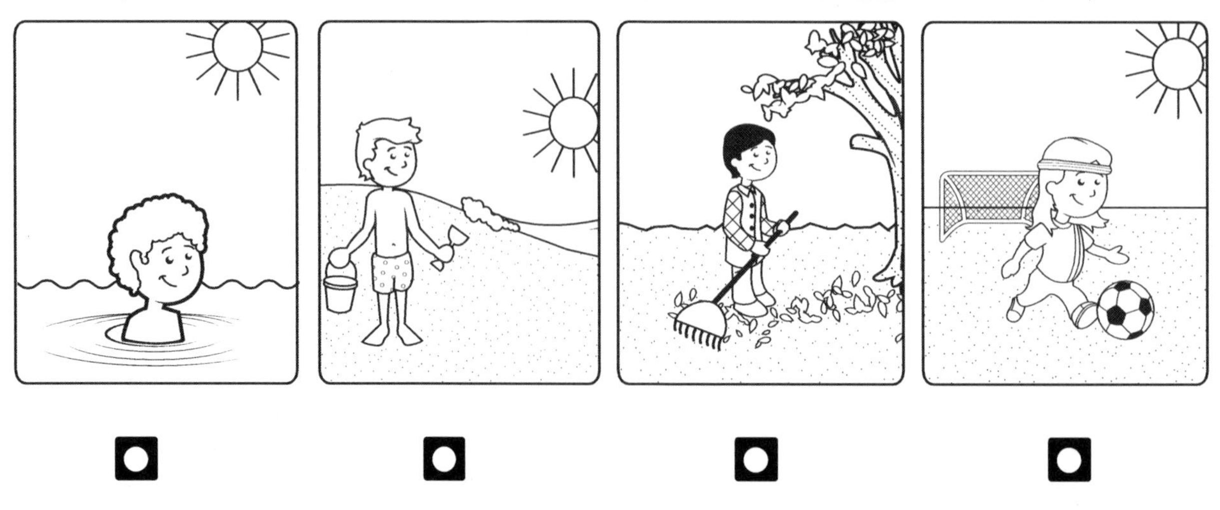

 Bright Kids NYC Inc ©

25. Mark the picture that shows day.

26. Mark the picture that shows night.

27. Mark the picture that shows before the party.

   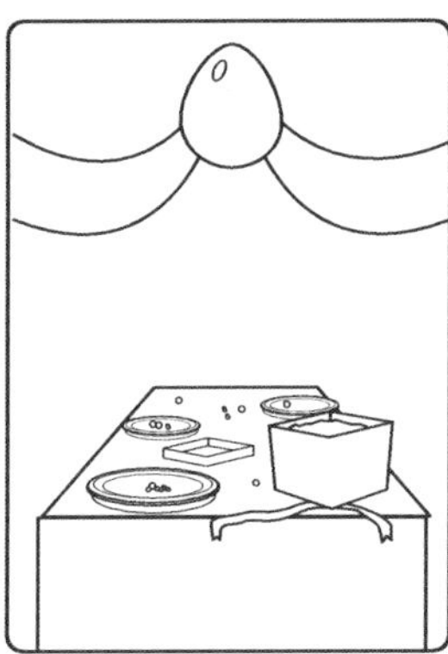

 Bright kids NYC Inc ©

ANSWER KEY

1.	Picture 1	-	First child
2.	Picture 4	-	Fourth child
3.	Picture 3	-	Third child
4.	Picture 1	-	First turtle
5.	Picture 2	-	Second duck
6.	Picture 4	-	Fourth child
7.	Picture 1	-	First pear
8.	Picture 2	-	Second turtle
9.	Picture 3	-	Third child
10.	Picture 4	-	Fourth plane
11.	Picture 3	-	Third child
12.	Picture 1	-	First child
13.	Picture 4	-	Running child
14.	Picture 1	-	First boy
15.	Picture 4	-	Turtle
16.	Picture 3	-	Third child
17.	Picture 4	-	Fourth party scene
18.	Picture 2	-	Towel
19.	Picture 2	-	Boy with soccer ball
20.	Picture 2	-	Girl with snowman
21.	Picture 1	-	Scene with butterfly and flowers
22.	Picture 1	-	Bare tree in snow
23.	Picture 1	-	Girl sunbathing on beach
24.	Picture 3	-	Boy raking leaves
25.	Picture 3	-	Row of houses
26.	Picture 4	-	Trees under the moon
27.	Picture 1	-	First party scene